FUGITIVE DENIM

D0168340

FUGITIVE DENIM

A MOVING STORY OF PEOPLE AND PANTS IN
THE BORDERLESS WORLD OF GLOBAL TRADE

RACHEL LOUISE SNYDER

W. W. NORTON & COMPANY

New York | *London*

Copyright © 2009, 2008 by Rachel Louise Snyder

All rights reserved
Printed in the United States of America
First published as a Norton paperback 2009

For information about permission to reproduce selections from this book,
write to Permissions, W. W. Norton & Company, Inc.,
500 Fifth Avenue, New York, NY 10110

For information about special discounts for bulk purchases, please contact
W. W. Norton Special Sales at specialsales@wwnorton.com or 800-233-4830

Manufacturing by RR Donnelley, Bloomsburg
Book design by Judith Stagnitto Abbate / Abbate Design
Production manager: Andrew Marasia

Library of Congress Cataloging-in-Publication Data

Snyder, Rachel Louise.
Fugitive denim : a moving story of people and pants in the borderless
world of global trade / Rachel Louise Snyder. — 1st ed.
p. cm.
Includes bibliographical references and index.
ISBN 978-0-393-06180-2 (hardcover)
1. Clothing trade. 2. Denim. 3. International trade. I. Title.
HD9940.A2S618 2008
382'.45687—dc22
2007024335

ISBN 978-0-393-33542-2 pbk.

W. W. Norton & Company, Inc.
500 Fifth Avenue, New York, N.Y. 10110
www.wwnorton.com

W. W. Norton & Company Ltd.
Castle House, 75/76 Wells Street, London W1T 3QT

6 7 8 9 0

FOR ANN MAXWELL AND PAUL BURTON.

THE BEST STORIES OF MY LIFE ALWAYS INCLUDE YOU.

"THE PUBLIC BOUGHT THE PRODUCTS . . . AND ASKED NO QUESTIONS AS TO CONDITIONS UNDER WHICH THEY HAD BEEN MANUFACTURED. SHOPPERS REJOICED WHEN PRICES WERE LOW, AND DID NOT DREAM OF THE SOCIAL COST OF THESE CONDITIONS."

The National Consumers' League pamphlet:
The First Quarter Century, 1899–1924

CONTENTS

PART THREE

PART FOUR

PART ONE

1

THE SUBVERSIVE ECOSYSTEM

IN A DOWNTOWN NEW YORK LOFT, INDUSTRY AND WHIMSY dominate the landscape in the form of two items: orchids and skateboards. But not just orchids—many, many orchids. Orchids dripping from a desk and clambering toward the windows. Orchids vying for light, and taking root where they find themselves. Fuchsia, ivory, lemon. And not just skateboards, but many, many skateboards, wheelless, waiting for the freedom of movement. They are piled under chairs like diner trays, stacked against the desk and atop bookshelves, lining walls like skirting board. Paint has been splintered and splattered on some, carefully swirled and brushed on others. Orchids and skateboards. Beautifully sloppy, full of light and life, and always inviting movement. In this office, they are Rogan Gregory's perfect foil.

Rogan is a fashion designer. An accidental designer, in fact, who could just as happily be planting trees in the north woods of Canada, one of the few landscapes he probably wouldn't feel the urge to redesign. A founder of the clothing label that bears his name and another called Loomstate, he is the creative visionary in a business partnership with fellow New Yorker and good friend Scott Hahn.

Rogan made a name for himself with his own high-end clothing line; he'd worked at Tommy Hilfiger, Levi's, Calvin Klein, the Gap, Daryl K, and others. He was known for his funky jeans, his upscale menswear, his urban style. "Anonymous," Scott called it once, meaning it was both familiar and new. But he also became known, through Loomstate, which uses only organic cotton, for a business model that was environmentally conservative, ethically conscious, and aesthetically progressive ("subversive, sustainable agriculture," Scott calls it).

One afternoon in the fall of 2004, Rogan and Scott got a visit to their small showroom in Manhattan, a rustic space painted a weathered white; the room is all light and windows, big timber beams carry scars from old tenants—rusting nails, splinters, carved-out fissures. Scott and Rogan received lots of visits from buyers and sourcing agents and stylists and deliverymen and models, but this one was different. This one was a panic-inducing, pressure-cooker of a visit, if they were the type to betray such things, which they aren't. This visit was from Ali Hewson, an elegant, earthy Irishwoman known for her activism whom Scott had met the day before without knowing who she was or any of her particulars. Today, she also brought her husband. Bono.

ROGAN LAUNCHED HIS CLOTHING LINE IN 2000 AND garnered a reverent, almost overnight, cult following—particularly for his denim, which was all soul and style. Details matter in a Rogan pair of jeans: the exactitude of the stitching, sometimes from lime-green thread, sometimes another color, sometimes even silk, the sideways back belt loop, the patterned fabric lining inner pockets and the yolk, savvy style minutiae that isn't seen by anyone but the wearer, like little secrets. They sell for hundreds of dollars and are worn by actors and musicians and the kind of people for whom the term "red carpet" has real meaning. But success took Rogan away from some of the things that mattered most. "I made a name for myself and I was making a living, but it just didn't seem like . . ." he pulled back, thought about what he meant for a minute. His feet vied for space with a stack of skateboards spilled under his desk. "I was designing stuff and I was like 'What am I doing?' Rogan is just an aesthetic. It's *my* aesthetic, but it's still just . . . It's hard for me to talk about Rogan, but Loomstate's easy because there's something there."

Scott and Rogan started Loomstate in 2003. They wanted this line to be more affordable than Rogan and more wearable than hippie dippy hemp, and as beautiful as anything you'd find in the best stores. Loomstate was the place they found a mission, the place where they proved what they could do and how and for whom. Sales were brisk in the first year and the fashion media wrote glowingly about them. "We aren't on a path to save the world," Rogan said, "but we were doing our part, and making a serious commitment to it."

This may be an obvious point, but it bears mentioning anyway. It's *pretty hard* to start your own clothing line. It's even harder when you're young and new to the scene and when you have to convince, say, one of the biggest fabric mills around—and by around I mean around Turkey, the world's biggest grower of organic cotton—to invest their resources and their time into an environmentally sound product that may sell. Or not. Or a little, but not enough. And then you have to convince retail customers that they should buy it, and media that they should write about it, and critics that they should take it seriously. Scott was the numbers guy, the entrepreneurial spirit with no formal business school training. Rogan was the creative genius who set the course of the aesthetic, who also had no formal design training. But they each took on their own and the other's role at times, and the facts on paper, the particulars of their lives, didn't add up enough to keep them from trying. All of which is to say that Rogan and Scott were a little crazy to take it on and the crazy worked for them. They offered Loomstate. And Loomstate brought them Ali and Bono. Ali and Bono would bring them Africa.

Rogan, who is thirty-five, grew up in Kent, Ohio. The very first thing he says of his mother and father is this: "My parents are good people." From his father he got the skateboards, learning how to fix and build things. From his mother, the orchids. He says she began the community's first recycling program. His father teaches at Kent State University—in sociology (deviant behavior for undergrads, social psychology for grads)—but he also has a workshop in which all manner of product is laid bare, reworked, created, rethought. His mother is an administrator and fund-raiser, a woman of action and activism. "They're both into efficiency," he said. "I grew up nature loving, [but] they're not hippies or anything. They're just way ahead." (They sound exactly like hippies, of course.) From his sister, he learned about self-sacrifice. She was a Peace Corps volunteer for two years in the Dominican Republic, helping to build aqueducts. "She's noble," Rogan says. "I'm not that noble. She's still struggling to make it happen. It's grass-roots shit. I don't have the tolerance for people, so I kind of picked another avenue. A selfish industry."

But it's those very components—the selfish part and the industry part—that he believes are so ripe for change. (And perhaps it's not a far stretch, the son of parents who fundamentally foster change and understanding. And deviance.) The garment and fashion industry is, as he puts it, "a huge contributor to the problems I see in the world. So it doesn't even take that much of a change to make a difference."

For Rogan, the fashion industry also has one other distinct advantage. It allows him—his vision and his message—to reach many more people than he would if he were, say, planting trees in the wilderness or building aqueducts with his sister. "I have a big opportunity to touch a lot of people," he says. "If you can get someone to spend money on something, in some ways it's almost more valid than voting. It's much more difficult to spend your hard-earned money on something than it is to check a box . . . A lot of times you're sacrificing something else, or you really want to support something. I think it's significant."

Rogan met Scott through an ex-roommate in 1999, and they shared an immediate camaraderie. They have a similar aesthetic, a pull toward industrial or architectural redesign and an affinity for nature and conservation. They both had a desire to affect change in a community larger than the one they inhabited. Scott spent about half of every year of his life growing up on Fire Island, a spit of land about an hour's ferry ride from Manhattan that cultivates a strange blend of hedonism and natural wonder. In college, he worked summers at a seafood restaurant called Matthew's that was something of a weekend magnet for islanders. The restaurant had a twenty-four-slip T-dock, and on a busy night, each slip could turn four boats. Scott called it a "rodeo" for watercraft. "You'd park them in the middle of wind and wake cracking off the bulkhead. There was current. You'd have to know hitches and bends and do it all really fast," he said. "It was dangerous." But he imagined it was also entertaining for the patrons watching all those dock boys jumping around trying like hell not to destroy anything, including their pride. And it was political. The kind of place where high rollers tipped C-notes to get a good slip on a busy night. The dock boys were what Scott called the gatekeepers, deciding who was in and who had to wait. In this way, it foreshadowed the work he would someday do with Rogan. The frenzy of it all, the pressure, the hip crowds and endless cash, but most of all the fact that he was the one in the thick of it, surrounded by the watchful eyes of those customers who perhaps had no stomach for this sort of action, who left the hard part to those who knew better. But the point wasn't their inaction, the point was they were still interested. They took note.

Scott's grandfather built the Sailors Haven marina on Fire Island and ran it for forty years. In the summertime, Scott worked wherever he was needed: tying up boats, doing maintenance, flipping hamburgers, working the register in the gift shop. The park rangers taught him about the land, the birds and trees and dunes. The lifeguards taught him about the sea. The beach parties taught him about free love, homosexuality, and heterosexuality. And his grandfather taught him to see man's footprint on the earth, the destructive evidence often left behind.

The ecology on Fire Island includes a curious geological phenomenon that Scott thinks about sometimes. Predominantly, the island's vegetation is pitch pine, salt marsh, shadbush, bayberry, beach grass. Harsh wind and salt spray typically keep island growth, like trees, to a minimum. But on Fire Island, a second set of dunes acts like a canopy and gives protection to the trees and shrub life behind it, allowing a forest to develop. Called the Sunken Forest, it is a sixteen-hectare oak-holly maritime forest hundreds of years old, a fragile ecosystem shortlisted for extinction, say environmentalists. Similar island forests of its type are very rare and a host of endangered species germinate or breed in the area. They are all, like the Sunken Forest itself, globally imperiled.[1]

Scott's grandfather's marina was the vanguard of the Sunken Forest. It had space for maybe forty boats. You could tie up your boat and sleep there, but only for a few days at a time and only if you'd gotten permission. Those in Scott's orbit could track when people went in and came out of there. The rangers, the park enforcement, people whom Scott once described as his surrogate parents. There was the second set of dunes and there were the surrogate parents and there was Scott the kid. Guardians of this fragile, imperiled place.

I asked Scott once if he remembered long walks with his grandfather pointing out birds or owls or types of trees. I had visions of kid wonder and adult wisdom, a Wilford Brimley arm slung over the thin shoulders of a small, wide-eyed boy. The walks he said he'd had, "but it was more about pointing out the trash and litter left behind, papers on the ground that needed to be picked up," the unnecessary sullying of an otherwise magical landscape. These are the memories he carries with him. You have the beauty of a place forever juxtaposed against the responsibility. That the former won't last without the latter was Scott's lesson.

For Scott and Rogan, environmentalism and social responsibility aren't the point in their line of work. The point is more like *why not?* "If it were a huge pain," Rogan says, "maybe it wouldn't be worth it. But it's not *that* much harder to grow organic cotton." Of course, it's probably not entirely beside the point to remember that this is a man who can get orchids to bloom in the middle of a Manhattan winter.

Scott says the point is that you don't have to sacrifice everything to do the right thing. You just have to do a little tweaking. One morning, he introduced me to a friend of his named Mehmet Ali, a legend in the Turkish denim world who encouraged their Loomstate vision early on, and who made the point using a familiar story. "There's a story about the starfish on the shore," Mehmet said. He had a thick white mustache and the kind of ironed, cosmopolitan air of a character in a Thomas Crown movie. He told the story with as much aplomb and vigor as if he'd been the point of origination. "A guy on vacation in the morning wakes up early and sees these starfish along the beach after the tide goes out . . . And he sees a guy walking along, throwing them all back, one at a time. He asks why, and the guy says, 'Otherwise they will die.' But surely, the vacationer says, surely there are millions, what you're doing can't matter. 'Well,' the man says, tossing another into the ocean, 'it mattered for that one.' "

SHARON BLANKSON WAS RESPONSIBLE FOR SETTING up that first meeting between Scott and Ali Hewson in the Rogan/Loomstate showroom. Sharon is a stylist and a longtime friend of all three who'd used the Rogan line from the beginning. U2 were her clients. She'd dressed the band in Rogan clothes for photo shoots and public events and she needed to pull samples for the following day. This time she brought Ali with her, though she never told Scott who she was. "Ali wasn't introduced to me as Bono's wife, and I thought maybe she was a writer or a photographer or a fellow stylist," Scott said. "She had a very powerful quality about her." Ali, who'd always kept a low profile, particularly given the global fame of her husband, asked a lot of smart questions, and she spent a while checking out the collection. Then the two women left.

The following day, Sharon called Scott and told him who Ali was, told him that Ali and Bono knew all about Loomstate and really appreciated what they were trying to do with the brand. Sharon told him Bono wanted to come in to meet them. So he and Ali came the following day. "Bono walked in and said hello and told me he was a big fan," Scott says, "which I found quite . . . comical. I mean, you want to talk about a fan!" It was sweet, really. They sat together and chatted for a long while, and then Bono started to talk about this vision he had of creating trade in Africa, and people needing help through employment. "He had a consumer product vehicle in mind," Scott said, "the campaign of a brand." They didn't know it yet, but they were talking about what would soon become the Edun brand, high-style, high-end fashion made by and for people who cared about labor conditions, responsible consumerism, and ultra-trendy chic garb. It would also carry the name Bono, thereby infusing it with as much social capital as an emerging brand could possibly have at the outset. Edun would be like Loomstate with organic, only the idea was to have a different social consciousness as the nucleus—economics and poverty alleviation. But social responsibility and environmentalism are really two avenues that arrive at a common destination. "He was so excited about it," Scott said, "and I just remember grabbing his arm and being like 'We share this vision with you!'" Bono and Ali wanted to start a clothing company that would be socially progressive and economically sustainable. They wanted it to be taken seriously in the fashion world. They wanted to source entirely from Africa to contribute to solving the AIDS crisis in that continent, and help lift individual communities from dire poverty. And they wanted Rogan Gregory and Scott Hahn to help them lead the charge. Bono told them he wanted them all to do it together. Scott remembered this phrase: "Let's shoot a rocket into the sky."

They were also starting to build that rocket at the worst possible time. Global trade rules for textiles and apparel were two months away from what people in the industry believed was going to be a worldwide catastrophe.

OF COURSE, DREAMING OF SOMETHING AND MAKING it happen are vastly different things. Scott had already been educating himself on trade law and what it all meant, and he received almost daily advice from a lawyer on how things had to be done. Early on in Loomstate's evolution, he learned things couldn't go from Point A to Point B. If you wanted to source something from Turkey and have it sewn in, say, China, you had to make sure your order wasn't going to disrupt a trade system that was so convoluted and so tangled up that hardly anyone actually really understood it. Sometimes thread had to be purchased from a mill in the States, then sent to Turkey for weaving, or the cotton had to come from Turkey and be milled in Turkey, but the finishing had to take place in the States. It all depended on what country a "Made in . . ." label would reflect, though the real truth is that most garments carry labels with a single country but handprints from a multitude of nations. "Made in Peru" might have cotton from Texas, weaving from North Carolina, cutting and sewing from Lima, washing and finishing from Mexico City, and distribution from Los Angeles.

In a mad dash to fulfill their first orders, Loomstate accidentally ended up with a geographical concoction whereby the cotton came from Turkey, where it was also milled into fabric, but then it was sent to Mexico for cut-and-sew operations. After it was shipped there, Scott visited the Loomstate factory in Mexico and found it didn't meet standards he was comfortable with, so at great expense, they sent the fabric to Los Angeles for cutting and sewing, and then afterwards again sent the garments to Mexico for "washing" (the process by which jeans get ripped, beaten, sand-blasted, overdyed, or otherwise chemically treated). It was an inauspicious start, but these days the Loomstate supply chain (which is not the same, geographically, as Edun's or Rogan's) sends Turkish fabric to Tunisia for cutting, sewing, and finishing, and North American fabric to the Dominican Republic for the same.

Once you had all these logistics figured out as best you could, you still had tariffs to wade through—how much did you have to pay to whom if your thread came from North Carolina and your cotton from Turkey and your fabric from Italy? Or your cotton from China and your fabric from China and your sewing from Cambodia? Or Lesotho? Or Mauritius? Or any one of the sixty or seventy countries that each has a piece of the overall global garment industry? Were you disqualified from trade benefits if your buttons, zippers, and fabric came from a place other than the factory where it was all sewn?

You could decide you wanted to do everything right, support the people who would grow your organic cotton, and mill your fabric and compile your design vision. You might also want to pay them well, listen to their needs, create a system that would keep them fairly happy, but it didn't mean you could actually do any of it. You might want to give business to Mozambique, but it didn't mean you could find anyone there qualified to sew your designs. Or if you did, you might have to organize with three other countries just to get the raw materials you needed into the country—materials that would likely disqualify you from trade benefits, making it ultimately too expensive for you to hire the Mozambique factory. If the raw materials could be made there, it would all be so much easier. It was a Catch-22, and it required so much organization and thinking and planning, it ended up costing too much to be worthwhile, in economic terms, but also in terms of administration. Unless of course consumers would someday be willing to shell out $500 or more on their everyday jeans.

All of this is to say that even the vision and enthusiasm of Bono could perhaps not penetrate the deep, dark heart of twenty-first-century worldwide trade law.

Scott says they did their best to learn it all. Ultimately what you really pay attention to is just the part that applies to you. "We were trying to figure out the duty gymnastics," he says. "It was insane."

Part of the problem, at least as it pertains to global trade, is something known to the industry as the quota system. On January 1, 2005, a few months after Scott and Rogan's meeting with Ali and Bono, a decades-old system called the Multi-Fibre Agreement (MFA) expired, in accordance with rules established by the World Trade Organization under something they called their Agreement on Textiles and Clothing (ATC). Members of the WTO were signatories of the agreement to end the MFA. In place for the better part of the post–World War II era under various aliases and auspices (the WTO took over the administration of the quotas when it was created in 1994), this system evolved as borders became more porous, consumers more aware, and organizations more global. Basically, the MFA set limits on the amount of textiles and apparel any one country could export to the United States. For example, of the roughly 365 million sweaters imported to the United States every year, the Philippines got to manufacture and export 4.2 million of them.[2] The quota given to each country varied, and for the bigger manufacturers like China and India, a void was left when they reached their quotas—a void other, smaller countries like the Philippines gladly stepped in to fill.

From 1974 to 1994, the MFA dictated the global terms of the textile and apparel industry. It began as a way to protect manufacturing in industrialized countries in the face of competition from textile industries first in Japan, South Korea, and Taiwan after World War II, then in China, India, and other developing nations. The quotas ensured that no single developing country ever captured a monopoly of the developed world's market by limiting what could be exported to countries like the United States. What this meant, in real terms, was that countries like Cambodia, recuperating from decades of war and genocide, had a clear entrée into a market that otherwise might have been prohibitively competitive. The same applied to Mauritius, Nepal, Laos, Lesotho, Peru, Honduras, Guatemala, Mexico, Indonesia, Tunisia, and dozens of other countries. Left on its own, the textile production market may have concentrated in just a handful of countries, rather than the sixty or so that compose it today. Ending the quotas was an attempt to rebalance our first attempts at, well, rebalancing. We would eradicate the trade laws we'd written and revised to partly protect the impoverished countries and thereby give the impoverished countries a chance to make it on their own, with not much more than their own pluck. What the World Trade Organization is doing by eliminating the MFA and eradicating the convoluted quota system is, in essence, pretty simple. It's a giant do-over, sort of like God and the great flood.

The trade rules weren't a bad idea. They were supposed to keep jobs in the United States. They were supposed to help Europe rebuild and give a helping hand to Japan after the United States devastated Nagasaki and Hiroshima. We even bought Japan a slew of sewing machines. But then Europe rebuilt, Japan went high-tech, and we lost our jobs anyway to countries in Central America, Southeast Asia, and China, among others. The trade rules didn't evolve so much as simply proliferate.

As a result of the ending of quotas, starting January 1, 2005, consumer clothing prices were expected to plummet by as much as 30 percent. In a free market, so went the logic of the WTO, all countries are created equal and consumer savings is what it's about. If they can keep up, small countries like Cambodia and Lesotho will have the same access as big manufacturers like China and India to giant consumer markets like the United States and western Europe. But access is hardly the end of it; one needs customers as well. And the competition promises to be fierce, while the free-trade proponents promise it will be fair, from the Big Troika (China, India, and Pakistan) to the relatively small producers like Haiti, Sri Lanka, Slovakia, Tobago, Israel, Lebanon, and many others. What's more, eliminating the quotas means all countries in theory will have equal tariffs to pay to export their goods to the United States—tariffs that run anywhere from 19 percent to 30 percent. Many European countries are exempt from these tariffs, as are 70 countries in Africa, and the Caribbean and Latin America, under various trade agreements. No promises have yet been made to offer to the poorest countries of Asia these same duty-free benefits, so the ending of the quotas is particularly ominous to them. One prominent newspaper called 2005 the "dawning of the [industry's] death sentence."[3] It wasn't just a potential death sentence for countries like the United States, it was a death sentence for any country anywhere that couldn't compete with the biggest producers.

In economic terms, it is anyone's guess what may happen long term. Industry predictions varied wildly, with the very best projecting that twenty-five to thirty countries' apparel industries, out of a worldwide sixty to seventy total, would survive. The worst projected a mere eight to ten.[4] For countries like Bangladesh and Cambodia who have banked their economic survival on textiles for the last decade or more, the potential fallout is staggering. Lobbyists worked around the clock to find new stopgaps and trade agreement extensions that the U.S. and European Union (EU) governments might exploit to keep the flood of Chinese goods at bay just a little longer. In the months before January, textile and apparel Web sites, from governmental to private, Atlantic to Pacific to Indian coasts, all showed clocks counting down the days and sometimes even the hours, minutes, and seconds to the ending of the quotas. It was akin to the frenzied months and weeks leading up to the millennium, when private citizens stockpiled water and withdrew their bank savings. From the buyers to the designers, the factory owners to the workers, the industry held its collective breath—all under the unknowing noses of the consumers. And all eyes were fixed on the economic runaway train that is China. China can do it cheaper, better, quicker, and in greater quantity than anywhere in the world. Rarely had so much seemed at stake in this vast expanse of the commoditized world.

Countries panicked in their own quiet ways. Italy mourned the death of its manufacturing sector. The United States tried to revive a moribund union movement. Cambodia joined with thirteen other countries to lobby for duty-free status in the United States. Central America and the United States passed a free-trade bill called the U.S.-Central America Free Trade Agreement (CAFTA). Africa tried to extend its duty-free privilege. Most of these efforts continue, three years after the ending of the quotas, and though some countries have suffered—Nepal, Laos, Lesotho, Mauritius, Mexico, and many others—the cataclysmic changes that were predicted have yet to happen. It is, instead, a slow unraveling. In the first months of 2005, a series of stopgaps were put on China to slow its growth; they were basically a fancy way of re-creating portions of the quota system. Thirty-four categories of clothing and household goods, including bras, cotton trousers (but not denim jeans), sweaters, swimwear, underwear, cotton towels, and socks—the latter of which seem particularly contentious to trade negotiators—all have limits on how much China can export to the United States.[5] Europe has safeguards in many of these categories as well for China, though generally the restrictions are more lenient than those negotiated by the U.S. trade representative. The stopgaps have sheltered many dozens of countries, and by the end of 2008, when the stopgaps run out, the panic will start again (until 2008, the numbers allowed for export will increase slightly each year). This is the framework under which Ali and Bono and Scott and Rogan and many, many others in the industry around the world are operating. Some buyers just threw up their hands and made a dash for China. Others promised not to give up on the countries they were already in. And others vowed to increase their manufacturing in the most impoverished countries on earth.

Rogan and Scott started Bono and Ali Hewson's ultra-trendy, ultra-thoughtful Edun line in 2005 with the hopes of alleviating a little poverty and bringing the realities of the impoverished world to the doorways of Barneys, Fred Segal, Saks Fifth Avenue, Nordstrom. Places where those who are least likely to find themselves in sub-Saharan Africa might in fact be forced to acknowledge the place in some small measure. The message is simple: If you don't know, we'll tell you, and once we tell you, you can't not act. Of course, the acting is the trickiest part of all. Thirty percent of the cotton Edun uses is organic, and the line is sold in many of the world's high-end stores and luxury boutiques. The company is watched closely, not only because of who runs it, but because of what they're doing and how they're doing it. If a company with a designer like Rogan Gregory, and a backer like Bono, and a mission like saving an entire continent fails, it will speak to much more than simply the failed bottom line of another fashion house startup.

Scott talked to me about the pieces of the vast trade network that affect him. Clothes for Loomstate, Rogan, and Edun are made in Lesotho, Tunisia, Peru, Turkey, India, and the United States. "Tunisia ships to our distribution center in Ireland," he said, trying to remember what countries fit where and what duties were assigned. "Turkey has a duty. Africa doesn't, unless you're bringing in fabric from somewhere else. Then it doesn't qualify for AGOA [the African Growth and Opportunity Act, which essentially gives 7,000 products in 38 African countries duty-free status[6]]. I think the average is about fifteen percent on the product." He went on, but there was something wearying about it all, like working your ass off to cure some disease that's been busy killing off the people all around you while you've had your head down, trying to figure it all out, trying to beat the hell out of it. The rules are dizzying. You can, for example, use a label that says "Made in Bangladesh" even if the shirt is sitting on a hanger at a factory in China. If the back and front panels of the shirt and the sleeves were sewn in Bangladesh, then shipped off to China to have the cuffs, collars, and finishing done, you can circumvent the fact that China has perhaps used up all of its shirt quota, and under current trade law you'll be allowed to use the "Made in Bangladesh" label. It's as if John Cleese and the Monty Python gang got together and wrote the global trade rules for garments. A sleeve in Turkey! A fly in Laos! A rivet and button in Kenya! And a label in Suriname!

"The haves are more protected than the have-nots," Scott says. "It's restrictive in terms of existing laws, [but] it's all about opportunity. Opening up trade rules is a huge part of allowing the development to occur, and you have to be part of it, as a company, in the global community. It's not about short-term profit; you have to be involved in the government decisions that are going on." Edun has a distinct advantage. Bono is one of the few people walking the earth today who can convince world leaders to change rules, to establish different priorities. He's a lobbyist of the highest order; a salesman whose greatest tool is himself, his own belief. Other companies lobby for change as well—the Gap, Levi's, Patagonia, many socially responsible buyers and brands—but Bono is a singular force, and in this way Edun, even as a tiny company, wields enormous influence. "Someone like Bono can at least get your pitch in the door to hear why something needs to be [changed], to support trade out of a certain region," Scott says. "This whole paradigm of altruistic commerce is catching fire, and the competitive side of altruism is showing its face. It's like who can do better for the world? That's what your cape has to say, how you're doing things for other people as a company. If that's what it takes, inducing ego into why people want to be associated with one company or another, I think it's great."

Scott compares the garment industry, which employs somewhere between thirty and forty million people around the world, to a vast ecosystem that has, at its heart, balance. If you order too much fabric, you'll be left with stock in the warehouses; if one of your sewing lines moves more quickly than another, it'll throw the production off; if you order too much for Barneys but not enough for Nordstrom, sales will be skewed; if one factory runs out of orders and another has too many and some people lose their jobs while others suffer through overtime, the social and economic costs will be high. Or if your trade rules have run out of steam and a redirect is in order, the entire manufacturing system might have to be relocated. The balance is needed everywhere, on every level. "Nature itself is probably the best analogy for looking at how to be inspired creatively, and how to check the rules," Scott says. "Nature has a lot of rules; if you pay attention, there's wisdom there. It's an important example, because a lot of ecosystems are out of balance, or abused, or in danger.

"Art, fashion, music," Scott believes, "[these have] the emotional connection to so many important things, like science. The failure of scientists to communicate climate change is because they don't have a way to tell the story. People miss the origin of the fiber, how far things travel to get to them." For him, fashion tells these stories, and many others as well: the garment industry and its own vast, imbalanced, imperiled, impervious ecosystem; the stories underneath the skin. It's a picture, he likes to think, of "what everyone's doing and thinking in the world."

The rules are like Fire Island's second set of dunes. Protection for a forest—an ecosystem—that would have otherwise died, assuming it'd lived at all. People like Scott and Rogan and thirty million of their counterparts are in the swale, trying, even as the dunes disappear, to keep the forest alive. This is their story.

II

THE VEGETABLE LAMB
CONQUERS THE WORLD

MEHMAN HUSSEINOV LOVES COTTON. IT PUNCTUATES his colloquialisms, his jokes, his stories. When he holds a wad of raw cotton, his fingers caress it as if it were fine silk. The day of the 2004 elections in the United States, he said: "I don't care about George W. Bush. I only care about cotton." Then he paraphrased Churchill: "Politics is just a lie that is found out later."* Mehman loves cotton so much that he aced a course in cotton classification and testing at the Gdynia Cotton Association in Poland, one of the few places on earth to offer such a course. It's famous in the industry. His teachers remembered him from a visit he'd made there with his father, who also worked in cotton, when he was a young boy. Mehman learned how to grade cotton, how to recognize high-quality from low-quality, how to define it by color,

---

*The Churchill quote is: "A politician needs the ability to foretell what is going to happen tomorrow, next week, next month, and next year. And to have the ability afterwards to explain why it didn't happen."

strength, uniformity, fineness, and consistency. On his lapel, he occasionally wore a gold stickpin, evidence of achieving the top score in the class. Though he doesn't do it, he knows how to grow cotton and pick it and weave it into textiles. He can look at a world map and tell you where, in the northern and southern hemispheres of the globe, cotton is growing, and when it will be picked, ginned, classed, and sold to the world.

Occasionally, he ridicules his own love of cotton, knowing that not many people in the world are likely to share his passion. He studies clothes hung on racks or folded on shop shelves, and clothes people wear on the street, and he tries to define the quality of the cotton. "If it claims a hundred percent cotton, I feel it," he says. "Egyptian cotton is said to be the best. Armani uses Egyptian cotton in their men's shirts. But if you ask me, I will tell you Azeri cotton is the best." He grins, comes close to a laugh—he is often close to but rarely quite arrives at laughter—then to prove his point he feels a white lab coat from his own office and says, "Not one hundred percent." It is, in fact, ninety-five percent cotton, five percent polyester. Mehman, the Cotton Classer, top in his class, is never wrong.

Mehman (pronounced Meck-man) is one of ten cotton classers in Azerbaijan. They are the first stop for cotton from the countryside that gets sold on the international market. Classers analyze the grade and quality of cotton—factors that eventually translate to price. Mehman earned a bachelor of science in economics and merchandising from Baku State University, but it was his time spent in and around gins and cotton that formed the basis for his professional life. He sees himself as the first stage in a global process and one that is, in fact, not all that foreign to him. During the Soviet era, when he was a child, the Azerbaijan economy was based on the ruble; now the country has its own money, called shirvans or manats. By his mid-twenties, Mehman had traveled to Poland, Italy, Russia, Germany, Uzbekistan, and Soviet Georgia. But he also believes that "global" is a state of mind. In these two regards, he is perhaps as cosmopolitan as any well-traveled professional. The world may still be an object of mystery and curiosity, but the idea that one could not explore it would be as foreign to him as the idea of a borderless state would be to his father's generation.

Mehman lives in Baku, a city of curious improbabilities in a country that borders Iran and Russia on the Caspian Sea. Once-glorious buildings awash in peeling paint and crumbling corners stand beside grand European-inspired edifices and soaring bronze monuments to history and folklore. Ancient stone towers teeter near square communist structures, which themselves sit near new residential and commercial construction sites burgeoning from the country's post-Soviet oil boom. Smokey basement jazz clubs, a weekend philharmonic, and regular opera performances attest to the elevated status of art and culture during the Soviet era, but tucked away in corners of the city squatter villages abound. Families living under corrugated asbestos roofing and sharing a common courtyard for cooking and washing are the fallout from the upheaval to capitalism—a system that many Azeris grow ever more resentful of. It is a country of moderate Muslims in the midst of a tiny civil war between Azeris and Armenians over a speck of land in the far southwest. Azerbaijan sits at the fulcrum of a fundamentalist theocratic regime and a brand-new secular democracy.

I had come to Azerbaijan because I'd heard that it was the cotton capital of the world. It's not. It's not even a close suburb. It is, say, what Dayton is to Los Angeles: technically speaking, an urban center but hardly comparable. This approximation is not entirely accidental. Uzbekistan lies just across the Caspian Sea and is one of the largest cotton producers in the world. It's also infamous as the country that drained the Aral Sea of its water precisely through its use of irrigation for cotton fields. During the Soviet era all cotton from the region was sold as Uzbekistan cotton, whether it came from Azerbaijan, Kazakhstan, Turkmenistan, or anywhere in the area that grew the crop. Today, many people maintain the mindset that Azeri cotton is Uzbek cotton; Russia labeled it Uzbek cotton partly because Uzbekistan's geography was known for growing high-quality cotton and partly because it made paperwork easier.[1] Those in the cotton industry in Azerbaijan could not be more keenly aware of the difference. They also know that their precarious place on the world stage means continual efforts must be made to gain a more substantial foothold. The Azerbaijan/Uzbekistan conflation is evidence of the continually blurry line between the states of the former Soviet Union and today's independent countries of the former Soviet Union. The people haven't changed, the borders (mostly) haven't changed, the languages haven't changed, but lots and lots of paper has changed. In Azerbaijan, the people speak Russian but call themselves Azeri. Or they speak Azeri and call themselves Russian. Or they speak both and call themselves Russian one day, Azeri the next, depending upon who is doing the asking. It is a state of being that is constantly reflected in the daily lives of those who feel both freed by and subjected to a system that is at best confusing to them and at worst economically, socially, and politically cataclysmic.

Mehman, who is twenty-eight, works within this system, full of ideas, but hampered by realities. He loves his job, such as it is, but he loves other things as well. What he wants more than anything in life, he said, is to be happy. He equates happiness with freedom and money, among other things. In Poland, at his cotton classification course, he was very, very happy. He was free from familial obligations. He could eat at cafés whenever he wanted with whomever he wanted. Paradoxically, in Baku, he believes the question of happiness is irrelevant. Only beyond his own geography does he pose this ontological inquiry. It does no good to ask it in Baku. There is inevitability when one comes to live his life here; a place where sons still walk in the footsteps of their fathers. Mehman loves cotton. But what he loves more is choice, even if that choice were to lead him right back to where he is today.

Mehman also knows not everyone is as excited by cotton as he is, but he can't help it. Cotton is in his blood, knowledge passed down from his father. In the cotton industry of Azerbaijan, his father was once the go-to guy for cotton. Hussein Husseinov, Mehman's father, was a cotton trader in the Soviet era. He lived for a time in India and Bangladesh but longed to return home. He traveled the world as a cotton expert and helped determine what the Ministry of Agriculture's cotton standards would be for export. Now he's a sociology professor at Baku State University and a coauthor of sociology textbooks. He is still an occasional cotton consultant and can remember the industry's details even from years ago. "I was in Odessa in '95," Hussein said, over a chicken Caesar salad at a restaurant in Baku called the Sunset Café, which paid homage to the gilded age of American cinema. Cary Grant and Katharine Hepburn stared from enormous celluloid prints. "Cotton was two thousand three hundred dollars per ton." Today, it is around $1,200.[2] "Bah," he waved his fork through the air, "The price is set by the cotton mafia anyway." Hussein's cotton mafia are fast-talking Liverpudlians. According to Hussein, they set the daily price of cotton for the rest of the world at the Liverpool Cotton Association. In fact, however, cotton prices are set by individual buyers based on market conditions and global crop surpluses or deficits, but the folks in Liverpool do collect prices and send the averages out daily to their subscribers.

Even though he doesn't work full time in cotton anymore, Hussein discusses it with a certain passionate insouciance. He is probably the only non–cotton industry person in the world who loves cotton so much that he still monitors the price per pound on any given day and tracks how much his country can expect to export any given year. It is not difficult to see how the passions of the father were genetically programmed into the son. "Turkmenistan is developing a rose-colored cotton," he said. The United States already has one—Sally Fox of Foxfibre is generally credited with growing a variety of natural cotton colors. Cotton comes in white, cream, yellow, light brown, or pink. There are also organic growers experimenting with colors like blue and brown.

Mehman had joined us for dinner, and we sat at the table

together, watched over by Bogart and Bergman. When Mehman talked about cotton, his blood pressure appeared to rise. His dark hazel eyes lit up, thick eyebrows lifting and falling animatedly, and he sat on the edge of his chair, with a hangdog grin. Mehman has an expansive brow and a record-setting dimple in his chin. At the age of sixteen he was offered a job as a cotton inspector, in part because he'd been loitering on the edges of the industry with his father since he could walk. At nineteen he was the quality control inspector at a gin, or cotton-processing factory. He took a new job in 2003 with an international testing company called Intertek, to create and run their new cotton-testing lab.

Part of what makes Mehman able to predict cotton content in finished garments is the weave. Nubs and naps, in particular, are exciting because they allow him to guess whether he is seeing long staple or extra long staple or middling or long middling cotton. It is as if cotton were a wonderment, a miracle. Which, in some ways, it is.

GROWN IN NEARLY EVERY REGION OF THE WORLD AND the second largest crop grown for oil, cotton has more than 1,000 uses. It is second only to hemp in utility, though many Azeris argue somewhat ineffectually that hemp's got nothing on cotton; but they have little experience with hemp. Billions of people use cotton daily around the world as a natural fiber and a food staple. Cooking oil, automobile upholstery, gunpowder, cattle feed, varnish, celluloid, parachutes, lotion, paint, dye, airplane tires, honey, paper, industrial pipes, nets, manufacturing belts, and electrical wire coating all rely on cotton.[3] An agronomist at the Ministry of Agriculture in Baku told me that for Muslims cotton "is the crop of God. We take cotton to the grave, wrapped in a shroud."[4]

Weaving cotton for fabric clothing began more than 7,000

years ago, though some believe it to have originated around 12,000 BC in Egypt. Archeologists have identified textile fragments made from cotton in 3,500 BC in Mexico, 2,500 BC in Peru, and 500 BC in the United States. Today, it is the single best-selling natural fiber in the world, and in the United States cotton outsells all synthetic fibers combined. (There was a blip on the cotton radar briefly when John Travolta and the Bee Gees shimmied through their disco-infused night fevers in polyester leisure suits, but the crop soon recovered with the advent of the leg warmer.) Many of the woven cotton fabrics that we recognize today have origins in the military. Cotton T-shirts were first used by the United States Navy in the late nineteenth century. Khakis, originally wool and named for military trousers in India, became the standard pants for U.S. soldiers in World War I. By the mid-twentieth century, civilians had adopted them for light sport and generic leisurewear.[5]

People on nearly every continent have an almost spiritual reverence for cotton. During festivals some Southeast Asians place bands of cotton around each other's wrists in hopes of fostering good luck and protection against disease (in Cambodia, this is done at weddings). In the Antilles, the bones of great men were once wrapped in braided cotton and placed inside woven baskets, to be revered as powerful talismans. In India, the agriculturalists of the Punjab region created a female figure from the most beautiful cotton plant of the harvest as a symbol of the Cotton Mother, who some believed controlled the reproduction of harvested plants. They also prayed and sprinkled buttermilk and rice water on the largest plant in the field, just before the flower dropped off and the cotton tuft emerged, to entice the rest of the plants to grow as tall and strong. In China, cotton was once called the "treasure of the ancients," or *ku pei*, and used as currency for barter. The Hopi of North America ascribed special power to cotton as a symbol of male sperm, and slaves in the colonies believed cotton bark could stimulate the body and induce abortions.[6]

Cotton is one of the world's few crops that was found growing on unconnected continents concurrently: South Asia and Central America. Its value was immediate to anyone who saw it. Alexander the Great brought cotton back from his conquest in India, as did the British many centuries later. During the Hellenistic Age people believed cotton came from a plant that grew a certain type of Scythian lamb they called a vegetable lamb. This lamb allegedly grew from the pods of the cotton plant and was just like the little field rompers we recognize today, but they were attached to a stalk coming from the soil, which was flexible and allowed them to graze—like a stiff umbilical cord. When the grass around them had been consumed, the lambs would conveniently expire, and both the wool and the flesh would then be available to the ancient consumer.

Other civilizations revered cotton as well. Cotton robes were once the vestments of the aristocracy, rather than the wardrobe of the masses. The ancient Incas and Mayans grew cotton and wove cloth long before the colonialists from England and America took up residence on newly planted cotton farms in the Caribbean, in Africa, and in the southern United States. In Japan, cotton is said to have begun growing when a Chinese junk carrying cotton seeds blew off course and shipwrecked on the Japanese coast. Cotton was, in no small measure, responsible for the extinction of England's vast wool trade, which spurred the Industrial Revolution. It became so popular so quickly that in England, for several decades the importation of cotton was outlawed and the government attempted to fine anyone wearing cotton clothes rather than wool. The British discovered the pleasure and comfort of cotton skivvies, whose breathability resulted in a marked decline of jock itch and yeast infections. The fabric quickly found its way into every home in the United Kingdom. In the United States, cotton was equally beloved. In the nineteenth century, a certain David Cohn wrote: "Cotton is more than a crop in the Delta. It is a form of mysticism. It is a religion and a way of life. Cotton is omnipresent here as a god is omnipresent. It is omnipotent as a god is omnipotent, giving life and taking life away."

Cotton has also drained lakes and rivers, polluted bodies of water across the world, and incited trade wars. It has nestled itself in the lungs of mill workers and caused them slow, painful deaths. Its new corporate farming structure and old government subsidies in the West ensure that cotton farmers around the world will remain destitute. The cotton subsidy issue, of course, has been around for a century and a half. South Carolina Senator James Henry Hammond declared in 1858, "You dare not make war on cotton. No power on earth dares make war on it."[7] He just as easily could have been speaking to farmers in Africa, in Central Asia, in India today. He wrongly believed that the South could secede from the North and be economically viable simply from cotton, but he also predicted that one day the entire world would purchase cotton from the United States. History has proved him right in the latter. To slaves in America, of course, cotton picking was sheer drudgery, though it was also the single greatest rallying force for the abolitionist movement. David Christy, an antislavery writer from the nineteenth century who coined the phrase "Cotton Is King" in his seminal work of the same name, warned that slavery wasn't going to end if people approached it on a moral level. To Christy, slavery had to be seen as the economic issue it was. ". . . as long as people keep buying the cotton products, made plentiful and cheap by slave labor," he wrote, "they are encouraging the useless and superficial attempts to solve the slavery problem." The parallels to similar issues today, like environmental degradation and sweatshops, are striking. Where a market exists, someone will be there to fulfill it, often, sadly, with little regard for any consequences.

Today, cotton exists in nearly every aisle of a drug store, in every fashion show, in the cars on the road and the money in our wallets. It has brought fortune and misfortune to people across the ages and it continues, in the twenty-first century, to be a cause for technological advances and environmental devastation; it remains both demon and deity.

ON THE WORLD STAGE, AZERBAIJAN COTTON IS A BLIP. In 2002, the country exported 30,000 tons of cotton, compared to 4,420,000 tons exported by the United States.[8] By 2004, it produced roughly 100,000 tons,[9] though according to Mehman's father, the actual figure was more like 60,000 after the cotton was processed. Cotton is processed by rolling it through a ginner, which takes seeds, leaves, and dirt out of the fibers—elements referred to as "trash content." For Azerbaijan, which is smaller than Portugal or Pennsylvania and has more than twice the number of Azeris living outside the country than in,[10] cotton is a lifeline, the country's fourth largest export and the largest agricultural employer in the country. (Oil is 85 percent of Azerbaijan's export market.) For every one of the nearly half a million agricultural workers in the country, another eight to ten people live off income generated by the cotton crop.[11] In 2005, however, in spite of the rising cotton harvest, the market price plummeted to less than $1,200 a ton.[12]

The cotton industry in Azerbaijan in some ways has changed very little since the days of the Soviet empire. The scientific and agricultural institutes created by Russia have remained exactly as they were, for the most part. This communist-era hangover means there are way too many people on the payroll. The country, whose population is about seven million, has nearly a thousand agricultural scientists or agronomists, which is commendable, but would be even more commendable if there were something for them to do. Whereas before the scientists used to share research across state lines, today there is too much overlap, with only meager resources. Mechanical pickers purchased by the post-Stalin governments have long since broken down and been left as rusting hulks in far-off fields. Dependency on irrigation is rampant—87 percent of Azerbaijan's fields use irrigation—and the systems are deteriorating, with no money to fix them.

Indeed, when I visited the agricultural library in Baku, a room on the top floor of a building with only sputtering electricity and broken elevators, I found a single drawer housing the cotton archives, which consisted almost entirely of records written by hand on yellowing cardstock. Like the agronomists, the agricultural librarians seemed to have little to do. They ran out to greet me wearing bedroom slippers and spent much of their time hovering over my table and offering me tea. Occasionally, they would point out a book of interest: *Party Management for Developing Industry Production in Uzbekistan, Genetic Cotton Embryos and Changes for Future Generations, Hero Labourers of Cotton Women in World War II, Communist Party of Soviet Union as Organizer for Developing Cotton Production*. There wasn't a post-Soviet title in the drawer.

In October 2005, an American company named Valmont Industries out of Nebraska announced plans to invest in tiny, oil-rich Azerbaijan in a pilot program for cotton and sugar beets, the exact nature of which is apparently clandestine—likely something to do with irrigation. When I called Valmont, I spoke with a man named Jeff, who could neither confirm nor deny that the company was doing something with irrigation—even though it is their passion, according to the company Web site, which features many pictures of smiling men in hardhats atop great scaffolds of watering contraptions. A company in Azerbaijan named MKT, which owns a majority of the country's cotton gins (there are fourteen) announced that Valmont would build irrigation systems on more than 700 hectares of land and would offer MKT revolving credit of nearly three million U.S. dollars out of an "American" bank called ExImBank.[13] Jeff seemed to want to get off the phone quickly, and he could not say whether Valmont was working on cotton, or any crop, for that matter, or even that they had ever been to Azerbaijan, or knew where the country was. Valmont seemed a jittery bunch.

UNDER THIS UMBRELLA OF ECONOMIC DISENFRANCHISE-ment, Mehman goes to work each day and faces just one problem: because of the market price, the farmers aren't selling, and because no one is selling, there is no cotton to test, and nobody is interested in risking their precarious livelihood with a brand-new firm. "We have people, sunlight and water, but no markets," he shrugs. He says this as if he is offering up a mantra. *Sunlight, water, people, markets*. He says it sardonically, quilted in a sort of "crazy kids these days" vernacular. It makes him seem older than he is. His lab is competing for business with two other established labs, and many cotton gin owners promised him future business but have so far failed to provide any. "Inshallah," Mehman says. God willing, there will be cotton to test. He has worked, already, at the two testing competitors—SGS and Wakefield—and he believes cotton will eventually come. But this is where he begins to say, like every other person I met in the cotton industry of Azerbaijan, that even with the cotton, what Azerbaijan really needs is to get into apparel. That's where the real money is, turning raw cotton into fabric and fabric into garments. The more finished a product, the more money it brings in world trade. This, in fact, puts Azerbaijan in the same place as Africa—where cotton is grown, but then generally sent elsewhere to be woven into fabric or spun into thread. Without the ability to develop more finished products, poor countries can plan to remain poor.

What no one in Azerbaijan seemed to know much about, though, was how the quota system and the ending of the MFA was shifting everything. When I pointed out that markets were not a guarantee for a given commodity, I was most often met with the kind of gaze that opposing team members use on foes just before they crush them. There may not be a great market for raw cotton, the Azeris all seemed to believe, but creating the markets for finished products was simply a matter of getting Azerbaijan into the action. Dozens of countries around the world are terrified of what will happen to their own garment industries, and Azerbaijan just now wants to get into the game. Forget the global shifting—no one here, for the most part, had even *heard* of the quota system.

"Azerbaijan has nothing to lose by joining the textile market. I'm young and I have ideas," Mehman argued. "I have a PhD in cotton." He paused to fan a pad of sticky notes on his nearly empty desk. Outside, it was rainy and cold, a dark, gray day. His mobile phone jangled somberly and he picked it up, pondered it a moment, then set it back down and let it ring.

The fact that Mehman showed up at an office where there was very little to do did not seem odd to him. It was still his job, he maintained, even if his job offered no particular task at the moment. He was paid to have his mind and body at a certain specific place in the universe each day. It was neither his fault nor anything beyond a technicality that there was not work at this moment. It was one of the more obvious holdovers from Soviet times, when everyone held a job, no matter how necessary their actual labor might have been. His small, three-room office had four or five men just like Mehman; they showed up daily, sat on padded metal chairs drinking tea, and waited for something to happen. "Waiting is my job from nine A.M. until six P.M.," Mehman said.

Lately, Mehman's ideas during his long days of waiting have involved coffee more than cotton. How to make the perfect cup; how to serve the perfect cup with a slice of cheesecake at the perfect café, which Baku is desperately in need of, according to him. Coffee and cheesecake: the twin jewels of a cosmopolitan environment.

MEHMAN'S LAB WAS A HUMBLE AFFAIR. AWASH IN GRAY, it was a single room with a large cabinet on one wall and several very small pictures of cotton fields in plastic frames dwarfed by the size of the walls. The pictures were not from Azerbaijan because they had enormous picking machines in them and Azerbaijan does not have enormous picking machines. Mehman did not know where the pictures were from, but he liked them because they had cotton in them. Along one wall, a large whiteboard had a hand-drawn chart entitled "World Markets Production."

"That's just show for a magazine. They came here and took a picture. It's meaningless," he said. "The chart. Not the magazine."

Underneath a flimsy white lab coat, Mehman wore a button-down poly-blend peach shirt and corduroy jacket. He had on a silver necklace from a friend that he said was the Egyptian symbol for aspiration. He'd been talking coffee and cafés all morning. It was the first time I'd seen him without a tie configured into an oversized knot. A co-worker of his told me that for a long time, Mehman wore ties like cravats, half knotted and hanging.

A large black table stood in the middle of the room. The drab colors were necessary, Mehman said, because one mustn't have glare in a cotton testing room and black eliminates glare. In the cabinet, twenty-one black boxes of raw cotton were packed for use as comparison to Mehman's samples. They were labeled "AZ 1/3," "AZ 1/2," and so forth: Azeri: Grade One, Third Upgrade; Azeri: Grade One, Second Upgrade. The best-quality cotton is 1/1, and it goes down from there. "You need to feel cotton to see if it's perfect," Mehman said. "You can't just look and compare." Actually, Mehman is so good it *does* seem like he can just look and compare.

He took a wad of sample cotton from a large brown bag, held it under a sharp light, and compared it to the sample in one of the boxes. He kept several of these bags around for training his small staff. Then he measured out 300 grams by sight and put it inside something called a micronaire. The micronaire was the only item in the lab that could even be called a machine in that it had a power cord. A small apparatus with a glass cylinder measured the size of a single fiber of cotton. The life and use of a textile depends on the length and width of a *single* cotton fiber. Single cotton fibers, for the most part, are much less wide than single human hairs. "I brought commercial ideas back from Poland," Mehman said, watching the micronaire's gauge in front of him. He was referring to cheesecake, to coffee, to a café where friends could come and sit and talk for hours. He noted the fiber's thickness and turned the machine off. The room suddenly hushed.

Today, Mehman is by his own definition caught between the modern world of his generation and his profession, and the world of his family. His mother was both a chemist and a traditional wife and mother in charge of cooking and cleaning. His sisters, who are 25 and 26, both quit their jobs after they were married and as the eldest brother Mehman grew up with a certain amount of control over what they could and could not do. When they married, he approved their husbands. He calls himself "retro-modern" and alternates between the lessons of his religion and his father and the demands of his life as a link in a much larger global chain.

One morning when he was six, Mehman's mother came into his bedroom just as he woke. She insisted that he make his bed and clean his room before school. He had not yet responded when his grandmother, who'd overheard, stormed into the room and yelled not at Mehman but at his mother. "This is the woman's domain," he recalled her saying, "not the man's. *You* will clean his room." It was a pivotal scene for him, shifting power from mother to young son, woman to not-quite-man. He later called it "the moment he became a man." It was when he began to understand the difference between his father and mother, between himself and his sisters. He carries that responsibility with him wherever he goes.

The tension of being a retro-modern is always there, always around him. "Maybe it is a problem for me," he said. He quit drinking alcohol at the age of twenty-one, after six years of moderate usage, because he said one's mind must always be clear. He would pray five times a day—as his father does—if his work life permitted it, but the ablutions required before a Muslim can pray are not practical with an office career. Imagine, he laughed, "if someone went into the bathroom at my office and I was there washing my feet?"

At the same time, he has an open-mindedness not typically seen in the generation that preceded him or in the more doctrinaire believers of Islam. He follows Islam now as much as he can—during Ramadan, for example, he typically does not fast because it is too difficult to work and to go without nourishment—but he is not afraid to reflect upon the idea that some other religion could also be appealing. "If Islam did not work for me," he said, "of course, I would change. But right now, in my life, it fulfills me." Because Mehman is both a modern man and a traditionalist, he often abuts what might seem like paradoxes to outsiders. If his future wife wants to work, she can, but as a Muslim man, he cannot touch her money. He is expected to provide for his family and his house. But if she wants to buy things for the house with her money, she is welcome to do so. He expects her to cook and to clean, but if she needs help in these endeavors—if she has just given birth or gotten over an illness, for example—he will be more than happy to help. If she chooses to wear a headscarf, as many Azeri women do, that is okay, and if she chooses not to wear a headscarf, that is also okay. As a man, if he wants to yell at her it is his right, but she mustn't yell back, and in any case, it's best not for either of them to yell, but to talk. He would prefer, he says, never to yell at anyone. It is a life born of two worlds, two cultures, two economic systems, two generations, in which Mehman stands in constant, shifting balance.

"I found things in Poland I couldn't find here. Coffeehouses with music, cheesecake, a place to rest . . . But in this country," he smiled, seated in front of the silent micronaire, "when your father says 'This is black' and you know it is white, you say, 'Okay, Father. It is black.'"

III

WHITE GOLD AND
ALL-TEX QUICKIE

WHILE MUCH OF THE REST OF THE COTTON WORLD mechanizes, Azerbaijan, like all of Africa, still handpicks its cotton before sending it to a gin for processing. This is where Mehman comes in; he traverses the gins collecting samples for export—or at least he will when the market is ready and when he manages to get some contracts. Based on his assessment, cotton's end usage will often be decided and the price set. Azeri cotton is known to make, among other things, vast quantities of denim because denim as a general rule does not use high-quality cotton and Azerbaijan as a general and also as a specific rule does not produce high-quality cotton. It goes to numerous countries, including Russia and Turkey, and to parts of Europe and beyond. Textile companies tend to make thread and fabric with multiple types of cotton from multiple areas so that the material they create is consistent from week to week and month to month. It also means a single foot of thread might contain fibers from farms in Texas, Azerbaijan, India, Turkey, and Pakistan.

There are five main types of cotton, each with six varieties. The main types are short staple, medium staple, medium long staple, long staple, and extra long staple, all of which refer to the length of a single cotton fiber. Within these, there are a finite number of varieties with a seemingly infinite number of names: 133, 108-F, Kirgis-3, Namangan-77, Bukhara 6, Kirgyzskiy-3, ZETA 2, Sindos 80, Eva, Corina, Si Mian 2, Ejng, Zhong Mian 17, Van Mian 48, Gauzuncho 2 INTA, Gringo INTA, Deltapine 41 20/U0280, Cedix, Acala GC-510, CPSD Acala Maxxa, PIMA S-6 and S-7, Varalaxmi, Suvin, DCH 32, Hybrid 4, Shankar 4 and 6, 1007 Variety, Bengal Deshi, Jaydhar, Aleppo 40, Rakka 5, Deir 22, Boomi, Sahel, Varmin, Sicala V-2, Siokra V-15, Giza 45, 70, 76 75, 77, 80 and 83, Barakat, Shambat B, Nuba/Acrain, Hyperformer HS 23, All-Tex Max-9 and All-Tex Quickie, and Paymaster HS 26.[1]

These are only some of the names. Many more well-known and lesser-known monikers are cultivated around the world. You can sometimes decipher the origins based on name. Aleppo 40 comes from Greece. Bengal Deshi from India. Zhong Mian 17 from China. Gringo INTA from Latin America. All-Tex Quickie and Paymaster from the United States.

Unlike the United States, where cotton is a commodity managed almost entirely by ever-newer technologies on fields often owned by megalithic corporations using the latest machinery, Azerbaijan cotton is owned almost entirely by small-time farmers using their families or neighbors as laborers on plots five or ten hectares in size (a hectare is about 2.5 acres). In the 1970s, Azerbaijan grew heaps of cotton for the Soviet Union. But after the fall of the Soviet Union, the cotton industry, like all other industries, was privatized, and individual families suddenly found themselves in the curious and unsettling position of being landowners. Land was sometimes doled out according to family size, so some got as little as two hectares while others got ten or fifteen. Still others got nothing, or scraped together enough funds to rent land that had remained state-owned.[2] In the Soviet cotton industry, 1997 is generally agreed to be the Year Everything Changed, and so in less than a decade the enormous cotton fields of Communist collectivization became the tiny fields of capitalist individualism. In this way, Azerbaijan in general and cotton in particular is in its infancy, full of owners still trying to figure out their way in an emerging economic world where competition, suddenly, means this tiny country must contend with the likes of China and the United States, the world's two cotton leviathans.

In Azerbaijan, as in other places, cotton is called White Gold (another book at the agricultural library was *White Gold of a Hungry Plain*). In discussions of cotton-as-commodity here, it is linked with oil, the Black Gold of the country. Most exporters are in one or the other, though the country is also known for its carpets, its saffron, and its beluga caviar (someday it will also be known for its pomegranate molasses, if I have any say). Among the White Gold peddlers, MKT is the largest, with as much as 65 percent of the market share of exported cotton. With a worldwide reputation, MKT acts very much how a bank might in a country with longer roots of capitalism and self-sustenance. It offers credit where debt is a wholly new concept to the farmers. Azeri cotton farmers, like many of their international developing country counterparts, can't make enough to survive off their land. Many Azeri farmers are also taxi drivers, teachers, factory workers, or fishermen. Then again, many Azeri economists and professors are also taxi drivers or factory workers or fisherman. Unlike U.S. cotton farmers, who receive subsidies from the U.S. government and whom global trade laws generally favor, the Azeri farmers are on their own, trying to protect futures based on an uncertain present and getting used to the unbelievable idea that the state will not provide in times of trouble. The owner of MKT, Ikram Karimli, is alternately referred to as the Godfather of Cotton and the Cotton King. But he is an accidental king. He didn't get into cotton until 1997 and now he can't get out, even when the prices are what they are. "Everything in the world grows except cotton prices," he moaned one day. "Cotton is like an illness: once you get it, you can't get rid of it."

THE HISTORY OF MECHANIZATION, WHICH IS REALLY the history of cotton in America, has a long and often tragic past. Between the time of the Civil War and World War II, when mechanization was spurred on by a lack of human labor, more than 1,800 patents were granted for picking machines that wheezed, burbled, trampled, and blazed through fields. Men lost their hearts, their livelihoods, their humble fortunes, and even occasionally their loved ones from failed attempts at mechanizing the picking process.* It is no wonder that in Azerbaijan, which was on the road to mechanization in the 1970s and 1980s but was blindsided by the collapse of the Soviet Union, many believe that only human labor can pick cotton thoroughly and cleanly. Azeris say the quality of cotton depends upon the hand that picks it. Perhaps no one would argue with them in theory, but the difference between hand picking and machine picking is the difference of many hundreds of thousands of pounds every single day.

Cotton had long been one of the world's most labor-intensive crops. When slavery was abolished in the United States, farmers were forced to pay wages to their black field workers. The pay was abysmal, the work grueling, and the hours long and arduous. What Eli Whitney had done for the gin—a device that quickly separated cotton lint from cotton seeds—many dreamed of doing for the cotton harvest.[3]

Cotton is a devilishly difficult crop to mechanize. It grows differently according to climate and variety; some plants grow less than a meter, while others can sprout up to become trees. Some

---

*Historical rumor has it that Eli Whitney, of cotton gin fame, was himself caught up in a love triangle with his best friend's wife—or lover, depending upon your historical reference—a wealthy young widow. It was her friendship with local cotton plantation owners who brought the problem of separating seed from lint to Whitney's attention, and legend has it that he created a working model in just twenty-four hours. Some women get songs and poems; others get deseeders.

plants are thin and scrubby while others bush out wildly. Bolls vary in size and ripen at different times, while the pre-bloom pods are very fragile. As early as 1820, one mad Louisiana farmer imported a large brood of Brazilian monkeys with the misguided but charming aspiration of training them to pick cotton.

Many of the early harvesting prototypes were drawn by mule or horse, though generally speaking they used pneumatic extractors, electrical devices, chemical processes, threshers, or other available technologies of the day. One 1957 industry book illustrates hundreds of failed machines that resemble upright vacuum cleaners, train engines, or basket/conveyor contraptions atop a set of wheels. Some even looked like early cartoon drawings of multi-legged aliens or, if you're a child of the 1960s and 1970s, oversized hookahs. The first attempts all had some sort of suction device and ran either on gasoline or electricity. One determined man named L. C. Stuckenborg spent more than two decades attempting to make a viable machine for the open market with a set of electrically operated brushes attached to individual sucking tubes. He was said to have been inspired by a cow's bristly tongue, after he allegedly watched a cow work seeds from unplucked cotton bolls one afternoon. His life's passion, as it turned out, never worked well enough to produce and sell.

Other suggested methods involved cutting the entire cotton stalk and then separating out the lint—though this required machines of inordinate weight and expense. Still others thought of chemically treating the entire cotton plant and eliminating the need to separate the lint at all. (It is probably good that this last method was never perfected, as environmentalism was just a few decades around the corner.) Many experiments were made along these lines, including one machine that allegedly could turn the plant into wood pulp. Some other early models involved flanges that would "comb" the lint from its pod, but these tended to pick up dirt, leaves, burrs, small rodents, and anything else lingering nearby the cotton boll, which resulted in cotton full of trash.

One of the more influential designs at the time came from a

Scot named Angus Campbell, who would eventually spend nearly forty years on his cotton machine (and who may well have been the first to use "cotton picking" in a slanderous manner). Campbell's model used spindles to separate the lint from the pods; the spindles were rodlike structures that were stabbed into the cotton boll and then twisted upward to pull out the fiber, much like spaghetti twists around the tines of a fork. Though Campbell had some limited success on various tests he conducted in the field, the real conundrum was how to make a serrated spindle that was strong enough to pull out the cotton yet smooth enough to remove it with relative ease (think of removing hair from a bristle brush and you'll get some idea of the problem). This dilemma dogged inventors for decades. Over the next twenty years Campbell, who'd settled in Chicago, used his vacation time to travel to the cotton growing regions of the United States to test his latest models. Though he garnered some early media attention, it would be twenty-five years of work before he finally had a product he could offer on the market, and even then it was clunky and expensive. Farmers remained unconvinced, and were unwilling to spend significant amounts of money on Campbell's picker. And by this time fears of mass unemployment had gripped agricultural communities in the South. Tennessee at one point considered the possibility of enacting a law that would keep mechanical cotton pickers out of the state. The governor of Arkansas, Carl Bailey, declared that he was "scared of the human consequences"[4] of mechanization. Angus Campbell died in 1922, heartbroken and, presumably, a little bewildered. Eventually, after World War II, International Harvester, who'd bought the patents to Campbell's picker after his death, set up the company's first successful shop, outside Memphis, and made many, many mechanical pickers. Ironically, Campbell's model was the basis for the first commercial cotton picker on the market, which appeared in 1948.

Individual and corporate experimentation continued through much of the first half of the twentieth century. In early 1929, in a spectacular case of ill timing, International Harvester announced plans to introduce a trial machine only to watch the stock market crash *just* after their announcement and *just* before any of the machines could be field-tested. The company had begun experimenting with mechanized pickers in the early 1920s, but it would be nearly three decades before they'd garner any kind of success. A 1957 report quoted the company's chief engineer as saying of those decades, ". . . Many cotton farmers were skeptical. . . . At the end of every harvest season we returned with a little more expertise and a little more ridicule."[5]

Undoubtedly, the greatest story to emerge from the age of mechanization came from two brothers. John and Mack Rust grew up on a Texas cotton farm at the turn of the last century. Though Mack went on to become an electrical engineer, John was a laborer and sharecropper with an outsized sense of social responsibility and the humble education of correspondence courses taken in automotive engineering and mechanical drafting. He began to think of machines as a way to alleviate the arduous labor of cotton picking. As a child, he and his brother had picked cotton, so he spoke from the broken body of experience.

One night in bed, John recalled how the morning dew would make the cotton he picked stick to his fingers. Then he remembered how his grandmother used to make cotton stick to her spinning wheel by wetting the spindle first. John later told *Reader's Digest* magazine how he'd jumped out of bed and "found some absorbent cotton and a nail for testing. I licked the nail and twirled it in the cotton and found that it would work."[6]

Joined by his brother, John left his job in Kansas and set up shop in his sister's garage outside of Fort Worth, Texas. Their first field tests were with cotton stalks nailed into a plank and set in their sister's backyard, but by 1931 they'd invented the first machine that was able to pick an entire bale in a single day—perhaps four or five times what the average man could pick. Two years later, they introduced an improved version and two years after that, they announced that commercial production would begin.

The Rust brothers, however, being socially progressive, told farmers that rather than buy the machines outright, the brothers would lease them in exchange for promises from farmers to forgo the use of child labor, to pay a decent minimum wage, and to ensure maximum hours for soon-to-be underemployed field hands who were still needed to plant and weed. Predictably, the farmers refused. By 1937, the brothers conceded that leasing their machines wasn't feasible, and they instead vowed that they would sell them on the open market, but not take profits of more than ten times the salary of their lowest-paid employee. Remaining profits, the brothers decided, would be put into a foundation intended to help displaced farmers and encourage cooperative farming.

Still, no one bought their machines. It wasn't until World War II and the country's vast labor shortages that cotton farmers' attention turned toward mechanization. By then the Rust brothers had parted ways and sold off their shop equipment for parts in order to pay off debts. A designer named C. R. Hagen working for International Harvester eventually designed the first viable commercial picker based partly on the Rust brothers' innovations, and partly on thirty years of their own research and development, and by 1948 the plant in Tennessee devoted itself entirely to the production of mechanical pickers and built more than a thousand machines. Though the South took several postwar decades to mechanize fully, John Rust's patent royalties eventually paid off modestly, and by the time of his death, in 1954, he had realized his dream of setting up an educational and charitable foundation.

IV

THE LITTLE VOLCANOES WE CARRY

THREE HOURS SOUTHWEST OF MEHMAN'S BAKU LAB, cotton grows in abundance in a province called Bilasuvar. Driving south out of town, oil rigs dominate the view. It is impossible to escape the reality of oil in Azerbaijan. The smell permeates the city; there are so many oil pumps that houses have been built around some and as a result have enormous metal apparatuses in their suburban yards. In the spring of 2005, the United States and Europe celebrated Azerbaijan's new 2,000-mile pipeline, the world's longest, which runs from Baku west all the way through Georgia and Turkey, thereby effectively avoiding both Iran and Russia—two countries the United States, in particular, would prefer not to have an oil dependence on.

With the glittering Caspian Sea to the east and mountains to the west, Baku and its surrounds would be reminiscent of the beauty of southern California minus the development were it not for the skeletal pumps, platforms, and metal scaffolds—immense contrivances colloquially referred to as "nodding donkeys" by oilmen. Salt fields and mosques spread across the horizon, and along the roadsides men sell fresh-caught perch and sturgeon from bath-tubs, and pomegranates and apples from the trunks of their cars, so packed the red fruit bursts onto the gravel shoulders, and the back wheels of their Ladas are flattened by the weight. There are few traffic lights or kilometer markers or directional signs along the road, but flocks of ducks, herds of cows and sheep, and occa-sionally darting roadrunners immobilize travel. Small stands sell jars of strawberry jam and candied cherries, and every few miles a sink and faucet appear in the middle of a field, there for the needs of cleansing before prayer and one of the few reminders that this is, for all its Western influence, a Muslim country.

Billboards of President Heydar Aliyev, who died in 2003, and his son, Ilham Aliyev, who took over the family business in what he maintains was a free and fair democratic election, inundate the towns, villages, and roadsides of Azerbaijan. They are everywhere, smiling at the minions. One billboard shows the elder smiling benevolently at the son, who is deep in concentration, hand on chin in a parody of political gravitas. Sometimes the Caspian is Photoshopped in behind them, and sometimes it is Baku, or the countryside, as if each depiction illustrates well-developed social, political, and economic policies.

On a crisp October morning I went to Bilasuvar during the cotton-picking season, when field hands work fourteen- or six-teen-hour days, racing against the coming inclement weather. There are an astonishing nine climate zones in Azerbaijan, which means the country is forced to diversify agriculturally. By compar-ison, the United States has eleven climate zones and is perhaps twenty-five times the size. Much of what Azeris grow in the way of grains and fruits and vegetables is sold domestically for less than half the price of cotton, so even with world prices paltry, cotton is a better option than pomegranates or wheat.

The rain came early in 2005 to Bilasuvar and some of the cot-ton molded. Many harvests had to be dried out after the picking. This is accomplished by laying the cotton like a blanket across the earth until the moisture dissipates. Many people in the cotton industry told me about how the Soviet Union took college students out of class every fall to help pick cotton. They say this with a hint of irony: the labor was easier then, and cheaper. Under Stalin, much of the rural peasantry was organized into collective farms called *kolkhozy*. The average *kolkhoz* encompassed more than six thousand hectares with nearly five hundred families. Though there was great resistance—and the loss of great numbers of human lives in the *kolkhozy* formation—this system persisted until the collapse of the Soviet Union. The government leaders called the *kolkhoz* a self-governing cooperative made up of "volunteers," (though presumably the Russians, being the hilarious people they are and Stalin in particular coming from that long line of Georgian quipsters, meant volunteers tongue-in-cheek).* Today, most cotton pickers in Azerbaijan, many of whom spent their early years on a *kolkhoz*, receive roughly thirty cents a kilo, which means anywhere from US$75 to US$300 for the season, depending on how fast and furious they collect.

- -

THE VILLAGES OF BILASUVAR SURVIVE ON COTTON. THE majority of the country's cotton is grown here on farms owned by single families or by MKT. Vasif Iruizou is a cotton farmer of sorts, though he rarely sets foot in his own fields. Instead, he is one of MKT's directors, charged with running an enormous gin on the outskirts of the town of Bilasuvar (the province and town share the name). Ikram Karimli is his boss. Like Mehman, he comes from a family of cotton workers, though Vasif's family lived most of their lives on a *kolkhoz*. His twin sister, he says, was legendary for being able to pick 200 kilos of cotton in a day when the average was about 70—perhaps an exaggeration, since some slow

---

*Lenin believed that capitalist agriculture would be the downfall of family farms. A drive across rural America today makes it hard to argue with him.

workers might well pick this in half a season, but the point sticks. His mother worked in cotton fields, and his two brothers, and all three of his sisters; he studied to be an agronomist at university during the Soviet era. He is only partially joking when he says, "I was born in a cotton field."

But Vasif is no ordinary farmer or gin director. He is wildly rich, the most powerful man in the province, and perhaps even beyond. In addition to his 400 hectares of cotton, he owns 15 water buffalo and 40 horses. On days when he is particularly filled with melancholy, he goes and watches his horses; they are his favorite animal. It would be easy to distrust him, to lump him in with the country's hordes of corrupt officials—Azerbaijan is rated as one of the world's top ten most corrupt countries[1]—but Vasif's money brings to him a fitful reality. "In the Soviet times, we did not have money, but we had lives. Now, we can't think about life, only about money." He maintains an almost desperate desire to return to what he saw as a much more meaningful life under the old Soviet regime—even without his substantial fortune. "I am a little capitalist now and I leave my house every morning and see people with so many problems."

Vasif and I are sitting in the private room of an upscale Bilasuvar restaurant drinking wine and peach juice from crystal glasses. The restaurant is made up of about a dozen of these stand-alone "dining cabins." Like most Azeris, Vasif's concept of hospitality involves dropping whatever possible plans, deadlines, and responsibilities he may have had for the day and taking care of me and my translator—which includes an attempt to pay off my driver so that Vasif will be free to offer me the use of his gleaming black Mercedes for the day, or two days, or however long I want to stay. His driver turned out to be a man who assumes all manner of road clutter—be it a bus, a Lada, a flock of geese, or a herd of cows— will heed our venerated transport and leap from the path as we speed along two-lane country roads at 100 miles an hour. Indeed, I'm not entirely sure he is aware that brakes, in addition to being useful for a full stop, can affect an occasional decrease of velocity.

Vasif grabs hold of his wine glass as if it were a chicken neck; in his grasp, the entire stem disappears. There is nothing small about him, in stature or idea. He stands at nearly six foot four, with over-sized features, a large midsection, and hands that could palm a beach ball. He has a mouthful of golden teeth, an enormous and ready smile, and a prominence that suggests royalty. Sometimes, when he talks, he lowers his head and seems to look through his eyebrows on a particularly heady point. Other times, he sits with one elbow on the table, one hand clutching the arm of his chair, as if he might take flight. Like many Azeris, he requires his full upper body for conversation. On his forearm is a faded tattoo—one single letter in Russian. It stands for a past love, upon which he does not expound.

He plucks a raw tomato and a whole cucumber from one of nearly a dozen plates in front of us, then rips off a piece of Turkish bread. Spread along our table, which seats a dozen, are mutton, steak, and chicken kebabs, fresh basil, cilantro and dill, radishes, kidney, aubergine salad, sturgeon with pomegranate, feta cheese, chicken and rice soup, potato salad, salami, liver, orange slices, carrot salad, grapes, and sugared cherries. He barely eats anything. I pretty much don't stop eating. All the food in the world, it seems, is before him, and in all the times I dined with him—probably half a dozen—he never ate more than a few mouthfuls of food. "Everyone has two lives," he says. "The life which they want in their soul. And the life which they want for their families."

Vasif is forty-six and looks at least a decade older. He has always felt, he says, like a salmon swimming upstream. In the countryside, rules and customs are mandatory and anyone who does not follow them is significantly more scandalous than he would be in an urban environment, where diversity—even in a homogeneous culture—is much more common. "Even when I was small, my parents thought there was something different about me," he says. "They wanted me to wear the same clothing other kids wore, and participate in the same activities other kids did.

They wanted me to behave like everyone else in society. But I always had my own opinion."

By the time Vasif was an older youth, Leonid Brezhnev was in power and the rigidity of the Soviet system had slackened. Vasif was free, for the most part, to speak his mind, to formulate ideas and desires and tell his friends about them. "Freedom of the soul is the most important freedom," he says. "Yes, we did not have everything then, but it was better. I don't think there's such a huge difference between social systems, socialism and capitalism. A country's system does not matter; what matters is how people are treated. We have a different mentality to America; we just hope for the top to change things."

As a teenager, my only images of Russia involved women in subfusc headscarves and clunky black shoes waiting in bread lines, or black-suited religious heroes sneaking bibles beyond a colossal, country-sized wall of rusting steel. Vasif laughs at such images, says things may have been like that elsewhere, but not in Azerbaijan. "We heard bad things about America from time to time, but we never understood what was bad, what the *bad* felt like," he says. He chainsmokes West cigarettes. "Now we feel the bad along with the good.

"We don't believe an individual should be on his own; now we have only ourselves and our homes, but no community. Rich countries have human rights problems, too. People are trampled. We have riches, but no human rights. We are not part of anything bigger now."

It is an idea perhaps lost in the individuality of the West, in the pursuit of rising above the pack. Vasif understands that the world is moving in ways he doesn't like; what bothers him most, it seems, is the spirit of ennui that he feels has overtaken his peers, his neighbors, all those who, like him, have lived both sides of the political and economic spectrum and have grown, in his view, apathetic. "You can call me socialist, but I don't want the same for everyone. Just *enough* for everyone," he says. "I can't say I love my country because now I feel I have no motherland. A country should be like a family, everyone taking care of each other. You should have a relationship with your country. Who are we waiting for to bring art? To bring dignity? We must do it. We are here. Even Lenin used to say if you have a good economy, everything else begins to work."

He stands and closes the door to our private dining cabin, lowers his voice. He pours hot water into an empty wine glass to warm it, dumps the water into a glass at one of the other nine empty place settings, and refills it with wine. "We had Russian imperialism, now we have American. What's the difference?" Outside, roosters crow and the thin walls of our room tremor slightly from a nearby stereo blaring frenetic, treble-toned Azeri music. In a good wind, this room would never hold. "I believe great people have no nationality," Vasif says. "Only little people fight over borders." His own country is enmeshed in a civil war with Armenia over disputed territory in a region called Karabagh. Then he takes us away from all the losses he mourns in his own country and, without provocation, offers up a toast to the people of Iraq.

- -

AFTER LUNCH, VASIF AND HIS DRIVER TAKE ME TO Vasif's gin. It is an enormous expanse of five hectares with four or five bright blue buildings and half a dozen niveous glaciers of cotton covered by canvas tarps. When he was a child, Vasif and his siblings used to collect cotton and help take it to their local gin. By early evening, all the farmers would have brought their cotton and great hills of it covered the field. The kids would jump and play in it much like kids from the northern United States play in piles of leaves in October. The piles stretch more than 15 meters into the sky.

Vasif's gin can process 100 pounds of cotton in 24 hours—if the electricity doesn't fail, which it often does. During the three-month harvest there are 230 employees, but the rest of the year he has just a third of that. By the end of 2004, his factory had processed 12 tons of cotton. "Agriculture is our stomach," he says, citing a popular leitmotif in the country, "and oil is our blood." Farmers bring their daily crop to Vasif's gin, where it is weighed and tested by a gold-toothed woman named Sveta who has worked at this gin for twenty years. She has a friendly relationship with most of the farmers, who earn roughly US$300 for one ton of high-quality cotton, but she is keenly aware that her categorization will set their profits for the day. She wears embroidered slip-ons with red socks, a pinstriped pleated skirt, a brown and black Aztec sweater, and a sleeveless leather zip vest. During the harvest she works from 9:00 A.M. until 1:00 A.M.

Behind her there are ten brown paper bags of cotton like those in Mehman's lab to grade—samples from different farmers. The farmers hover at the doorway of her lab and sometimes watch over her shoulder. She pulls a handful of cotton from one bag and eyeballs it, saying, "Third quality." One farmer steps into the room and protests. She smiles but doesn't meet his pleading gaze and puts the cotton into a giant machine that resembles a waffle maker. Suddenly the room fills with a smell approximating microwave popcorn. When the machine stops, she says "Second quality; trash two." Another farmer sidles up and asks her to give him a grade of best quality. She tells him not to joke, despite the fact that he doesn't seem at all to be joking. Last night a farmer was so angry with her pronouncement that he drove his tractor away in a huff, the cotton still atop the wooden trailer attached in the back. She shrugged coyly, "He'll be back today." She was right. Another farmer comes and whispers to her; she doesn't answer, and he trails her from her desk to the testing table to the waffle-maker machine, all the while whispering earnestly. She smiles, never looks at him, and says after he leaves, "His arguing was like singing." Soft, but ineffectual.

Outside the lab, pipes that run from the cotton piles to the gin tower ten meters overhead. Cotton, with seeds skittering like rabbit pellets, passes through them. A woman in a babushka and ankle-length skirt punches a pitchfork into cotton piles and loads it batch by batch into the pipes, which suction the cotton up using voluminous amounts of air to dry and fluff it before it is dumped into an enormous drum, which further dries out any excess rain or dew or humidity. "Opening" the cotton in the next stage means basically cleaning it, removing dirt and leaves, sticks or other trash embedded in the fluff. Afterwards, the cotton goes through one of fifty ginning machines that clean it and separate the seeds. These days there are two kinds of gins. Saw gins, like the ones Vasif uses, utilize circular saws to separate the lint from the seeds and suck the lint through narrow openings too small for the seeds to fit through. Roller gins, on the other hand, are used for high-quality cotton and involve a coarse roller that pulls the cotton under a rotating bar through slits too small to allow seeds. Cotton emerges from the gin matted into a sort of longish, flat wad, like a large loaf of Middle Eastern flatbread. This is called a lap. From here, cotton is "carded," or arranged into parallel fibers. High-quality cotton is "combed" after the carding stage, which removes short staples and creates longer, uniform card slivers. This is what is meant on labels that say "combed cotton." Drawing is the next stage, which begins to twist the slivers of cotton, and then roving completes the operation of twisting and elongating the yarn, and winding it onto bobbins, where it will be nearly ready for dyeing and use in a fabric weave.

For Vasif's gin, though, the cotton is just cleaned and compressed into five-hundred-pound bales four and a half feet tall, which are held together with canvas and thick wire. A sample from each bale—the size of a couple of fistfuls—is retrieved and sent to the classer's office, where someone like Mehman measures the fiber characteristics of each bale for export against globally recognized general classifications. A single bale can make 325 pairs of jeans.[2] Vasif's phone rings every few seconds. He glances at it each time, but rarely answers. It is a land of ringing mobiles that go unanswered half the time, making me think that people prefer to be the finders rather than the found. He wears a suit and tie and looks elegant beside the oversized garb of the farmers and factory workers.

The ginning room is so torturously loud that we cannot hear ourselves even if we scream. It is so loud I hear it inside my own body, machines and engines roaring as we wander past, hands clapped to ears. Tufts of cotton float in the air, and many of the workers wear bandannas tied around their faces. If they were in the United States or Europe they would be wearing respirators, not only because of the cotton lint but also because of the chemicals used on cotton. In the United States, the medical community reports ten to twenty thousand chemical poisonings a year among agricultural workers. Here, workers would simply get sick, quit, and either get better or die.[3] Cotton sticks to our shoes and clothes, it dries out my eyes, and we all sneeze and sneeze.

An occupational hazard known as byssinosis, or brown lung disease, is often associated with cotton textile work. Caused by inhaling cotton dust—which contains pesticides, fungi, bacteria, and soil—byssinosis affects numerous workers still today, leaving them with chest pain, shortness of breath, and even severe respiratory problems. The campaign to recognize byssinosis in the United States eventually led to the creation of the Occupational Safety and Health Administration in 1971, but in many countries, including Azerbaijan, OSHA does not exist. Vasif's gin is new and so has relatively good ventilation, with high ceilings and open-air doors and walls, but another ginning factory I was in had been in operation since the 1930s. Both gins probably employed any number of candidates for byssinosis.

Vasif has turned this factory into one of MKT's most financially successful, and the region is the country's most important for cotton due, in no small part, to Vasif. Earlier, he told me the World Bank wanted Azerbaijan to sell only raw cotton and would subsidize this, but Vasif feels if the World Bank really wanted to help the country, it would give subsidies to start small factories to weave fabric or make finished garments.[4] Ready-made thread sells for nearly double cotton's price on the world market. Vasif and other Azeris who put forth this argument may never have heard of the quota system, but they all knew about the subsidies paid to U.S. cotton farmers by the American government. It's a system that has helped keep farms in America afloat since the 1930s and which infuriates farmers around the globe, from Burkina Faso to Uzbekistan to Brazil. "Basically, the World Bank doesn't want you to improve," Vasif says. "The more finished a product is, the more money it demands from the global market. The World Bank gives credit if we do what they want, but we lose our freedom." Recently, without the help of the World Bank or any other entity, Vasif took advantage of his freedom to build a medical clinic in the town so his employees, and other townspeople, could see doctors without having to go all the way to Baku.

THE PROBLEM WITH COTTON SUBSIDIES IS THAT THEY were created for a world we no longer inhabit, like the '57 Chevys that still occasionally ply the streets of Havana: they're painted nicely and they harken back to simpler days, but they also guzzle gas and hog the road. In 2004, the U.S. government spent 264 million on cotton subsidies, and every single dollar was, according to the World Trade Organization, illegal. The vast majority of those subsidies, which were created to keep the family farm in business, went to agribusiness or corporate farms—80 percent. Tandy Ogburn of North Carolina, whom I've never had the pleasure of meeting, received $5.00.[5] Tandy's neighbor, Ronald Olive, received $17.00.[6]

Globally—and it should be noted here that both the European Union and Japan pay substantial agricultural subsidies as well—the reason the world hates subsidies is that many believe they suppress the price of cotton by enabling the United States to sell its cotton to the world at below-market prices. Brazil claimed U.S. subsidies cost its farmers over $600 million in lost revenue in 2002 alone. The United States, on the other hand, says subsidies don't affect world prices by more than 2 percent.7 U.S. cotton often undermines the prices in someone's own backyard: For example, cotton from the States may sell cheaper in Mali than cotton *from* Mali. The Brazilians took a case against the United States to the WTO, won, and threatened sanctions. The Bush administration has repeatedly promised to reduce subsidies but has not acted. In November 2005, Congress announced that a certain portion of cotton subsidies would be eliminated, including much of the money that went for conservation, and to small farms. The wealthiest corporations remain relatively unaffected. Republican Senator Saxby Chambliss has agreed that "the next farm bill will have to be WTO compliant. We know what the parameters are and the next farm bill will have to look different in certain areas." *Look different?* Chambliss is the former chairman of the Senate Agricultural Committee; I will assume he meant the subsidies will eventually disappear, as opposed to getting folded into some future creative accounting or filing wordsmithery. Did I mention that he was from Georgia? They grow heaps of cotton there—in 2005 the state yielded over 2 million bales worth $504 million.8 Between 1995 and 2005 they received 1.4 billion in cotton subsidies.9

Within the United States, the problem with subsidies is that they are concentrated among a handful of recipients, like Allenberg Cotton (a division of Louis Dreyfus Corporation), Dunavant Enterprises,* Cargill Cotton, and Parkdale America, which have all received hundreds of millions in subsidy payments over the last decade and which sound very different to me when you say them out loud than, say, Mr. Ronald Olive. More than 60 percent of family farms received *no* subsidies. Between 1995 and 2005, the

---

*In Memphis, they are headquartered on New Getwell Road. Really. *New Getwell.*

United States paid more than $19 billion in cotton subsidies, and in spite of the WTO ruling against the subsidies, payments have increased every year since 1995.

One of the common arguments for maintaining subsidies is that U.S. labor prices and living costs far exceed those of South Asia, Africa, and Latin America. The subsidies protect our farms from volatile markets, where we are competing with people who make pennies an hour. War, famine, and natural disasters can be charted by looking at cotton crops (you could also just read history books, but it wouldn't be nearly as convoluted as determining historical movements by harvests). During World War I, for example, the cotton harvest in Russia fell nearly to nothing and then built up again in the 1920s. Likewise, during the American Civil War, the lack of cotton production in the South—from 4.5 million bales at the start to three hundred thousand by the end[10]—was so substantial it was called the Cotton Famine, and the Brits, for one, were on the verge of meltdown at the thought of having to return to woolen undergarments. Such catastrophic events compelled the creation of the U.S. farm subsidy programs.

The United States occasionally offers to repeal subsidies if other countries promise us greater access to their markets. Most countries are unwilling to promise this. There is a difference between *free* and *fair* trade, and the United States generally claims to make policies based on the former. To someone in the developing world who's searching daily for his family's next meal, however, the fair part is just as important as the free.

As early as 1985, when corporate farming began to boom, the USDA warned that eliminating subsidies would mean "supply and demand forces would determine farm returns" and that adopting this alternative "would have significant and far reaching impacts on farm operations, the agribusiness sector, the general economy and ultimately the world market." More than 60 percent of farm output in the mid-1980s came from the corporate-owned top 10 percent of producers. It is hard to argue that subsidies lead to anything other than overproduction and below-market prices.

VASIF TAKES ME DOWN A DIRT ROAD FULL OF SOFTBALL-sized rocks and scooped-out ruts. There is something he wants to show me. Along either side of us are endless cotton and wheat and alfalfa fields, and occasionally fields of five-foot sunflowers. The earth is dry and fissured, the sun beating through a cloudless October sky. In another month, icy winds will have overtaken these fields, and the hunched bodies of field workers—all women—will have disappeared for the season. The road curves sharply to the right, and at the curve there is an enormous fence with electrified razor wire circling the top. Shirtless Iranian men play a game of barefoot soccer while a couple of guards stand sentry with machine guns at the gate. It's difficult to reconcile the picture of Iranians as a nuclear threat when I see them whizzing around after a ball in a field of weeds, laughing their asses off.

"Stalin moved my family from here in 1937," Vasif says, climbing out of his Mercedes. He does not look at the border; it remains in his periphery, parallel to the position in which he stands. "Most of the Iranians on that side don't even speak Iranian," he says. "They are Azeris." Vasif's family ended up with the Russians, and many of today's Iranians in the north are actually second- and third-generation Azeris. It was fortune that kept his family on one side rather then the other. Fortune or misfortune and probably a little of both. Iran has the largest population of Azeris in the world—even greater than Azerbaijan itself. To Vasif, a border is a thing of wonderment, completely arbitrary and yet sacred in some geopolitical sense. A border does not and will never mean to me what it meant to him. I've crossed borders for most of my life and feel a moment of shame about this. I've long taken pride, like many, in my travels, but I've never had to fight for them. I've never had to live with boundaries. All around us are flat expanses of earth in every direction. Vasif hikes his leg up on the runner of the car and I ask him what compels him more: ocean or mountains.

He thinks about this for a little while. And then he says, "Fields."

There are people, of course, who work on one side or the other of the Iranian border and so cross it daily, but they are the exceptions, and Vasif, like most who lived the bulk of their lives under the Soviet Union, had never left its borders. He hadn't gone abroad until 1995, when he went on his first visit to France. "I didn't know how to talk to people," he says. The guards at the border have begun to eye us, a sleek Mercedes, doors open, engine running, and a tall, regal man facing the sun with his arms resting on the car door and the roof. "I didn't know their customs; I didn't know how to act."

Vasif likes that he lives within an hour of an international border, that there is a mystery beyond it which is at least in part reachable to him today. After France, he went to Germany and stayed in a Turkish area where he could speak the language and knew the customs, and in this way, he began to live a life where travel existed in some small measure, where borders were something not to hold you in but to propel you out, and welcome you back again.

Vasif also wanted to show me a sanatorium two hours north of the Iranian border. Popular during the summer months as a health resort, it had a natural hot springs that smelled like sulfur and individual soaking rooms in varying sizes. It was built up along the side of a mountain and had small wooden cabins surrounding it that families could rent for the day or for several days or as long as they needed. Unlike what most Westerners associate with sanatoriums, those in the former Soviet Union are natural health spas of a sort, places to relax and perhaps get help for chronic health conditions. Some sanatoriums have medical staff and are very exclusive; others, like this one, are available to anyone. The water in the springs and in the soaking rooms is so hot that steam rises from it and dissipates in the clear air. Save for three employees who were lounging on plastic chairs as we drove up, the place is devoid of customers. In Soviet times, Vasif remembers, hordes came here to relax and recuperate. "We used to bring packages of food for ourselves and for others," he says. What he means is that no one has time to go anymore. He seems inexplicably sad and wanders down the craggy hillside toward the clear stream that runs down from the mountain. He is alone, a little hunched over, and he looks toward the land, but not in awe. It is as if he is looking through it to see something on the other side, as if the mountain were an impediment to a view he'd once witnessed. He doesn't say anything for a long time.

Earlier in the day, as we were finishing lunch, he'd picked up a piece of bread from his plate and said, "I swear on this bread, I would never leave anyone without money. In 1990, people were crying in the streets. I helped as much as I could, but I could not change the situation. People lost their dignity." He seemed to grow angry, color blooming in his face. I think of this moment as I watch him at the mountain. The hot stream of water hisses and gurgles. The cloud cover is thick and oppressive, dampening everything below. With the bread still clutched in his hand, he had leaned forward, lowering his voice in a sort of growl. "I have a volcano inside me," he said.

Six months later, when I tried to find Vasif again, I learned that he had been admitted to an unknown sanatorium beyond the borders of his country for undisclosed reasons. He was completely unreachable to anyone.

V

THESE GALOSHES WERE
MADE FOR WALKING

GANIRA ALIYEV WORKS IN AN EIGHTEEN-WOMAN TEAM picking cotton in a field thirty minutes outside the town of Bilasuvar. She is thirty-three and has worked in a cotton field for seventeen years. She is a wisp of a woman, thin and strong like a band of steel, with hip bones prominent under her jeans. She laughs callously, a blend of ridicule and joviality intersecting in that laughter. Lines from the sun are just beginning to form around her eyes, and she has cheekbones reminiscent of Cate Blanchett. She wears jeans that are too short and patched in several places and faded; she wears red socks and ankle-high galoshes over her shoes, a blue polyester shirt with "London" printed across the chest, and a plaid wool headscarf that protects her from the sun and which she is constantly pulling forward or pushing back on her head. When she speaks, she looks around the field and rolls a ball of freshly picked cotton in her hand. She finds it difficult—and the difficulty is funny to watch—speaking and picking concurrently, so she often stops to talk. She has a reputation for being the slowest picker in the team and this seems to make the other women giggle rather than scowl at her. They are paid by what they pick individually rather than as a team, so technically speaking she is probably allowing them to make a little bit more money every single day.

Between her legs is a burlap bag tied with nylon cord around her waist. The bag dangles lightly at the beginning of her days and by the end it drags between her legs and a little behind her like a massive bladder. Her hands are enormous and thick with hardened skin and fingers that dwarf the tube of her copper lipstick, which she reapplies every hour or two. She has agreed to talk to me if I help her pick and if I wear her bag around my waist, thereby freeing her up to pick and wander. The bag is a third full and gets caught on branches as I walk down the long rows next to her. She pretty much laughs at me all day. It makes me think of a novel I stumbled upon, the 1942 children's classic *The Bobbsey Twins in the Land of Cotton*. The Bobbsey twins learn how to pick cotton on a plantation owned by their cousin's family, where they encounter such naturally-occurring phenomena as "singing Negroes." They sing because "they are happy," explains the kind-hearted Colonel Percy. He also explains that the field-workers, who are adorned in brightly colored clothes, enjoy their work because it is "healthful exercise" and because they like Colonel Percy. I feel pretty confident in assuming that the writer didn't spend much time working in a cotton field or she may have allotted the Bobbseys a vastly different lesson.

Ganira has worked in the same field for six years. "We make each other laugh [out here]," she says. "It's probably like a hairdresser's salon. We joke about men." Then she tells me a common adage in Azerbaijan, which I hear over and over again in versions that vary only slightly. "Men are the head of the house, and women are the neck. But the neck turns the head."

Picking cotton is women's work in Azerbaijan, as it is in many parts of the world. From the farmers to the classers to the gin owners, everyone in Azerbaijan found the idea of a man out in the fields harvesting the crop, a sack tied around his waist, wildly amusing. In some parts of the world, entire families pick together. Ganira believes that the earth is a woman and that picking cotton is one way for her and her fellow pickers to "stay in touch with the land." (It sounds to me like a supposition drawn up late one night by a misogynistic marketing firm in the employ of several grangers.)*

It is a brisk fall day in Bilasuvar. The only sound is the crackling of leaves under our feet. The cotton bolls we pick seem to suck the moisture from my skin. My hands, in little time, are both strangely numb and itchy. Sharp branches poke at my ankles and I can feel a mild ache beginning somewhere in my lower back. The leaves are brittle, brown on the edges and hanging half dead from their branches. Every once in a while I retrieve my notebook from my pocket under the guise of jotting down Ganira's words, but really it's to give my back a break. Apart from the physical drawbacks, it is incredibly, mind-numbingly boring. I'm grateful to have Ganira nearby to chat with (and also, of course, to blame).

"I know women," Ganira says. "Women all over the world are the same. Land is the heart of a woman."

I ask her why she believes this and she looks at me curiously, then laughs in a way that says I am asking a question as dumb as why humans need potatoes.

Cotton fields around the world have a silence, as if the cotton swallows up the sound. It is not a particularly beautiful sight to see vistas of cotton. Not like, say, golden wheat fields as they sway

---

*Slaves in America also had interesting beliefs about cotton, such as: "If cotton falls from the wagon on the way to the gin, the cotton will decrease in value." "If a baby is carried to a cotton field, it will grow up to be a cotton picker, and that person's children will be cotton pickers also." "Anyone who dreams of a cotton field will be compelled to pick cotton soon." "If cotton be left in the boll for a year, there will be a death in the family of the owner of the cotton." Another favorite: "If one starts picking cotton in a row and leaves it uncompleted to pick another row, one is in danger of being bitten by a snake." Though the historical record doesn't say it, I feel pretty confident that these "beliefs" originated not in the fields but in the fine dining halls of wealthy plantation owners.

gracefully under a setting sun. The ancient Egyptians and Greeks grew cotton plants for decorative purposes in the pre-Martha age and they are almost surely the only ones. Cotton is a straggly plant, with dry, brownish leaves and balls of dusty yellowish fluff springing forth sparsely from bare branches. It is impossible for me to look only at the aesthetics of a cotton field now without seeing the terrific consumerism and environmental catastrophe that it often represents.

In Azerbaijan everyone from Ganira to Mehman to the Ministry of Agriculture's office in Baku told me that cotton is good for the land and good for the soil. The farmer who owned the field Ganira worked told me how pure cotton was for the earth. It is not.

THOUGH COTTON MAKES UP ONLY ABOUT 3 PERCENT of our global agricultural land, it consumes nearly a quarter of the world's insecticides and 10 percent of the world's pesticides — more than any other crop — with cost estimates for the pesticides alone totaling $2.6 billion. The average pair of jeans carries three quarters of a pound of chemicals.[1] Pesticides, of course, allow for the global cotton empire by killing the pests that would otherwise kill the cotton; but in short order, these pests build up a resistance and farmers need ever-increasing amounts of chemicals to combat the insects. Most of the conventional cotton in the United States is genetically modified, or Bt, cotton — with insecticides contained inside the seeds. Much of the rest of the world, particularly developing countries, can't afford the proper safety equipment needed for chemical use, nor do they tend to understand the precautions, which are often written in English or another foreign language. Ten percent of fatalities in the agricultural sectors of developing countries come from pesticide poisoning.[2] In California, cotton is the third highest crop responsible for agricultural workers' illnesses. The West African nation Benin reported seven deaths from endosulfan poisoning, an organochlorine pesticide, in just one season, 1999–2000.[3] In India, more than seventeen thousand farmers committed suicide in 2003 alone.[4] The majority come from cotton-growing areas, where expensive pesticides and genetically modified seeds have not only *not* worked for farmers but have left them deeply in debt. The weapon of choice for these farmers tended not to be a gun, or a razor, or a rope. They swallowed the very pesticides that had, in one way or another, failed them. Pesticides kill more than sixty-seven million birds in the United States alone each year. The Aral Sea, once the world's fourth largest body of freshwater, lost eleven thousand square miles of water to irrigating Uzbekistan's cotton fields and is now so polluted from pesticides that it cannot support marine life.[5]

In 2006, the Environmental Protection Agency (EPA) completed a ten-year study of pesticides and ultimately banned one, leaving thirty-two others approved for use.[6] Malathion, for example, was given the green light in spite of the fact that it has been linked to cancer, fertility problems, and neurological disorders in developing brains, and despite the fact that excessive malathion spraying in 1995 led to significant secondary pest outbreaks and eventually cost Texas cotton farmers $150 million.[7] Aldicarb, phorate, methamidophos, and endosulfan were pesticides developed during World War I as toxic nerve agents; all are allowed under the EPA's ruling.[8] Another particularly nasty organophosphate called chlorpyriphos was also a World War I nerve gas and is used in more than a hundred registered products in the United States alone.[9] While the EPA has banned it from home use because of "its negative impact on children's health," it remains commonly used in agriculture.[10] Methyl parathion is also common, though it is listed as "extremely hazardous" and nineteen countries have banned it, while another forty-three make importing it illegal.[11] The United States is not one of them. Nor is China, which has become the world's biggest user of pesticides.

Much of the scientific community is not behind the EPA. More than nine thousand federal scientists and their colleagues have written to the EPA commissioner in response to the ruling, asking him to "prohibit organophosphates and several other pesticides." In their letter, which was made public to a number of newspapers across the United States, including the *Los Angeles Times* and the *New York Times*, they stated: "Our colleagues in the pesticide program feel besieged by political pressure exerted by agency officials perceived to be too closely aligned with the pesticide industry and former EPA officials now representing the pesticide and agricultural community. . . . [the EPA] is bending to political pressure and ignoring sound science."[12]

This does not preclude the United States from exporting products that it considers too harmful for use in American homes. The EPA has even ruled that banned pesticides are not prohibited from being imported into the United States so that they may be repackaged for export. Between 1997 and 2000 forty-five tons of pesticides that were either "severely restricted" or "forbidden" altogether were exported *every hour*, totaling roughly 3.2 billion pounds. More than half these products—many of which are classified as extremely hazardous by the World Heath Organization—were shipped to the developing world. According to the *International Journal of Occupational and Environmental Health*:

> The following is a description of the personal protective equipment recommended for workers applying aldicarb: "Coveralls over short-sleeved shirt and short pants; Waterproof gloves; Chemical-resistant footwear plus socks; Protective eyewear; Chemical-resistant apron when cleaning equipment, mixing, or loading; Chemical-resistant headgear for overhead exposure; Approved respirator." More than 70% of aldicarb exports were destined for developing countries . . . where it is extremely unlikely that this level of protection would be available to applicators.

This being said, however, the report also noted a dramatic reduction in the export of banned chemicals from the United

States since 2000, though high volumes of hazardous chemicals, unfortunately, continue to be exported.[13]

THESE DAYS, ORGANIC COTTON AND BIOENGINEERED cotton seem to be charting the apparel future. Turkey was the first country to certify organic cotton. Today, it is the world's leading grower, followed by India, then the United States and China. Still, less than one half of 1 percent of the cotton grown around the world today is organic, though the Organic Cotton Exchange claims that each year organic cotton fields grow by more than 20 percent. Consumer demand for organics has increased by 35 percent annually,[14] and dozens of brands now offer wholly organic cotton clothing lines, or blended lines—a concept first pioneered by Nike, which claims to be the leading buyer of organic cotton for apparel.[15] They're followed by Patagonia, which aims to have its clothing line made from 100 percent recycled or recyclable products by 2010. Wal-Mart also claims to be the world's biggest buyer of organic cotton.[16] (I toyed with the idea of searching for other leading world buyers of organic cotton but realized it was likely to be an activity infinitum.)

Organic cotton, however, is not necessarily a panacea for the dangers and destructiveness of conventional cotton. Yields from organic cotton tend to be smaller. Controlling weeds and pests is a significant problem normally handled by pesticides or defoliants and as a result there is more labor involved. Sometimes, boll weevil or other pest infestations produce lower grades of cotton, which can mean significantly lower revenues.[17] In order for a field to gain organic certification a transitional period of roughly three years is needed, which also means lost revenue, and once certification is granted, only organic products can be planted and harvested. Additionally, the associate director of Cotton Incorporated's agricultural research department claims that conventional lawns use more water than cotton and that people generally misinterpret "organic" as "sustainable." In particular, he says organic cotton requires "more labor, more land and more water," and that using manure as a fertilizer may well pose pollution problems for the environment that are every bit as serious as those from synthetic fertilizers.[18]

Advocates of organic cotton don't necessarily dispute these issues, but the point is to leave, perhaps, the lightest footprint possible on the earth. The Sustainable Cotton Project, based in California, has partnered with local growers and with the agricultural extension offices of the University of California at Santa Cruz and at Davis to offer a viable alternative to conventional farming in a program called BASIC. BASIC, which stands for Biological Agriculture Systems in Cotton, uses integrated pest management, or IPM, in its cotton fields. Essentially, it's a blitzkrieg: the good bugs against the bad bugs. Planting crops like alfalfa, sunflower, fennel, buckwheat, black-eyed peas, cilantro, corn, and others alongside cotton fields or in neighboring fields encourages beneficial pest populations who feed on boll weevils and other cotton-damaging insects. Weekly monitoring of cotton fields ensures that the soil has balanced nutrients along with the right levels of nice bugs. One farmer said he basically divided his field into thirds and grew grain, beans, and cotton, rotating the crops every season so as not to deplete the soil of nutrients.

The downside of the BASIC program, according to organic purists, is that it does not wholly eliminate the use of chemicals, particularly those used for defoliation. But overall, program administrators say it results in a 73 percent decrease in pesticide and insecticide use.[19] They believe that in the long run it surpasses organic in the amount of pesticides that can be reduced over greater volume, but that rather than an alternative to organic, BASIC should instead be seen as corollary.

Genetically engineered cotton seeds are another alternative to conventional pesticide spraying. They were first marketed by the worldwide agro-tech firm Monsanto. The company managed to integrate the insecticide right inside each seed, thereby eliminating the need to spray fields multiple times—also thereby cornering more than 90 percent of the genetically modified cotton seed market. Interestingly, their seeds came with a built-in resistance to the chemical glyphosate, which happened to be the active ingredient for Monsanto's best-selling herbicide, and which had been marketed by Monsanto as biodegradable and environmentally friendly, until the New York State attorney general sued them and won.[20]

Probably just coincidence.

Monsanto's Bt seed rose to dominance in the United States and around the world very quickly. But, like the Rust brothers, the company didn't want to "sell" their product. Unlike the Rust brothers, this was not because they had a predilection for social welfare. Monsanto insisted that farmers using their modified seeds sign a contract that the seeds were ostensibly "leased" and had to be repurchased each year. In other words, farmers could no longer use the logical, cost-effective methods they'd used for millennia—saving the seeds to replant new crops each year. Farmers would heretofore be obligated to buy new seeds each year.

Monsanto's seeds do indeed decrease the need for spraying, often by more than 50 percent, but many predict it won't take long for the bugs to catch on. The Pesticide Action Network does not support the use of these seeds, not only because they still contain insecticide but because they carry a significant risk of genetic contamination. At least one type of insect has already worked its way past the chemical wall, and at least one entomologist gives just a few years for bugs to adapt.[21] Monsanto's little miracle may well be nature's next victim.

- -

IN AZERBAIJAN, EVERY FARMER I SPOKE WITH WAS under the peculiar assumption that what grew in his fields was "organic" cotton. While it is probably true that Azeri farmers have a difficult time affording pesticides and insecticides, none of Azerbaijan's cotton is certified organic and much of what I saw had clearly been treated. The leaves were dying or falling from stalks—often a result of defoliants. The cotton bolls were spilling from their pods—organic cotton tends to hold together in its pod until it is picked. At the end of the day I spent picking cotton my hands were covered in a dusty film.

Drip irrigation, which waters crops in the Bilasuvar region, is possible from a shared agreement between the Azerbaijani and Iranian governments. It is fair to say that cotton fields are among the most schizophrenic of the agricultural community. They need lots of water and lots of sunlight, but not necessarily at the same time and not too much of either or they will drown and die or shrivel and die or never grow and therefore just die. But the effects of a lifetime of cotton are visible most clearly in the faces of the pickers who work alongside Ganira; they are stooped and aged, missing many of their teeth, and thin as stalks. They work hard and die young. Though they range in age from fifteen—the minimum working age in the country—to forty-five, they look many, many years older. Ganira's sister-in-law looks twenty or twenty-five years beyond her age.

Ganira and many of her countrymen, however, want not larger fields of cotton, but a textile factory that could give them year-round employment. They want security. "We get paid very little and we work very hard for this so-called freedom," she says, referring to the breakup of the former Soviet Union. "Freedom is good. We need freedom. But life was better then."

Ganira comes from an agricultural family. "All [of us] has something to do with soil," she says. Her brother drives the truck that takes them to the fields every day, and he also drives a tractor for a neighboring field. Her father worked in a *kolkhoz* in the Soviet era and he received four commendation medals. Besides her sister-in-law, her niece also works in her team picking cotton. Ganira, despite her hard work, is vibrant and curious and sarcastic. But she says her family are now "slaves to money." Like most Azeris I met, she harbored a rage toward Gorbachev (one translator I worked with warned the man had best never show his face in Baku). Hailed as a hero in the West, he is universally despised here. Ganira says her family never had much, but they didn't have to worry about paying for the house, and for an education, and for the doctor. "If you have money, then you are alive," she says. "And if you don't, then you die."

I do not last long in the field and I make Ganira look down-right brisk. In the end, I have earned her less than a dime for my efforts, according to my calculations. Later, we sit in her house having tea and jam. It is pale pink and built up from the ground so that chickens can live under the house. There are ten people living here and sharing two main sleeping areas. Her father, who is bedridden, lies on one of three mattresses on the floor in a back room and he coughs and coughs. Ganira cannot afford to send him to the hospital and no one knows what's wrong with him. It occurs to me that he may have brown lung disease.

At home, Ganira is transformed, as if her personality were a cape she wore only out in the fields. She puts sugar cubes in her mouth and sips her tea, allowing the cubes to disintegrate slowly. She says little, but allows Aliofsat, who is married to the sister of *her* sister-in-law, to speak for her. Aliofsat lives in the house with his wife and two daughters, and like everyone else I meet here, he talks about how hard life is now, how Russia still feels like a relative rather than a separate country, how worried he is about educating his daughters. While he talks, Ganira wears a thousand-yard stare in the general direction of the unpolished wood floor while her father wheezes and coughs. Later, I offer her a silk scarf from Asia, where I live, and she takes it with a melancholy smile, but seems disinterested. "I wanted a pair of jeans," she says. I feel like another in a long line of disappointments in her life, and the only thing I can think of when I walk away is that if I return in 20 years' time, I fear I will find her lying on the bed like her father, victim to the same unnamed fate.

VI

THE PARTICULAR DREAM
OF CHEESECAKE ENDS

I SEE MEHMAN AGAIN SIX MONTHS AFTER MY FIRST visit. When I walk into his office, one of his co-workers is head back, feet propped on desk, fast asleep. Startled, he nearly falls off his chair when I enter. Mehman has recently gotten his first contract with one of the country's fifteen or so gins. It is also one of the largest. He tests cotton fairly often now, but he seems to have lost his wry humor. His face is serious and he tells me he's tried a number of hobbies, including music and art, but found he didn't have the desire to devote much time to them; he reads books on philosophy and economics and tries to connect their ideas to his own life. His office building now has a coffee shop—Filicori Gourmet—where he can buy watery cappuccino and occasionally cheesecake, as well as Turkish coffee or banana coffee, whatever that is. The day I arrive, cotton is just beginning to grow in the fields of Bilasuvar. Mehman is dressed all in black and secures his wallet in the front waist of his pleated pants, which are belted tightly so that his wallet doesn't go sliding down his pant leg and end up at his ankle. A single gelled curl cascades down his forehead. His computer is off and the lights in the office are off, and small, neat piles of folders and binders cover the desk, along with three small flags: one from Azerbaijan, a Union Jack, and one from Intertek. "Work never ends," he sighs. The office phone has rung only once, and Mehman stared at it through five or six rings before he reluctantly picked it up, spoke for a few seconds, and hung up, then leaned back in his chair, smoking a Kent. "If waiting is your work," he says, logically, "then there is a lot of it." On the wall above his desk a New York Futures chart follows the price of cotton from December 2004 through December 2005, with one long sloping line downhill across the page. Prices are US$200 per ton lower than they were last time I was here.

A friend from Tanzania who is also "in cotton" e-mailed him earlier this morning, and Mehman's been laughing about it on and off for the past several hours. "He said, 'How's it going Down There?' Down? *Down There?*" Mehman says, cracking up. "Doesn't he know Azerbaijan is *up* from Tanzania? We are *UP!*" He laughs a minute longer and then says, "I'm very interested in Africa, because it is very close to nature." By contrast, Mehman is not very interested in America because "there is no history there." It's a common refrain from many people I've met who come from places where their central squares were built a thousand or more years ago. Outside, bricks and mortar career down from several floors above us, pieces of a city in a constant state of construction and reconstruction. Mehman reaches into the trash can, pulls out a wad of raw cotton, and uses it to open an ornery screw-top water bottle. He is reading a book by a writer named Napoleon Hill.

"If you have a bridge behind you, you can't reach your goals," he says. He tells me the book is called something like *Stinking Rich.** "What is life?" Mehman asks, inhaling deeply on another cigarette. Atop his computer, a tiny plastic bull of the sort found dangling from the necks of Spanish wine bottles sits angry and

---

*It's actually called *Think and Grow Rich*, but I like Mehman's title better.

stiff. "A bridge behind you is a known entity and your natural instinct is to go where it is easier. You must move forward. Forward is always harder. The philosophy of this book is to burn bridges so you can't retreat." He picks up a Casio calculator from his desk as an example. "This works well, but if it breaks, I'll get a better one," he says. "However, I cannot do that until this one breaks. See?" Mehman says that Hill advises his readers to write down exactly how much money they need to earn not just to live but to live free of worry, and it's got him to thinking about how. "In Azerbaijan, everyone starts to think about how much money they'll need from age fourteen, more or less. Life is very expensive." Mehman figures he needs about US$25,000 to buy a house in the city and maybe US$2,000 to live each month without worry, and so that neither his father nor his future wife need work. Oil and its attendant well-paid expatriate employees have driven prices way up in Baku, and inflation in the country hovers around 14 percent.

When I ask about his coffee/cheesecake shop, he shrugs and gives me a serious look. "That particular dream is over. It cannot be realized," he tells me. "I think more realistically now."

Mehman has just come from a cotton conference in Uzbekistan, where it was confirmed that China is now both the world's leading exporter and the world's leading importer of cotton. Three hundred and seventy men, according to Mehman, sat around for three days wringing their hands over the falling price of cotton. The subjects seemed to revolve around a single theme: Why are prices so low? What's to be done about the low prices? Will the prices rise? How long should farmers hold on to their stocks hoping for better prices? No one had any ideas, he says. But I know he is being polite because I'm an American. There is never a meeting about cotton these days without talk of developed world subsidies and their effect on the global market.

Later, Mehman takes me to the gin he's been testing for. It's an hour and a half outside of Baku, and along the way we pass a mountain range that looks a little like a wet compacted sand dune. It is actually shale, made from mud that lies on the bottom of the vast sea that once covered the area, and the mountain is marbled with the red and white stripes of eroded shale formations. They're called the Candy Cane Mountains colloquially and invoke the landscapes I used to make at summer camp by layering multicolored sand inside baby food jars. As we drive, Mehman tells me about dancing. He has begun to study the Caucasus dances, or *lezginka*, and calls himself an Oriental dancer. Last month he was part of a troupe that performed at the cultural center. The dances are reminiscent of Russian folk dances, where the trunk of the body is held still but the legs and arms jut in and out from the elbow or knee. It is both wholly controlled and frenetic, the movement of the body at odds with the demands of the music. The dancers carry a proud stature on stage with them, an almost physiological attempt to be expansive. On the screen of his mobile phone Mehman showed me a video of himself performing at the cultural center. In it, his face is stern and his limbs move so quickly that tracers follow behind them. Later, his teacher told him his biggest mistake was not having emotion on his face. "I need to have fire in my eyes," he says.

We arrive at CTS Agro, where the recent harvest is held in bales in a three-story open-air warehouse. A nodding donkey churns in the yard while a handful of men in stocking feet clean train cars next to the warehouse. International standards for cotton include things like making sure transport will not add trash or water to processed cotton. Cotton is hydrophilic and gets wet easily, so that the same properties that make it ideal in bathrooms across the world also make transport on the open road less than ideal. Mehman greets the men from CTS Agro with a handshake and a single nod. Some of his co-workers are already there and they will spend several days at the gin collecting samples to bring back to the lab. Just before he walks away, he looks at me a moment, then says, "Be careful of snakes. They hide in the bales." I am not a great enthusiast of snakes.

Mehman's co-worker, who is also named Mehman and who

also warns me about snakes, takes a straight razor from his shirt pocket and unceremoniously cuts a small sliver into a canvas-covered bale. I half expect a copperhead to spring hissing from the tear, but instead cotton spills out the hole. A bale weighs four to five hundred pounds and the cotton is packed so tightly it is hard as a ream of paper. Men who deal with bales often have hunched backs by the time they are in their thirties. A forklift can only get the bales as far as the train doors. From there they must be hand-carried. Mehman takes a pinch of cotton and pulls it several times until he has a small one-inch uniform staple. Two pounds of raw cotton can make about two yards of denim, or about one pair of jeans (less for Americans since we're generally fatter than the rest of the world). "One and three-thirty-seconds of an inch," he says, referring to the length of a cotton staple. This crop is mediocre. The cotton is discolored, perhaps singed by a drying machine, and has a high trash content. It won't garner much of a price in the market.

In addition to collecting samples and inspecting the train cars, Mehman's group will also oversee the loading of bales onto the transport, checking the metal bands around each bale (there can't be more than two broken), the canvas holding the bales together (if the canvas is ripped, women in white lab coats appear with six-inch needles and darn them by hand in the warehouse), and the weight in kilos. Once they finish, they will bring the cotton samples back to the lab in brown paper sacks about the size of two grocery bags for further testing, and once it's been approved and categorized officially, they will ultimately grant an inspection certificate so that it can be sold internationally.

- -

DURING THIS VISIT WITH MEHMAN, I CALL VASIF AGAIN and again, but his mobile is turned off. Mehman knows Vasif by reputation and even joins in the search. Weeks pass. After a while,

I drive down to Bilasuvar and to Vasif's gin and learn that he is no longer running it, that he has been transferred to a different region two or three hours away. No one knows why or how to get hold of him. On my way out of the gin, a man recognizes me and he wanders over, surreptitiously handing my driver a phone number. He walks away silently. It is the number of Vasif's driver.

The driver meets my translator and me for lunch late in the day and says Vasif had health problems and needed to rest. He suffered from bronchitis and stomach ailments almost surely brought on by stress and a profligate love of tobacco. No one can contact him; not even his family. But the driver says Vasif will return that Saturday evening and can meet me in Baku. He would not want to have missed me, I am told, and I am leaving two days later.

We finally meet again at a restaurant in Baku's Old Town, housed inside a caravanserai—in this case an old camel stop from about the fifteenth century. It is made of pale sandstone and has carpets hanging from the walls. I had been trying to find him for a month and I realize, when he appears, that I had been profoundly worried about him.

Everything has changed. He was moved to a gin in another region, ostensibly to make it as successful for MKT as the one in Bilasuvar, but he'd also been moved, he believed, because he was too popular with the townspeople. "The goal was to take me away from the eyes of the people," he says. He'd joined a progressive political party and he felt he was threatening to an older establishment who'd consolidated their power in the immediate chaos of the Soviet fallout. "People fear change," he tells me. "They've had change already." He has decided to run for local office in Bilasuvar because he has long been interested and because he believes he can ignite something positive around him.

He reminds me of how the French fought for the lives and country they have now during the French Revolution. "Even as they were dying, they said, 'You can kill me, but the seeds around me will grow,' " Vasif says, taking a small sip of his wine. He still barely eats, and he has lost weight. "The French were true to their ideals till the end."

The Maiden's Tower, Baku's most famous building, looms above, with sparrows or bats—I can't tell which in the night sky—zipping around the air space over us. A striking eight-story stone fortress which from above appears as a giant comma, no one knows exactly who built it or why. Thought to be from the pre-Islamic era, some historians argue it was a military fortress (for a teensy army, I'd guess). Others attribute it to the fire-worshipping Zoroastrians, who devoted each of the first seven floors to one of their seven gods (the eighth story was added later). The story I like best, though, is that a king who wanted to marry his own daughter built it. She had asserted that only a refuge of her own would make her acquiesce to her father's amorous advances, and he ordered its construction. Higher, she demanded as each level was added. Higher and higher. After the eighth level, she climbed to the pinnacle and threw herself into the Caspian Sea below.

Vasif is heartened by the fact that in Bilasuvar things seem to be slowly evolving. Privatization was the most dramatic change in the region, and even though people were given land, Vasif feels they really didn't have a sense of ownership until the past year or so. He also is confident that despite his posting to another region, his home remains in Bilasuvar (along with his family) and he will not be forgotten. If the people there vote at all, they will vote for him. He doesn't say this outright, but I can tell he feels it. He grins self-assuredly and settles into his thoughts. I know now that questions for him don't elicit nearly such expansive discourse as when he is allowed to range freely, and we sit together quietly for a few minutes and watch the swooping black creatures criss-crossing above us. I think of that girl throwing herself into the Caspian, and what it takes to feel that sort of desperation around you.

After we pay the restaurant bill, but just before we say goodbye, Vasif threads his fingers together and says, "You can't keep principles like we have now: *Follow me and I'll give you bread; don't follow me and you will die.* If we close our doors, we will die. Just like anyone else."

ON MY FINAL NIGHT IN BAKU, MEHMAN TAKES ME TO a restaurant and dance club called Beirut where he goes to practice *lezginka* with his friends. The other Mehman from his office is there, along with a girl dressed all in white and visiting from Dagestan, and two other friends of the Mehmans'. A waiter serves black currant juice and we sit at a table six feet from the deejay, though Mehman phones in his song requests rather than walking over to the booth. He has programmed his phone to speak to him now: "Excuse me, Boss. You have a text message." It sounds like the same techno voice that spoke to David Hasselhoff from the console of KITT in *Knight Rider*.

As on every day I've seen him during this trip, Mehman is dressed all in black. Gone are the peach or white shirts he used to wear, though he also says black is a bad color for the soul. His mother won't wear black headscarves. "Even me," he says, "I am in black and do not feel so good." Since his clothes pain him in some way and he continues to wear them, I decide to refrain from asking him the obvious question.

"This is the most difficult dance," Mehman says of *lezginka*, because "there is simultaneous movement of your limbs. When your legs move left and your arms move right, it is very difficult."

A belly dancer in gold lamé emerges, stopping at tables full of men and sometimes hitting them with her hips. A Western woman several tables away from us rolls her eyes and the judgment is quick and fierce; she frowns and turns away. Somehow I feel sorry for the belly dancer, who is sweating profusely. She earns little or no money in tips that I can see. "Frankly speaking," Mehman says, "I don't like these dances. To earn money makes this beautiful dance worse. Before, you had to work to see a woman's body. For me, this is the reason the beach is not so interesting. You see too much." The music stops for a minute and Mehman slumps in his seat. "Oh, now my brain can relax," he says.

We are sitting on a low-slung squishy couch, the table roughly chest high, making me feel like an Alice in Wonderland character. Each table sits under a dramatic brick archway, which only adds to the effect. Between the tables, a rectangle of open space serves as a makeshift dance floor once the belly dancer has left, but most people just sit at their tables and watch. The brick and clay walls have carvings made to look like ancient bas-reliefs, and low lights glow on the tables and in sconces. The deejay plays old American tunes by the Beatles and Elvis Presley and Meatloaf and our whole table gets up to dance, though the songs don't ever finish, but instead bleed into one another so we end up with one long version of "Blue Suede Bye Bye Miss American Wake Up Little Twist Submarine." Mehman and his friends dance in their socks and watch to see what special American-style moves I might break out (I wonder at which point they were disappointed). Tables full of expats and locals watch us, but we are the only ones on the dance floor, we six, and remarkably, I feel more like an insider with this small minority, as if our gawkers were the ones really missing out.

We sit down after a few minutes, and the girl from Dagestan says she is a psychology student and has a quiz for us. She asks me to picture a house and describe it with animals. I offer dogs and horses and geckos, a large, cottagey-feeling place on a lake somewhere. She asks me if the horse is inside or outside. "Outside," I say. "In the shade." She tells me that my horse represents my partner (he was relieved to hear he'd been put in the shade). I tell her her test seems fundamentally flawed since no one, even metaphorically, is likely to put a horse in the house.

"A Georgian would," Mehman says. Then he picks up his mobile and phones the deejay. From the corner of my eye, I see the deejay answer. If he and Mehman both reached out, their fingertips could probably touch. They chat for a couple of seconds.

Several minutes later, Mehman is on the dance floor with the

Dagestani girl doing the *lezginka*. His friends join them. He is by far the best dancer of them all. The girls are supposed to be graceful and the boys are supposed to show strength and dignity and Mehman embodies this. He counts silently with his lips moving and concentrates on every movement he makes. The others form a circle around him and he preens, arms darting out at elbows, legs at knees, like he is a marionette, controlled by hidden maestros. The boys try to outdo each other in solos, and then after a while they all dance together as a group. Mehman and the Dagestani girl are the antithesis of each other, male and female, black and white, supple and severe. Here, dance does what drink cannot. It allows them to laugh together, to flirt, to stand an inch away and still not touch. It allows them a freedom, while still maintaining the rules.

Once they start, they never stop dancing. With their shoes off, they dance and dance, a Monday night turned Saturday. Their motions are without intimidation; they allow one another the alternating limelight. They cheer for each other, moving as if they are capable of stamping the very foundations into the ground underneath their feet.

PART TWO

VII

GOD'S NECTAR AND OTHER DENIM
YOU DON'T KNOW YOU WEAR

ON A FROSTY FEBRUARY AFTERNOON IN THE PLEBEIAN workroom of a northern Italian fabric R&D office outside Bergamo, the mood was quiet. Outside, winter fog nearly eclipsed Roncola Mountain in the Alps. Far more people than this office typically saw at once wandered in and out. They carried swatches of denim in blue, gray, ocher, pink. They brought color cards, market brochures, style specification sheets, or simply greetings. They were mostly the sales force of the company, usually spread out in more than twenty countries and five continents, brought partially together in anticipation of the season's fabric shows, the most important of which was just a week away in Paris, with a smaller show in Milan in the days beforehand. The company, Legler, is one of Italy's oldest textile firms, and though the shows had been everyone's focus for months, the final-day preparations on this Friday afternoon were strangely quiet. Just a few last decisions about fabrics to include and booth logistics had to be made. Each year the office unveils at least 110 new fabrics, more than half of them denim; the new fabrics are 40 percent of their entire annual collection, additions to the longtime steady sellers. The head designer, Pascal Russo,[1] has always worked twelve- or fourteen-hour days leading up to the shows, but this year he was surprised to find he had time on his hands. I sat with him in the conference room talking while his employees wandered in to ask questions every so often. He was relaxed, leaning back in a leather chair with his legs crossed, in jeans and a powder-blue sweater. Pascal had been to these shows dozens of times and approached them with the same level of quiet confidence that an aging rock star takes the stage: with an almost distracted perfection. For Pascal, there were more important things to worry over.

News that Armani, Gucci, and Prada were moving their manufacturing to Asia had shaken the industry in Italy, Pascal said. The country's high-end designer manufacturing has undergone such a profound change in recent years that it seems traumatized, enmeshed in a cultural state of disbelief at what is certainly its inevitable end. Pascal tried to articulate the effect of losing what has long defined you as a people. "Gucci, Armani, Prada, these are Italian," he said. The word *Italian* emerged as an appeal, as if he was stating not what they were, but what he yearned for them to be. Or, in this case, to return to. A day earlier Pascal's boss, Sergio, had called such moves "unacceptable for the Italian mentality."

Pascal keeps his hair cropped, and shards of silver alight from it in bright sunlight. Most days, he wears raw denim, cuffed at the hems, and pullover sweaters, often in variations of blue. He has a dry sense of humor that emerges in slow, volcanic waves. One day, during the following week's Milan fabric show, after an hour-long meeting with several Korean clients who neither laughed nor smiled a single time, Pascal claimed he understood their stoicism. "Tough life," he said, shaking his head. "I think they do not have salami."

Quiet and habitual by nature, Pascal appreciates ironic humor and the grandeur of global geography. He's crossed borders and lived near borders all his life. When something strikes him as

funny, he often does not laugh, but instead says, "This is funny."
Theez eez funny. When something strikes him as wrong—a political
situation, a rising crime rate, or a dearth of cheese or chocolate—
he will say, "It is a pity." Often he describes unexpected places or
things or events as "beautiful": the opening ceremony of the Turin
Olympics, a juicer that his wife bought, the belongings found by
an archeologist of an early hominid, the leather chairs in the conference room, paintings by Chagall, Klimt, Modigliani. They were
all, in his vernacular and his aesthetic, "beautiful." Such pro-
nouncements lend a sort of profound authenticity to the things he
incorporates into his orbit. Juicers, in general, are typically not
beloved for their aesthetic appeal, not at least beyond the moment
of purchase, so the fact that he finds the one in his kitchen
lovely is charming and impassioned and a little bit kooky, even
to him. Also beautiful is just about anything bearing a "Made in
Italy" label, which means Pascal's world gets slightly less beautiful
each day.

Even while Americans and Britons were clamoring for cheap
Chinese-sourced goods a decade or more ago, Italians still had the
majority of their consumer products made in their own country—
particularly when it came to fashion. This is no longer the case for
Italians, particularly in 2005 and 2006. Imports of denim jeans
rose by 260 percent between 2000 and 2005.[2] The sheer number
of "Made in China" labels hanging from the racks in stores from
Milan to the Marché had the entire design and manufacturing
industry in cultural and psychological chaos. Italians had long
taken pride in those things they designed and made.

Pascal absently doodled fabric patterns—weaves and prints—
on a blank sheet of white paper as we spoke. Thirty-eight years old
now, he has worked at Legler since 1990; it was his first job after
college, and now he manages the entire research and design
department. Armani and Prada were meant to be the stalwarts;
when everyone else had gone, they would still be there. It had
always been believed that no one but an Italian could make Italian
clothes, in the same way Italians are loath to accept the fact that

anyone other than an Italian can make an Italian shoe. "To see 'Made in China' on them is . . . ," Pascal struggled with the right words, "It is a pity. 'Made in Italy.' This still means something."*

PASCAL SAID ITALY BEGAN TO FEEL THE CONSEQUENCES of the lifting of the quota system almost immediately. Exports from Italy fell and imports rose. Given that the safeguards put on certain Chinese goods in 2005 were meant to protect countries like Italy from feeling too strongly the onslaught of cheap Chinese goods, that is, from feeling exactly like what they were feeling, this didn't bode well. Of course, many of the safeguards covered items that Italian design and manufacturing wasn't particularly bothered about, like socks or men's cotton trousers or T-shirts. Italy, as the purveyor of global couture and home to many of the world's most influential fashion houses, is neither mass-market consumer goods nor generic designer apparel. Because it is neither, whatever feeble and temporary protections in the way of trade safeguards that existed for much of the rest of the world offered little help to Italy. Pascal believed that not only was the country feeling the end of the quotas, but Legler specifically had begun to feel the effects in preparing their latest collection. "We must all work hard," Pascal said. "And we must all be worried." For all of them, 2008 loomed as a sort of death knell.

Part of the problem, I was told again and again, was tremendous overproduction. A Legler executive named Bruno Schilling said the industry needed restructuring and less production. Of course, he sighed, "to produce less, you need [fewer] people.

---

*Ironically, it may mean more in China, since the country has gotten so good at fakes that even the "Made in Italy" labels can be fabricated. China may have the world's manufacturing in its pocket, but Italy still has the reputation.

Everyone is free to produce or not to produce. That's a free market. But you can't do it without disruption." He talked about the English company Marks & Spencer, how everything they made used to come only from the UK. Now, he said, "no one in the UK cares where M & S makes their textiles. I'm sure it'll go the same way in Italy." The difference, of course, is that even he admitted that textiles are profoundly fused into the country's cultural psyche. "Italy IS textiles," he said.

Sergio said sometimes a company had to sell fabric without a profit to keep volume these days. "Volumes plummeted quicker than we expected," he told me. We were sitting in Legler's conference room, discussing strategies for the Milan and Paris trade shows. "In 2005, compared to 2004, denim imports [to the European Union] increased something like two thousand percent," he said.3 He insisted, though, that while manufacturing may disappear, styling would always remain in Italy. "Italy was one of the last countries to understand globalization and change. Finland and Sweden lost their manufacturing long ago, but they moved to technology, like Nokia. H&M also understood [globalization]," he said. He was wearing a pale blue sweater and red glasses around his neck. A second pair of glasses occupied his hands. He seemed resigned. "In Italy we are the tail of Europe because we still focus on manufacturing. On hardware."

Perhaps the most profound effect, though, was not the downturn in sales for companies like Legler and its competitors, but the inevitable layoffs. The main office for Legler had the uncomfortable task of cutting sixty jobs by the end of 2006, Pascal said. That's roughly 10 percent of the entire work force. Pascal was supposed to cut two from his department. It would mean a 30 percent drop in employment for his department, and it frankly didn't make sense to him. "If we could do the job with only four, why not have four all these years?" he asked. "From six to four? It's not possible." Italy is unique in that people tend to stay in their jobs; the newest employee on Pascal's team had been there nine years; the oldest, nearly thirty. Partly it is the Italian culture to stay at a job for one's entire life. If you had job security, then you stayed. But these days, it was also a lack of viable options.

But it also wasn't possible that things could stay as they were. In Italy, technical considerations were important in deciding who stayed and who went, but also taken into account were family situations and length of employment. Even if a five-year employee was the best in the department, she could still lose her job to a mediocre worker with a family who'd been there thirty years. It was the sort of civil law that seemed fair and maybe even progressive to someone staring down forced retirement, but in reality created multifarious real-life issues of fairness and egalitarianism.

- -

PASCAL'S MAIN TASK IS TO DESIGN DENIM. LEGLER takes raw, ginned cotton and makes Pascal's designs, which are then sold to brand designers all over the world. It is an increasingly complicated endeavor. There are methods of weaving, combinations and weights of fabric, many dozens of laundering techniques that all create different effects and looks. Pascal's dyeing lab has more than ten thousand colors. He studies slub effects in jeans, where the white threads are uneven within the weave and stand out against the blue. According to Pascal, slubs are particularly popular in America.* The average customers, he told me, see jeans in this order: color, feel, fit. Pascal sees jeans this way: color, treatment (like abrasions or stonewashing), feel. Style and fit are left to the designers. Laundering technique is of paramount importance, however. Pumice stones of varied sizes create different looks.

---

*One afternoon, I asked him what jeans Americans like. I was standing across from him, separated by a waist-high table in his office. Slub yarns, he told me, with a boot cut and stretch jeans. "American women always must have stretch," he said. When I looked down at my own jeans, I saw this: slub yarns, boot cut, stretch.

They also eat away at the metal walls inside industrial washers, which quickly shrink from seven to three millimeters thick before they are replaced. Diamond paper, glasspaper—both of which work much like different grades of sandpaper—and carbonium brushing all put a shine on fabric. Small plastic tags of the sort usually used to hold price tags on store garments act as laundering staples, holding small gathers of fabric around pockets and hips and seams, while the pants are dyed or bleached or otherwise color-treated. When the tags are snipped, they create paths of uneven color on the pants, in the same way sunlight honeycombs through a swimming pool.

Pascal and Ariana Contadino,[4] another manager in the department and also Pascal's wife, do not consider themselves artists. More accurately, they are textile technicians for some of the world's best-known retailers: Diesel, Benetton, Max Mara, Marks & Spencer, Earnest Sewn, Replay, Gap, and Levi's. The American sales agent for Legler's fabric often introduced Pascal as the "brain" of Legler—a claim that left him incredulous. "Really?" he laughed, shrugging. "Brain? This is crazy. Americans always ask who you are, what you do," he said. "They don't do this in Europe or Japan."

Retail designers rely on people like Ariana and Pascal to design and manufacture denim that they will then purchase and send to garment factories—also independently owned and contracted—to be cut and sewn. The shapes and styles come from the mind of a brand's designers, but the fabric—texture, color, pattern, finish, feel—often comes from the Arianas and Pascals of the world. They in turn rely on designers, retailers, industry rags, and trend forecasting companies to determine what's popular on the streets and suggest where style might be going. In this way, a world of fashion codependence and design recycling has been born. A Dutch designer for McGregor told me that he often finds inspiration for the designs of his garments in fabric created by a textile technician, and not the other way around, so Pascal may be more forecaster than he believes himself to be. In either case, Ariana and Pascal are the front line in the creation of a pair of jeans. "[But] we are not artisans." Pascal insisted, "Everything must be industrial; it must be able to be reproduced. Denim that might be nice today, in two years might be too old. It's not like art. Fashion is the general taste in a given period." He pronounced fashion "fay shun."

Pascal said that Levi's 501 jeans changed the industry. It marked the moment denim became mass market, what he called "the globalization of denim." From then, the West became known for industrial denim—denim that could be produced and reproduced in exactly the same ways, much like the fast food industry automated the French fry. (Though French fries, it must be said, never had the cool factor of a pair of 501s). Japan, meanwhile, built its reputation as the world's capital of fashion denim—that is, denim with expensive washes and finishes, progressive fashion-forward designs by avant-garde or postmodern textile artisans, or high-end specialized cotton and weaves. Denim, in other words, that could not be mass produced, at least not easily and not without significant expense. Pascal pointed out that the globalization of denim then gave way to the customization of denim—so many small labels, so many styles and colors and shapes and designs.

Legler is one of Italy's oldest fabric makers. Its corporate headquarters is in a small town called Ponte San Pietro, fifty kilometers northeast of Milan. The commute to Milan can take forty-five minutes or an absurd number of hours, depending on traffic. One day, when I drove to the city with several Legler employees, the fog coming off the Alps was so thick we couldn't see more than half a block in front of us. Pascal shrugged it off as "nothing" in much the same way a Minnesotan shrugs off half a foot of snow in February. Though rush hour had long passed, it took us nearly three hours to get to Milan. This industrial corridor is perhaps the most unsightly part of Italy, badly in need of more highways or public transportation. It is an area where traffic, consisting almost entirely of trucks, is lugubrious and unforgiving and perennial. Traffic jams at midnight are not uncommon.

Legler started as a Swiss company in 1834 but moved to

northern Italy in the late nineteenth century. It has always been a family-run operation.* In 1971, Legler bought an old textile factory in the town of Crespi d'Adda, and both the factory and the town now compose a UNESCO World Heritage site. Crespi, the family, had built up the factory and the town in the latter part of the nineteenth century. Long before Legler took up residence the company employed 3,600 people, and families in the Crespi village were required to have at least one person employed at the factory in order to live in the town. Workers' houses generally held two or three families; each family had four rooms. The families enjoyed large, airy spaces with small yards for their children, a far cry from the misery their English counterparts often experienced in the same period and an even farther cry from the dismal dormitories of today's garment workers in many parts of Asia.5

Legler employed six hundred people at the Crespi factory and eventually outgrew it, moving to their current location in Ponte San Pietro a few years ago. One of Legler's 375 modern looms can do what twenty looms in Crespi's nineteenth-century heyday did. Today, the Crespi factory is abandoned, save for a rare tourist, usually from the region. The day I visited, pieces of fabric littered the floor, along with an occasional machine. The warehouses were home to many dozens of pigeons and their accompanying flotsam and jetsam. Though people continue to live in the Crespi houses, it was not hard to imagine each red brick building of the factory complex buzzing with life, a neighborhood alive on the fulcrum of work and home.

Today, Legler is a series of unremarkable putty-colored, red-

*Its current owner, Eduardo Polli, bought it from the Legler family in 1989. One of Italy's most common phrases is "Conosco i miei polli." Translated loosely, it means, "I know my chickens." It is informally forbidden at Legler to use this phrase, which means employees snicker when they whisper it in the hallways, usually under the guise of warning me not to use it. Many, in fact, found it necessary to warn me again and again, several times in a single afternoon.

trimmed warehouses on the shore of the Brembo River, fringed by evergreens and cyprus trees. Despite its unprepossessing appearance, it has historical relevance to local residents whose parents and grandparents—of which there are a surprising number— worked there. Locals seem to hold the same tender regard for Legler that one might hold for an old pet. The area it takes up is so big that the company bought a collection of bright yellow bicycles for employees to get from one end to the other.[6] The bikes are often propped against walls and railings, disappearing and popping around randomly. After I had hung around for several days, the bikes seemed to me to take on cartoonish personalities, one in a warehouse office, another next to an empty desk, another leaning against a bolt of cloth, as if they were actually just one single bike in a kind of *Where's Waldo* game for interactive adults. They gave the place a jovial ambience.

The only clue that Pascal's office was a week away from Première Vision, the textile show in Paris, and one business day away from Milan's fabric show, was the constant ringing of his mobile phone—at odds with his thoughtful saunter and the hushed tones of his speaking voice—and the sheer volume of denim in view. Fabric swatches, black binders and multicolored samples of ready-made jeans hid every available inch of work area. Wooden spools with the circumference of barbecue grills had patchworks of denim covering them and served as makeshift seats. The mess spilled into the conference room next door, where hundreds of pairs of jeans hung on multitiered bars two and three deep around the room's circumference. A wooden conference table and hand-stitched leather chairs the color of saddles appeared almost suffocated by denim. It is impossible to fathom the infinite styles of jeans that exist in the world until you see what amounts to a fractional portion of them aligned together and vying for attention: red selvages, oversized pockets, bejeweled embellishments, threadbare knees, embroidered trim, wrinkles, fades, color washes. Before she had a baby, Ariana said she was the same size as most of the tiny samples (she still seems so to me) and sometimes she could take the old ones home. This probably accounts for how she came to own twenty-three pairs of jeans.*

In years past, there had been manic activity and long days leading up to these shows. Revenue at Legler was down, and manufacturing in the country was down, which basically mirrored what was happening in the rest of the European Union, to greater or lesser degree, and the United States. Costs and customer demands were rising, and tightened budgets across the industry meant the fabric shows had fewer exhibitors, and those who still came had smaller booths. There were even rumors that Legler might not show after this year—it would be the first time in the more than thirty years since the Paris show began. It was a general squeeze, and depending on who you talked to, times were either tougher than ever, or merely cyclical and in a slow period.

Pascal fell on the side of the bigger, noncyclical worrier. "It is stupid to buy fabric in Europe, then make it in the Far East and send it back to Europe," he said. "It's not cost effective. It won't be more than five or seven years before we have to move." He gave manufacturing another half decade in the country, give or take, before it was gone completely. If he wanted to keep the same career, he believed he would also someday need to move.

- -

THE MILAN SHOW WAS A LITTLE LIKE THE OPENING act to the headliner, Paris. Together, Pascal and Paolo, a co-worker, pulled a few pieces from the collection that they wouldn't have room for in their display. Dozens of pairs of jeans were laid out on a long red and white work table, and Pascal called their decision-making process "roulette." The jeans were held by their belt loops with a plastic cord, and each time he decided to nix a pair, the entire cord had to be slid out of each pair, then put back on. It was

*By comparison, Pascal owns a paltry ten.

absurdly time-consuming. One of the sales team wandered in and told Pascal that this year there had been a lot of interest in a caramel-colored faded look. White, too, had shown promise for summer. Months later, I would see both colors in nearly every store I entered—from the Gap and Levi's to Next and Eileen Fisher and Target and even Strawberry. Each time Pascal's phone rang he was slow to answer. Even on the first ring he would start a new sentence or thought with the person in front of him, as if his pants pocket weren't playing the shrill tune of an unanswered mobile. Then he'd stop midway and answer on about the fourth ring. It was as if he had to put his thoughts or ideas partially out into the cosmos to make them matter, even if he never returned to them. The phone cut his available preparation time in half. The people who worked with him all tended to bear the same cheerful manner of desperate patients in a doctor's office who know screaming at the nurses never helps.

PremièreVision is the Oscars and the G8 Summit of denim all in one; a showcase for new designs, a chance to size up the competition, potential for new business. PV, as it's called in the industry (and when you say it fast it sounds a lot like "peeved"), is a chance to make last-minute sales for the upcoming season, though Pascal called it an event to "shake hands." More than fifteen hundred exhibitors from over one hundred countries attend; visitors can number upwards of fifty thousand. In 2006, though, the exhibitors I chatted with believed both the Milan and Paris shows had fewer participants and most of the booths were slightly smaller than in previous years (PV's Web site suggests more exhibitors come every year). The industry trend seems always to be fewer sales, bigger worries. You were only as good as your last profit. Everyone in the industry, from country after country, seemed to feel the pinch that Legler was feeling. Ariana and Pascal, rather than leading a frantic pre-show office as they had in years past, found themselves, even with sample changes and phone calls, in the odd and uncomfortable position of having time on their hands. This was the first year they'd not had to work overtime to prepare for PV. Indeed, they even had time for restaurant lunches. They laughed at the incredulity of it. Every year they'd wanted to be this ready, but now they finally were and it was unsettling.

Down the hall from their office a series of glass cases contained samples of their best-selling fabrics, much like a movie studio hangs life-sized portraits of its biggest stars. Each pair was assigned its own peculiar name that signified what collection it belonged to, as well as the grouping and the style or treatment. Some of the best were karma, cayenne, beetle, and monster. Generally, what sold and what didn't sell was a mystery. Pascal said maybe 30 percent of each new collection won't sell for reasons indiscernible to him, beyond the common adage that markets are fickle creatures. Each year, they said, the clients wanted more and more from them. Sometimes, a customer requested as much as ten thousand meters as a "sample."* Rather than fabric swatches, now customers wanted entire garments before they committed to an order. Legler's outlay and risk continued to increase. One sales agent said that you always passed costs and risk on to the next person in the supply chain. But the fabric begins at Legler; there was no one else for them to pass the risk on to.

Perhaps the single most common theme among those who work with denim is the idea that it changes along with you, that it could be a map for future archeologists of our modern life. Denim has a near-religious following; it was spoken about not only by Ariana and Pascal but by everyone I met in poetic terms. Like an actual religion, it incites its fair share of insider wars over its origins, its care, its proper development and manufacturing. No other fabric has held the symbolic fortitude of denim—the rebellion, the antiestablishment rhetoric, the edginess—and no other article of clothing than jeans has been the focus of more literature. Ariana called denim a "living thing. You treat it differently than

*That's a little like me walking into a drugstore and requesting, say, seven hundred ounces of Colgate toothpaste as a "sample."

other fabrics. It's important because you know indigo changes, and fades. You understand its soul." Maybe the fleeting quality of it is precisely why it is so beloved; it cannot be fixed in place.

Pascal believes denim is beloved because it is so unpredictable and so versatile. Its behavior is erratic. Each season, there will be some new fabric designs by him that don't work at all, though he's been at this so long that fewer and fewer are rejected—maybe two or three each year. The texture is off, or the color combination is not what he'd envisioned. It makes his work interesting and, in its own way, risky. "After denim lives with you, it changes with you, as you are," Pascal said.

Pascal had not intended a life in fashion, or even on the periphery of fashion. When he was a teenager, he was obligated to declare an area of study in high school. He lived in a small town on the outskirts of Bergamo, as he does now, and textile manufacturing was a profession that surrounded him. Italy, still today, has regional specialties for textiles: Prato for wool, Como for silk, Bergamo for cotton. Pascal had thought first about computers or engineering, but textiles was a wide-open market back then, and the creativity of inventing fabric and its manipulations appealed to his artistic tendencies. Only twenty or so textile technicians graduated each year, he remembers being told. It seemed like a good idea. He studied at the Istituto Tecnico Industriale Paleocapa, where he learned about fabric as a scientist might: How will it behave under certain conditions? With certain dyes? With certain laundering processes? With certain blends of synthetic or natural fiber? Denim became his favorite fabric, the one that offered him many faces. As an Italian, he felt he was uniquely suited to working with denim. "Denim is linked with people and their life styles," he said. "You need a culture of denim, a culture of what it is."

He served his mandatory military year after school. The cold war was ending, and he was sent to the far north of Italy, in South Tyrol. Italy shares a border with Yugoslavia and kept bases on the border, so the area was strategic. His helmet had a plume. The area has long been the locus of a separatist movement; Tyroleans, who speak German as their first language, historically have sought autonomy from the Italian government. Today, Pascal and Ariana vacation there, and Pascal calls his military experience an unequivocal "waste of time." He was not a particularly good soldier, he believes. He operated within bureaucracies, like most of the rest of the world, but he never felt comfortable in them, also like most of the rest of the world. He left his post and came home to Bergamo and took a job at Legler. He got promoted, married, had a child, and then the world of his profession began its slow unraveling. Most of the time, Pascal didn't think about it, because when he did, the problem was too big and too complex to untangle and he found comfort in keeping a tight focus: weave, color, treatment, product. Wife, daughter, soccer.

ARIANA AND PASCAL HAVE WATCHED MANUFACTURING seep slowly eastward in much the same way New Englanders and then southerners in the United States once did. Legler was not immune to the attraction of lower-priced geographies. They planned to open a fabric manufacturing warehouse in Morocco in 2007. Quietly, most employees I spoke with referred to this new plant as the company's salvation. Twenty years ago, when Pascal was in school, Italy was still the world's fashion capital. It was a good time to begin a career in textiles. Now, as manufacturers struggle more each year and colleges like Istituto Tecnico Industriale Paleocapa churn out even more young professionals to a saturated job market, the situation worsens exponentially. One manager at Legler told me 1995–2005 had been the worst decade ever for the industry. The fact that Legler had a reputation for some of the best denim in the world kept it perhaps more insulated than most, but it was facing significant losses still.[7] One sales manager said the company had gone from making a hundred thousand meters of fabric a day several years ago to forty thousand in 2005 and 2006.

Italians have struggled with the loss of their manufacturing sector while concurrently tallying the biggest deficit in western Europe and enduring wild inflation, not to mention corruption and bribery scandals under the always colorful Silvio Berlusconi, who was mercifully relieved of his post as prime minister by Romani Prodi in the 2006 elections. "We suffer more than the rest of Europe because we have manufacturing," Ariana said. She was, surprisingly, not an opponent of globalization and saw the threat to the country's industry as an opportunity for Italy to "make something new." She is tactile and fiddles with anything in reach: paper, fabric swatches, her pen. "I think of myself as a very small, small part of what goes on in the world. It's not so important, but we all have a duty." Under the euro, the country has languished. They now find themselves at odds with the rest of the European Union, desperate to hold on to whatever manufacturing they have left while their EU colleagues clamor for ever cheaper and voluminous Chinese imports. Similarly Americans bemoan the loss of manufacturing while pushing overflowing shopping carts through Target and Macy's, Family Dollar and Wal-Mart, Bloomingdale's and Ann Taylor. In the summer of 2005, Italian newspapers suggested the euro was one of the country's worst economic decisions in recent history and charted the rise of a pro-lira, anti-euro movement in the government. The movement had almost no chance of realizing its goal, but its existence means something all the same, evidence of a deeply unhappy populace. Berlusconi claimed that the euro had "screwed everybody" and blamed it for Italy's economic situation. Of course, the fact that his main political foe championed the euro probably had nothing to do with Berlusconi's public rebuke of the currency. The truth is that Italy has been in decline for a while. It has high unemployment among the young, a huge deficit, and the lowest economic growth rate of all the EU countries.[8]

The status of family businesses like Legler in the Italian economic psyche is of profound importance. Family-run operations have long been the foundation for Italian business, and it's the family firms that are most affected by the influx of Chinese goods. Up until the early 1990s, Benetton manufactured nearly 90 percent of all its goods in Italy; today, the number is less than a third. In 2005 the World Economic Forum rated Italy's growth competitiveness just a tad higher than Botswana's (the countries ranked 47 and 48, respectively), which, when viewed another way, is really great for Botswanans. The convergence of textiles being one of China's big moneymakers and one of Italy's greatest sources of pride doesn't make for a happy ending. As the *Economist* wrote, "Italy is caught in a long, slow decline."9

Ariana said it another way: "China is on my doorstep."

ARIANA, WHO IS THIRTY-FIVE, HAS WINDSWEPT BANGS across her forehead and dark sloping eyes that suggest sad wonderment. *Vogue* magazines were piled up behind her desk and a tiny pair of jeans hung from the waist above a filing cabinet; they were so stiff it was as if an imaginary tiny human were dangling inside. Ariana is avidly fascinated with the world in a kind of mystical, ingénue manner. She moves with the same quiet immutability that makes you strain to hear a canoe glide through a lake—such little commotion that she appears and disappears without your realizing it. She met Pascal in 1997, when she got her first job at Legler. Her father had worked there in various departments for more than forty years before retiring, so it was a comfortable place for her. She studied literature at university and loves the English language, the way it sounds to her and how her mouth moves when she speaks it. She wrote her thesis on David Leavitt, but loved the stories of Raymond Carver, Ernest Hemingway, and Bret Easton Ellis. During school, she spent a year in Hull, England, on a scholarship studying American literature. When she was hired at Legler, she knew virtually nothing about denim, but after a while she began to think about it often, and the more she learned, the more the symbolism appealed to her, the idea that how a life is lived can be charted in some small manner from the things we wear. It's a poetic thought; we vanish but our imprints remain in a thousand tiny folds. Pascal taught her that denim lives with you. If you cross your legs, the color will wear; if you bend over car hoods, or vacuum stairs on your knees, or paint canvases on enormous walls, or sit at a keyboard all day, your jeans will eventually reflect these movements.

"Jeans imitate life," Pascal likes to say. His jeans will someday show a lot of pacing, hands tucked into front pockets, one faded rectangle outline of a mobile phone.

Pascal was a very thorough teacher—perhaps more thorough than he was with other employees, since he wanted to marry Ariana. She didn't notice at first; she was so caught up in the learning. She thought he was just meticulous. Very, very meticulous—which, in fact, is not an inaccurate representation of him. After a while, they started to run together. Pascal is a passionate footballer. "I never ran before," she said. "I told him I could run, but I couldn't. I don't know how I could do it back then. I had adrenaline or something." She was so good it was ages before Pascal knew she wasn't a runner and hadn't ever been a runner and, frankly, had no intention of becoming a runner. After they started dating, they used to work late together and order pizza for dinner at the office, because, as she put it, "Together at home or together at work was just the same." Gianna, their three-year-old daughter, changed all that; neither of them, but especially Ariana, worked late anymore. Pascal referred to their lives as BG and AG, which is self-evident to any parent reading this. Soon, Gianna would change even more.

ARIANA SPOTTED LEGLER'S DENIM DESIGNS ALL THE time—on vacations, on the train to Milan, in stores. Once, she and

I were at a shopping mall near Orio al Serio airport in Bergamo
and she excitedly reached for a pair of jeans. Sometimes she told
the sales clerk that she knew the fabric, that she helped design it,
but most of the time they didn't understand. Textile technicians
are hidden draftsmen, designers behind the designers. "These are
ours," she said, running her fingers over the fabric, turning them
over to look at the back pockets and inside the waistband. "They
are Karma."

Typically, a collection will have several group names, then the
fabric will get a name depending on the color, the weave or effect,
and finally the finish. In this way, God's Nectar and Delphi Oracle
were born. "We try to link one fabric to another thematically,
like king, prince, queen," Ariana said. "Genesis, ark, love, passion,
freedom." Chocolate, for example, is in a group with mint, milk,
and cacao. Sometimes names didn't translate in quite the way
Pascal and Ariana had intended. In a spectacular case of ill translation, they once named a group "dream" and dubbed a finish
"wet." All their native English-speaking colleagues love to remind
them of this faux pas. They have since learned to clear names lin-
guistically with English speakers before committing them to the
collection.

The groups can usually be traced to something in the lives of
Ariana and Pascal. World geography figures into almost every corner of Pascal's life. He paints pictures of places he's been; he reads
books about adventure and travel. In the basement of his house
was a half-finished canvas of vivid salt fields in Bolivia based on a
picture he took. In real life, he said, the fields were blinding,
squared off by ocher dirt that looked like suede and capped with
intense blue skies. When they visited the site in person, they
couldn't look at the fields without wearing sunglasses. Next to his
desk a *National Geographic* map of the world studded with two
dozen yellow pushpins marked all the places he wanted to go still.
Cambodia, Botswana, Tibet, Yemen, Jordan, Israel, India, Brazil,
Bolivia, New Zealand. "It's missing a few," he said. Their house is
full of pictures of them in Bolivia, Indonesia, Greece, Spain, Japan,

Peru.* So their ideas or groups—"stories," in Legler's industry vernacular—often reflect this global sensibility, and end up symbolizing not just the lives of two denim designers in northern Italy but an industry at large. There was Chicago, with blues, funky, and jazz fabrics, for example. There were nomad and gypsy, Rykers, Alcatraz, Eldorado, and Silverado; divali, nirvana, yoga, shiva; mambo, barrio, gotham, Brooklyn, Marin, Ceylon, samurai, karate, and gypsy vibe. One co-worker said you could always tell where Pascal and Ariana had been on vacation. Sometimes the collections were even more personal. Epic, fiction, and tale, Ariana said, were probably named by her. With the birth of Gianna, a Bugs Bunny devotee, cartoon characters emerged: Mickey, Bugs, Daffy. In 2006, the collection had an even wider angle: Europe, South America, Japan, the United States, Africa, and Australia make up the main groups, as if Pascal and Ariana were trying to capture the world.

Neither of them, however, claimed to remember where "desire" or "hug" had originated.

ONE DAY ARIANA AND I DROVE TO MILAN FOR A CONference put on by Cotton Incorporated, an advocacy group supported mainly by U.S. farmers and government funds to "build demand for global cotton consumption." It was, Ariana told me, an industry presentation about design trends that, generally speaking, helps her and Pascal when they're creating a collection: new colors, new fabrics, new treatments. Such presentations occur frequently and Ariana attends them sporadically. What they

*They've been to the United States many times. Ariana once described to me her one and only trip to Starbucks. The coffee is "big," she said, "but not substantial." She compared it to dirty water. She ordered a venti cappuccino and was shocked to discover it was roughly the height of her torso. She called it "lunch," and not in a way you might typically describe a memorable vacation moment.

really are, like so much of fashion, is a method for compartmental-izing the world and consumerism. Fashion, in this way, is brilliant. I once had a teenager tell me with utter conviction that she bought what *she* liked, not what was fashionable or popular at the moment. Industry professionals would have applauded to hear her say this. Not only does she, of course, buy what is marketed to her, but she does so under the conviction that it's because it's what she would choose on her own.

At the conference, held at Hotel Michelangelo, we were told that the season's new accent color was apple green (perhaps not coincidentally, it matched the presenter's sweater). Six themes were presented in what was called the season's "trend collec-tion"—the inspiration for what we would find on store shelves more than a year later, the slow-moving perambulations in a cen-tury of fashion from modern to postmodern to post-postmodern and beyond. These presentations foretold the indefinable reason why a certain purple from last season is just a shade too dark for this one. The themes had esoteric, suggestive names: intrigue, provocateur, muse, destination, triumph, and expression. Intrigue's inspiration came from James Bond and the fabrics con-centrated on what the presenter called "moisture management."* Provocateur was a departure from holiday reds, a mix of brown and red called, in the presentation, chocolate and roses. "These sexy colors make the heart beat faster," said the presenter, who had flown over from America and seemed a little jet-lagged.

"Hot beet?" whispered the Italian translator to the presenter. Her reading glasses dangled on a chain around her neck.

"Heart. Beat. Faster," the presenter clarified, touching her hand to her chest. "HearT. BeaT."

---

*I find this phrase utterly lovable. It means sweat, yes, but also the general moisture emitted by your body at any given time, which is so minute that nei-ther you nor I would ever notice it, but there are people in the world paid to notice it and, further, to invent new and better ways for us to keep on not noticing.

Ariana and I sat two rows back from the podium in padded metal chairs, behind a woman wearing a belt with tiny pastel-colored stuffed animals dangling from it. Later, when the woman walked in her black stiletto boots, the stuffed animals banged gently into her hips. The room was half full: thirty or so fashion industry folks who'd come for a presentation on cotton as it is used in consumer goods, cotton as stylish, sexy, trendy product. Cotton as clairvoyant. The apocryphal crop.

The presenter played a slide show, with techno music, about what inspired the choices this season. Ariana weaved in time with the music. In addition to James Bond, inspiration featured yoga (for the "muse" line; from a "Zen-like" state of mind), 1960s track suits, spices, graffiti, old cars, sports cars, sliced-off chunks of lipstick, Tibetan prayer flags, Latin American peasants, a Rubik's cube, sports, massages, monasteries, knee socks with stripes, fall leaves, and someone who looked suspiciously like Dwight Eisenhower. The slide show seemed to assert that everything you see at any part of the day, no matter if you are awake or asleep or even particularly lucid, is a possible source of inspiration and thus a trend to be extrapolated. Many of the sources of inspiration seemed, in fact, old to me, but later several people explained that fashion isn't about great innovative leaps but about redefining known commodities. I suppose this explains why some clothing from the 1980s peach and sea foam palette might today be called blush and evergreen, with shades just different enough to make your '80s holdovers dorky. Darker, lighter, more or less saturated. What this means is that in some way, shape, or form we are doomed to repeat the mullet. Trend forecasters aren't sibylline fashionistas as much as they are cultural and sociological anthropologists, minus the doctorates and the debt.

The next part of the presentation had to do with what were called surface trends: new ways to treat garments once they're sewn. It's the kind of thing that is responsible for the destruction of your jeans through various washing methods or treatments. It's the addition of embellishments, or overdyeing or finishing. We learned that one trend this year was 100 percent cotton dyed with urethane coating to look like leather; another, overdyed cords and blotch prints. One slide showed the face of an old woman embedded in a swatch of denim, an effect that seemed mildly creepy as a piece of apparel. There was ripped fabric and frayed plaids—items so trendy and fashion forward I feared they were already out of style by the time the slide changed. The presenter said this group was engaging the customer through "optical illusions."

Desire came next. "Desire is the driving force for consumer market saturation," the presenter continued. The slide showed cotton lace and luxurious women's wear. From time to time, Ariana jotted down a note. Stained glass was an inspiration for this line. To me, stained glass and intimate apparel have never seemed particularly compatible, but I'm not scouring the streets looking for trends, either. The presenter finished desire and said, "More and more we're finding rituals affect our lives even if we don't realize it." She showed a slide of an ethnic woman in cotton print who probably lives in some remote South American village. I tried to envision what the presenter meant, the rituals of my life, but I couldn't come up with anything. I live in Cambodia; people there have rituals. If a white owl flies through your window you bring in the monks to cleanse the entire building before anyone can reenter. *That's* a ritual. I can't quite conjure anything similar in the Western world that is, in fact, a ritual "more and more" beyond perhaps morning coffee and e-mail.

One of her final slides was a collage. Eisenhower's smiling face appeared again. Maybe she included it as a means of harking back to what Americans imagine were better times.

In all of this—the new fabric abrasions, the multilayered prints and new technologies for dyeing and weaving and washing—were tools with which Italy would try to save itself. They could not compete with China in price, but Ariana and Pascal believed they could (at least for now) compete with quality and inventiveness. When I asked Ariana if Italy, who along with Japan produces the world's highest-quality denim, had fallen a little behind in innovation and a little behind as the focus of the industry, she didn't say anything for a long time. I sensed a tiny battle being waged inside her: the desire to be wrong and the need to tell the truth. "Maybe. Yes," she finally said. "A little."

On the ride home, Ariana said she sometimes referred to these presentations as "smoke."

JEANS ARE OF COURSE THE UNIFORM OF CHOICE AT Legler. Even the executives wear jeans most days. Across the developed world, there has been perhaps no greater reason for the renaissance of cotton after more than a decade of dismal sales in the 1980s (polyester was king back then) than casual Friday. One industry executive told me denim had ridden the cotton comeback/casual Friday wave. He claimed that while denim was popular in the 1980s, it tended to all look alike. The advent of different denim styles and embellishments, along with the movement of premium denim, helped spur the industry to its current peak. According to Cotton Incorporated, the average American woman owned one pair of jeans in the post–World War II period; now the average is eight, and for young girls, it is thirteen.* Denim accounts for $55 billion in annual sales, out of a $395 billion textile and apparel market.† In short, we are living in the Golden Age of denim.

*Cotton Incorporated's 2004 Annual Report also noted how "even though most women had lots and lots of clothes, they always felt good about shopping for more."

†That equals every person on the planet spending $61 a year on textiles. For the three billion folks who live on a buck a day, that would be about two months' salary. In America, it equals more than three grand a year for a family of four at the $18,810 poverty line. Wonky, but it gives a little perspective.

LEGLER'S PART IN THE PROCESS OF MAKING JEANS generally takes place in a pulley system of Italian geography: The design is created in Ponte San Pietro, the cotton becomes yarn in Sardinia, and then back again, where the yarn is woven and dyed. Legler claimed to produce the second largest amount of denim in the country—forty-one million meters annually, which was enough to make about 27.3 million pairs of jeans every year (it takes 1.5 to 2 meters of fabric to make a pair of jeans). Legler's warehouses can hold six million meters of fabric.* Cotton bales from any one of dozens of countries in Africa, America, Asia, or the former Soviet Union are woven into yarn in a process called spinning at Legler's plants in Macomer and Siniscola, Sardinia.†

The yarn is typically "ring spun" or "open-end rotor spun."[10] Ring spun means cotton fibers are twisted together to make yarn (a single fiber might be twisted from 20,000 to 50,000 thousand times with other fibers, which is how something as fine as filament yarn made of cotton can hold together at all). Open end rotor spun, a newer technology invented in the 1970s, produces yarn that is both less strong and much cheaper than ring spun. The cotton fibers are whirled together in a sort of cotton candy machine using centrifugal force. As the yarn is twisted into long strands, it is bundled together by cotton fiber wraps in much the same manner as sushi pieces are held by strips of seaweed.

The next stage involves turning single yarns—in this context

---

*If a roll of denim, which usually has 20,000–25,000 meters of fabric and is the circumference of a water buffalo, fell on you, your chances of survival would be nil.

†Technically, thread is used to hold a garment together at the seams, while "yarn" is the processed cotton that is actually woven together to make fabric.

yarn is basically a plied version of thread, as opposed to the thick skeins of yarn we all watched our grandmothers knit sweaters with—into what is referred to either as sheets or rope, about one half-inch wide, in a process called warping. The lengthwise yarn in any given weave is called the warp. The horizontal yarn is called weft or filling. A pair of jeans very often has two or three warp yarns for every weft. The warp is dyed in enormous vats of indigo for the average pair of blue jeans and the weft is left its natural color.* (Undyed warp yarns are separated on a warping machine, which takes 500 yarns at a time and winds them on a three-foot-long section beam. For dyed warp, a ball warping machine takes loose yarns—again, about 500 at once—and wraps them on a wooden core, after which the yarn is dyed.) Pants can also be "piece" dyed, meaning dyed as one finished garment after they're sewn together.

Warp yarn is where artistry starts when it comes to denim. In order for the yarn to be dyed, it must maintain constant tension to absorb the correct quantity of indigo dye paste and it must enter the vat vertically. The process requires a series of connected dye boxes and machines more than a football field in length that move tens of thousands of yarns per second into and out of the indigo vats. At Legler, an indigo vat or dye box is about the size of a small car, and the indigo inside it froths and bubbles and gurgles, reeking suspiciously of overheated molding cheese. The vats operate, like much of the rest of the manufacturing side of the company, twenty-four hours a day in three shifts, five days a week. It takes an entire shift change to change a vat color. The day I visited, the dyehouse was tropically warm and I had to dodge several speeding

---

*By natural, I mean entirely unlike anything found in nature. Much like Tom Cruise's teeth, it is taken from its natural beigeish and bleached to within an inch of its life. Cotton used to be more beige, but genetic modifications have made it whiter and whiter. This explains why you typically see white thread on the inside of your average jeans, though it does not, unfortunately, demystify America's fixation with alabaster odontology.

forklifts. Cotton fragments floated through the air.* Steam filled the air. Beside the vats, the few men I saw looked tiny.

Warp yarn is normally dipped between three and twelve times in indigo before it's ready to be woven. If you were to slice the yarn widthwise like salami, you would find that it has a white core surrounded by blue-dyed layers (like a Life Saver). Indigo is not water soluble and thus does not penetrate cotton easily or fully. This explains why jeans lose their color the more they are washed—the inside of a denim cotton thread always stays white. In fact, indigo is a wholly inefficient dye, relatively speaking, and cotton yarn is equally inefficient in soaking up indigo. Together, they are a partnership of inanity. But the imperfections, according to anyone who works with denim, are exactly why it is so beloved.

Once the warp indigo rope is dyed and each strand is separated on a beamer machine, it usually goes through a process called sizing, which adds starch, polyvinyl alcohol (which has been largely eliminated in the better laundries, for environmental reasons), or something called carboxymethylcellulose for strengthening. Paraffin then smoothes and lubricates the yarn. Mercerization is sometimes used to strengthen yarn and increase its ability to take dye by dipping the yarn into a caustic soda solution, and then later using acid to neutralize it. The yarns are also separated and aligned to prepare them for weaving into fabric. This stage is one of the reasons the use of organic cotton is, to the naysayer, a bit of a corporate feel-good policy. Once cotton is out of the bale, not much

---

*One of the big worries of textile manufacturers is fire. With so much highly flammable cotton in the air, they are particularly threatened. The Triangle Shirtwaist fire, which killed 141 workers (mostly women) in New York in the early twentieth century, is perhaps the most famous, but I read somewhere once that most garment factories will at some point in their existence experience a fire. Legler is no exception. In 1997, a refrigerator caught fire on a Saturday afternoon and destroyed large portions of one of the buildings, along with the entire fabric archive, which contained pieces from the earliest years of the company in the nineteenth century.

"organic" happens. Woven cloth is brushed and singed and dipped in a chemical finishing solution before being rolled up and shipped to a factory for garment production. The very processing of denim jeans is inorganic by nature. Even though vegetable dyes are growing in popularity, there is still no wholly organic piece of clothing today in the mass consumer market. Vegetable dyes are nice, but very limited in terms of color and, for large-scale manufacturers, both unavailable in large quantities and prohibitively expensive. Many dyes need what's called a mordant to affix them to fabric. Mordants lock in color. Mordants also often contain lead.

Reproducing meter after meter of fabric with exactly the same color and feel and weave has become a science; denim exactitude is as strenuously charted and calculated as any medical or engineering lab test. Most contracts allow for ten faults, or defect points, per one hundred square meters. At Legler, women who've worked at the company for decades still check grade and imperfections by hand, watching meter by meter as small conveyor belt machines run each roll of denim. Their hands turn blue from touching the indigo. Many firms these days have gone high tech and use cameras and lasers to find imperfections. The women at Legler, scanning for faults, are almost surely the last of their profession, like speakers of a dying indigenous language.

Once denim fabric is processed, it is sent away to factories where it is cut and sewn into jeans. Typically (though not always) jeans get treatments at what in the industry are referred to as laundries. Their only resemblance to the laundries familiar to the public is that they tend to contain washing machines. Most of the machines are about the size of a highway billboard and can fit hundreds of pairs of jeans at once. Laundries are the reason our jeans have become shorn, multicolored, frayed and bleached and patched and hammered and coated with all manner of invisible treatments. Numerous issues surround laundries—most notably environmental, since chemicals are used in many of the treatments.

One afternoon I visited a laundry in Los Angeles that makes

jeans for many of the high-end brands: Paper Denim & Cloth, 7
for All Mankind, Levi's Capital E (their premium label), J. Crew,
and Citizens of Humanity. An oversized man who drove an oversized truck and bemoaned his luck with women took me on a tour.
His laundry works with brands to design their own treatments,
though they also have their own designers on hand to create ever
new and wonderful methods of destruction. Though a number of
mass-market brands look to technology to do their malicious
denim bidding—dye-and-destroy machines, I call them—the
higher-end premium denim brands employ thousands of people
who sand, scrape, and grind jeans by hand. During a busy season,
they can treat fifty thousand pairs of jeans a week.

This particular laundry, which works often with Legler denim,
is made up of a series of warehouses cobbled together. Two large
rooms house what look like blow-up dolls severed at the waist
hanging from the ceiling. They're legs, really, "manikins" or "man-
drels" in industry lingo, that resemble two enormous hot dogs
joined together and sporting untreated jeans. Lots and lots of
blown-up hot dog legs dressed in raw denim jeans. Hundreds of
workers—mostly men—stand in front of the legs and sand thighs
and crotches, so that the indigo fades, and the cotton grows softer.

There are almost endless combinations of things that can be
done to treat jeans, using a surprising array of materials: glass,
sandpaper, diamond dust, pumice stones, enzymes, chemical or
mechanical abrasion, and many others. Stonewashing, which
requires the harvest of pumice from around the world, has come
under fire from environmental groups, particularly when stones
are first dipped in bleach and then used to treat jeans. Plastic balls
and enzymes are used more and more in "stonewashing," though
the effect is still often disappointing. This washing and finishing is
almost unquestionably the least environmentally friendly part of
the entire manufacturing process. Clothes are sprayed with chemicals to create a variety of effects, or overdyed (with one color layered over another or an excess of color applied to the fabric), or
coated in resin and baked in enormous ovens. Polymer resin is

commonly used to coat creases and folds in clothing, thereby making them permanent, and to set color; it also sometimes contains formaldehyde. Workers in the laundry industry must don an array of contraptions—special respirators, boots, coveralls, gloves, protective eyewear—to shield them from the myriad chemicals in use in nearly every operation. Buckets and buckets of chemicals with names wholly unrecognizable to me sat lined up in a warehouse where purple spray—potassium permanganate—was hosed onto jeans as they dangled on metal hangers from the ceiling. The walls and floor were covered in plastic, and the workers' gear had turned almost entirely purple from the spray. Potassium permanganate, when it's washed out using oxalic acid, gets neutralized and turns the area it's been applied to white, like a partial bleach. Sodium hypochlorite is used for bleaching an entire garment. Designers use these to create contrast.

Though it's almost impossible to know for sure which chemicals were used in the making of a specific garment, short of sending it to a lab for analysis, one way that suggests a laundry didn't have high standards is to check the inside front pockets. If they have a blue haze, it often means the jeans haven't been through the final wash stage properly and the indigo has bled.[11] Most garments have the majority of the chemicals used in their production washed off in the desizing stage, before they are sold in stores, so consumers, unlike textile workers, are generally safe from chemical residue. (I was advised many times, however, never to use sheets or wear underwear newly bought from a store without washing them first. When I asked why, I was never quite given a verbal answer, but rather a certain specific look. A look that suggested I just follow the advice I'd been given.)

IN LEGLER'S OFFICES, THE SAMPLES FOR THE SHOWS prepared by Pascal and Paolo were nearly ready. No one was doing much talking. A pall hung over the office. It was Ariana's final day at Legler. A month ago, after a season of anguish and indecision, she decided to leave Legler for a part-time job. Her leaving meant Pascal would only have to lay off one person from the department, but no one felt relief about this.

Gianna had had a series of health problems since her birth, which was equally traumatic for Ariana. She talked to me once about how pregnancy and childbirth taught her something she'd never known, something about how "your body betrays you." Gianna is a precocious child with an understanding of trauma far beyond her years. Ariana had suffered from postpartum depression, but she had also suffered through the anguish of having to tell doctors again and again that what made her child cry was not just a stomachache. Gianna had undergone a handful of surgeries.

One night, when I was at their house for dinner, I watched as Gianna, two and a half at the time, played with a nativity set she'd been given for Christmas. She tossed out the baby Jesus and inserted a tiny plastic tiger instead. It bothered Ariana that Jesus had been so coldly dismissed, and she stuck him on the corner of the table, which ruined Gianna's design aesthetic—and she had a strong one, understandably. When Ariana wasn't looking, Gianna relocated the entire cast to a wooden coffee table in the middle of the room and said the tiger had a stomachache and had to go to the doctor. The doctor performed an operation, Gianna said, and the tiger went home with his mom and played. It was one of several scenarios enacted that night, each ending in the same way: a child with a stomach problem, a doctor, a mom, a happy ending. Anyone who does not believe in the powers of the subconscious, the power of psychology, could spend a few hours with young Gianna. For Ariana, this made her decision: the happy ending. Maybe not for her, but for someone who now mattered more.

Surgeries for Gianna and the hospital stays and the stress of a toddler's pain took their toll. Even though Ariana died a little inside at the thought of leaving, she knew she had to do it, and so on this day she joined the world's many parents—mothers, most often—who make grand and painful sacrifices for their children.

Ariana has been crying on and off all day. She did not cry when Pascal proposed, or on her wedding day, but this day she had gone from office to office saying good-bye and then returning with her eyes red-rimmed and spilling over. There was a pull inside her not to go, and so even though there was nothing left for her to do, really, she stayed on past the morning and lunchtime and into the afternoon. Nine years was practically her entire working life. "My father worked here; I met my husband here," she said. "The place, the company . . . it is like a special monument. We have a saying in Italy: You have a chance to ride another wave." This is hers. Flight from her history.

By three in the afternoon, the moon was up and the sun had begun its descent. The windows in Ariana and Pascal's office allowed beams of light toward the upper portion of the room. They were odd, these windows, horizontal rectangles set high in the wall so that you can see the tops of mountains and trees but not the parking lot. Ariana's desk was clean and her computer was off and she said it was time for her to go. She stopped at the entryway and made a final phone call from an empty desk—someone she forgot to see. No one else moved. The sun lit a patch of her dark brown hair at the crown of her head so that she appeared suddenly illuminated, caught in this strange moment of no longer being there and not being gone either. She left a message and wiped at her eyes and I, like everyone else, looked away. A man came in and delivered an enormous wheel of Parmesan cheese, probably twenty pounds, to hand out at the Milan and Paris shows. We took turns trying to lift it; it was like trying to lift a tractor tire. When I turned back around, away from the Parmesan tire, Ariana was gone.

VIII

URINATING ON YOUR JEANS JUST MAKES GOOD SENSE

THE PRODUCT OF A NATURALLY OCCURRING PLANT called *Indigofera*, indigo is the most common dye material used in denim—and the world's oldest dyestuff. Indigo-dyed cloth remnants have been found by archeologists in Yemen, Indonesia, India, Vietnam, and Peru, some as old as 5,500 years. It was used in cave drawings and body decoration and even as a natural cure for liver problems and venereal disease (no one seemed to claim success in this latter). The Brits freaked out enemy armies by painting their bodies blue four hundred or so years ago. Indigo was once a major crop in the American South, but the Revolutionary War curtailed production of indigo in lieu of food. Still, there have been some sightings of this once vast crop still growing wild in places like Louisiana and South Carolina. Like cotton, indigo was believed to have magical qualities, understandable given its chemical composition.

These days, natural indigo is rarely used for clothing dye; it was replaced in 1897 by synthetic dye after its chemical properties were replicated in a German lab. Within a decade, sales of natural indigo dye fell to barely a fraction of global trade. Given that it takes about seventy pounds of plants to produce a pound or two of dye, the synthetic version's popularity does not surprise. (Surely, this ratio would dampen the spirits of even the most enthusiastic of farmers . . . the general equivalent of having to plant and harvest a city block's worth of veggies for a single evening stir-fry.) Using natural indigo is impractical not only because of its low crop yield but also because harvesting it is very labor-intensive, and it's often difficult to get consistency of color application. Today's textile market demands decreased costs, faster turnaround time, and mass replication, so the use of natural indigo isn't likely to return large scale any time soon.

The real magic of indigo, though, is how it ever became a dye crop in the first place. The plant, which grows to be six feet tall, has pale pink flowers. In order to extract dye the plant must be harvested just before it blooms and fermented in water for a week or so. After that, the liquid is drained and what's left dried into cakes. These cakes are combined with a chemical—usually hydrosulfite—or, in the old days, urine, to make what is called indigo white. Though this part of the process is the same for natural or synthetic indigo, I feel fairly confident that none of the denim manufacturers or brands I spoke with resort to using—even for the noble goal of corporate profit—urine to make your pants. Indigo white, like the indigo plant, isn't blue either. It's not even white. It's yellowish-green, a clunky adjective, of course, which may explain why chemistry texts never adopted the designation "indigo yellowish-green." Once the dye is made and the fabric dipped, it's not until oxygen hits the wet material that it turns, rather magically, pale blue. (Legler's frothing purple haze comes from oxidized dye at the top of the dye bath and is sometimes called a "head," like beer from a tap. This foamy head keeps the dye from contact with the air until the yarn has been colored.) Dipping and oxidizing multiple times creates deeper shades of blue.

One book I came across warned aspiring dyers that the process was complicated and they should take care to "remain humble" or they could be in for "a little fall" when using indigo. The very act of discovering that this pink-petaled, leafy plant would produce a dozen different shades of blue dye was assuredly an absurd bit of luck. One source I found noted how such a discovery might have taken place:

> If, by chance, some indican-bearing plant material found its way into a urine vat, the bacteria growing therein would render the vat in a reducing condition [use up the oxygen and release hydrogen], and the ammonia, being alkaline, would dissolve the resulting indigo white. Now, if some fiber fell into the vessel, and if it were retrieved later, the yellowish green material would turn blue before the eyes of the retriever, and the material would be dyed a permanent very pale blue.[1]

So, basically some ancient housewife dropped a flower bouquet of indigo into one of the large pots of urine that she kept lying around the house, and then some time later, perhaps while dusting, she also accidentally dropped a cloth into the same vat and didn't bother to retrieve it. Weeks later, then, in a spurt of inspiration, she decided a little spring cleaning was in order, retrieved her dusting cloth from its urine/indigo bath, and, as she lifted it to the air, watched it transform to an almost imperceptibly pale shade of blue.

Could happen.*

In the sixteenth century, Dutch traders brought indigo to Europe from the East Indies and it became valuable instantly; indigo cakes were used as currency. Of course, at the time indigo

---

*I found the real point to all of this, though, is how useful our urine is. The ancients, who seem always to have kept a few vats around the house, would think us mad for flushing with abandon.

began to be a commodity in global trade, the Brits wigged out much like they had with cotton, because up until this time they'd used woad, a plant similar to *Indigofera*, to dye their textiles blue. Free-market forces had yet to be embraced. Perhaps because of the threat indigo posed to woad dyers, it was associated for a time with witchcraft. Referring to it as a "fugitive dye" and a "corrosive and pernicious drug," France dealt with indigo users under a measured and reasonable rule of law during Henry IV's tranquil reign: They received the death penalty.[2] The law wasn't repealed until 1737, by which time indigo had also been outlawed—owing almost surely to economics rather than superstition—in England and Germany.[3] Up until the beginning of the twentieth century the same law meting out the death penalty to anyone using indigo was on the books in England, though by then it hardly mattered, since synthetic indigo had been put on the market. The demise of the natural indigo trade was particularly devastating for India. Today, more than fourteen thousand tons of synthetic indigo are manufactured every year. Few natural indigo growers remain. Japan is one, and certain tribes in Vietnam, Laos, and Nigeria.

Many designers today insist that if indigo had produced any other color—green, say, or red or yellow—it wouldn't be nearly as popular. Blue has an attraction that is universal; it's a color that evokes reflection, calm, warmth. It is also pretty much everyone's favorite color in the whole world. You might not think anyone has ever bothered to measure this kind of thing, but you would be wrong. The Dia Art Foundation in New York did a survey of fourteen countries and their favorite colors. With the exception of Ukraine, which ranked blue *and* green as favorite colors (18 percent each), every other country went with blue. The United States and Portugal, in particular, seem to have a particular passion for blue (44 percent and 48 percent, respectively).[4] Pascal believes that indigo, and thus blue, is the key to denim adoration. "We maintain the blue even when we work with other colors," he says. "There isn't a red or a green that works in this way. Only blue. It's something really magical."

It's also true that indigo, if untreated after dyeing, will leave blue stains on anything it touches: car seats, other clothing, furniture. Known as "crocking" in the industry, such leftovers have been the cause of a fair number of lawsuits, according to one industry professional I spoke with.5

Fundamentally, however, using any dye, including a fair number of natural dyes, is a polluting process. While indigo's sins are environmentally lesser than many other dyes used on garments, indigo does require multiple dips into dye vats, and is thus particularly demanding of wastewater treatment. Decolorization, as the undoing of the damage is called, typically takes color rather than chemicals out of mill water before dumping it back into the source. (Textile mills always need a water source nearby for breaking down dyes, washing, treatment, and other uses.) Residents who share water sources with textile mills would hardly be pleased at the notion of having purplish-blue water, after all. Nelson Houser, a chemist with Burlington Chemical, told me, "You remove the color [from wastewater], but you still have the chemistry there." The water might look clean, but it can still kill fish and insects. Environmental requirements for wastewater dumping vary depending on the size of the targeted water source.6 Smaller streams carry fewer nutrients to offset the waste products.

While industrialized countries have environmental regulations in place, many developing nations do not—or if they do, enforcement is weak or nonexistent. One industry consultant I spoke with said he believed a number of factories in Thailand and Indonesia simply shut down their water treatment systems after the factory monitors had left in order to save on electricity. Where pennies on the dollar could mean the difference between a contract or a factory closing, such activities hardly seem beyond the realm of possibility. Nelson Houser told stories of watching children play and livestock soak in untreated water outside textile mills in Asia. And both men talked about how most countries did not have safe handling practices like masks or close-toed shoes.

So why is this bad? In a word: chemicals.

Chemicals have a dizzying array of uses in textile manufacture these days. Dyes are usually classed either by chemical structure or by their application. All the clothing innovations we enjoy, like sweat management and flame retardants, not to mention antimicrobial, UV absorption, moth resistance, oil and dirt repellants, dust mite control, and easy-care fabrics, all rely on chemicals for their utility. Less well known are chemicals used as fixing and bleaching agents, lubricants, conditioners, tensile strengtheners, color leveling agents, and softeners. There are thousands of chemicals used in dyes, including in hair dye and industrial dye. The majority are harmless for those of us not employed in the industry; by the time our clothes hit store shelves the chemicals have been largely washed out of them. In denim production, sulfur dyes are particularly caustic. When used with indigo as a "sulfur bottom," these dyes create vintage denim looks by pretreating yarns prior to their being dipped in indigo, which casts a different hue on the finished jeans. This method can also be used after the indigo dye as a "sulfur top." Sulfur dyes, however, require the use of chemical auxiliaries that are particularly harsh on the environment. The most damaging is sodium sulfide, which is not only toxic but can cause contact dermatitis among textile workers if not handled correctly—think of it as having chronic poison ivy. Sulfur dyes, however—which typically come in greens, blacks, browns, and blues—are among the least expensive of dyes, making them attractive to manufacturers.[7] Sulfur dye residues remain in wastewater even after treatment.[8]

Because indigo is insoluble in water, it requires a chemical intermediary to render it usable to dye cotton. In the old days, this may have meant madder, ash, or of course our own handy urine. These days, hydrosulfite and sodium hydroxide are more common. Unlike the majority of most textile dyes, indigo does not require a mordant to set it, though it is also far less colorfast than most dyes.

"The environmental thing has kind of gotten lost in the merchandising side of things, because we're pushing for lower prices,"

Houser, who works on environmental issues at his own chemical firm, said. "There's pressure to make it cheaper, cheaper, cheaper. The message needs to be to merchandisers, retailers and consumers. Probably everyone in the process, those who work in factories or live near them, everyone gets touched along the path. Handling chemicals can be dangerous and everyone has a stake in textile safety."

Houser told me about a group called Oeko-Tex, out of Switzerland, that has established acceptable environmental standards and certification for textile manufacturers. Begun in 1992, the group labels environmentally friendly manufacturers. Generally, this includes the use of nonchlorine bleach, the elimination of heavy metals, and the reduction of formaldehyde in finishing agents. Yes, that's the same formaldehyde as used in high school biology class frog dissection. It's nice to know our clothes contain trace amounts of the same chemical used to keep dead frogs plump and pliable. Oeko-Tex focuses on what it calls "human ecology"—that is, making sure products used by consumers meet acceptable environmental standards. In the separate realms of "production ecology" and "disposal ecology," it admits the task of standardizing is much more difficult, first because global production involves myriad stages in multiple countries, and second, because there is a lack of consensus on the proper methods of disposal. Oeko-Tex has also not gained much of a foothold in the United States—with producers or consumers. From Houser's point of view, this has less to do with consumer desire for lower prices at any cost and more to do with the fact that environmental policies in the States are driven by local, state, and federal offices. Houser says—and this is true of environmental policies in general, not just as they apply to textiles—that Europe has simply been "more active than North America." Or, to put it another way, he said, "We do like our landfills."

The Oeko-Tex representative in the United States, Manfred Wentz, who works for Hohenstein Institutes in North Carolina, said the process had begun to gain some slow momentum here.

Wal-Mart declared recently that they were going to "go green," and many other high-visibility companies like Levi's have what he called "a very structured program." Surprisingly, China is second only to Germany in the number of outfits receiving Oeko-Tex certification (more than 700 plants certified, at the time of writing). Still, even he admits that there is no uniform restriction list as of yet, although Oeko-Tex's Web site lists hundreds of banned substances. Factories in Pakistan and Mexico were caught using banned substances, and China and Mexico do not yet have the wastewater controls that exist in the United States and Europe. The industry, as Wentz puts it, is very "vague."

Wentz's own father worked in dyes and died of cancer. It used to be that dyeing was an art, he said. You studied for years to become a dye master. These days, "people are trained on the spot." And the dye industry has moved with the textile industry. Sometimes, as was the case with Ciba-Geigy in New Jersey, they were compelled by the local populace to move. Sandoz, another big dyestuff maker in the 1980s and 1990s, was responsible for a notorious chemical spill into the Rhine River that killed wildlife for hundreds of miles. Dubbed the "Bhopal effect," it leached a 25-mile-long, red-tinted stream of chemicals and dyes into the water. Area residents had to get water for a time from enormous tankers brought down the Rhine. The spill eventually precipitated stricter environmental controls in Europe and the company never quite recovered its reputation. The big producers, Wentz said, can't stay in business, and the available data have shrunk with the industry's geographical movement to less well-regulated countries.

The European Union recently passed a 1,000-page law dubbed REACH (Registration, Evaluation and Authorisation of Chemicals), which will require all businesses producing *or* selling products in Europe to prove they've used safe chemicals in their production. They have until 2018 to implement the necessary measures. The hope is that the chemical industry will be compelled to search for greener alternatives. The 100,000 chemicals in use prior to 1981 have undergone little or no testing—even those still in use today—and are largely exempt from testing requirements in either the EU or the United States. Those developed after 1981, which number around 3,000, do have to conform to safety testing requirements, but at the moment there's not a lot of incentive for chemical companies to conduct tests on pre-1981 chemicals or develop new, "greener" chemicals. Such an effort would not only be expensive but could result in a company losing significant portions of an income-generating product.[9]

Over the course of a decade, REACH aims to change all that. The aim is to provide incentives for companies to develop environmentally friendly pesticides, solvents, and other chemicals while also giving consumers a fair level of confidence that the products they purchase will neither cause them ill health nor wreak havoc on the earth. The U.S. government and chemical companies oppose the law. Environmental groups like Greenpeace say the law doesn't go far enough, in part because it does not address companies that manufacture and import fewer than ten tons of chemicals a year.[10] Chemical companies say they're not against greener chemical alternatives, but that more time is needed to research and develop these alternatives and to "ease" the industry into this massive transformation. C. Boyden Gray, the United States Ambassador to the European Union, said in June 2006 that there was substantial concern over how REACH had been drafted, and he asked for a "risk-based" rather than a "hazard-based" approach. In his view, the legislation will force products off the market that are unlikely to be hazardous simply because they haven't been tested. He also said, "We are concerned that REACH will have a disproportionate effect on international trade. . . . The chances of trade disruption are too high to risk imposing such an unwieldy process on trade partners."[11]

HARRY MERCER, AN INDEPENDENT INDUSTRY ANALYST with his own consulting firm who has worked all over the world, is more blunt. Denim, he says, "is *always* contaminated with chemicals." Mercer claims he sees fake deportation systems—wastewater treatment—in countries around the world, or water diverted into storm drainage systems. Mercer says that even with the environmental controls, "clean water costs money," and a number of countries simply use polluted water for processing. There is no testing phase in place for this part of the process, he warned. According to him, many of the dyes now banned by Europe and the United States, like yellow sulfur, are still in use and simply kept off the Material Safety Data Sheets (MSDSs) that companies around the world are required to fill out. Mercer says these sheets make it easy to obscure data, particularly with benzidine in certain dyes; he named Direct yellow 27 and 28, as well as Red 1, as being benzidine-based, even if the data sheets don't reflect this.

Around the world, wastewater effluence is perhaps the single biggest environmental threat in textiles. Disposal of dyebaths and the cleaning of dye equipment is costly and complicated. High salt loads, toxicity, and lack of oxygen are all common problems in water where textile factories are unregulated or underregulated.[12]

In 2001, the United Nations Environmental Program (UNEP) asked Mercer to look into dye processes in the Indian state of Gujarat after the Indian courts threatened to shut down a group of textile dye producers for environmental pollution.[13] Mercer found that the dyers were simply dumping chemicals—particularly sulfuric acid, which is a common solvent—late at night, creating mass "wastelands." "They were avoiding treatment costs of the acid," he wrote in an e-mail to me. He went on to write, "all solvents used for dye manufacturing are poisonous or dangerous . . . chemical processes have not changed much in 100 years." And for the most part, washing hasn't improved in forty years.* Information, he said, is easily obscured. He warned against sulfur dyes, amines, and manganese, a heavy metal used in processing, as well as carcinogenic acrylic compounds, used in sizing and finishing agents. Mercer believes that certain denim is particularly offensive. Black denim, for example, is almost always treated using sulfur black dye (it is also often used in premium denim). Mercer accuses dye companies of recommending dye procedures using a far higher pH than is needed to increase their sales. As a result, half the dye is washed away during water treatment, where it "has to be flocculated with acrylics—which are made with carcinogens," he said. There are ways to use the dye with very little waste or pollution, though like Manfred Wentz, Mercer said there are almost "no qualified dyers left in denim companies anywhere that know enough to use the correct procedures." As a result, he believes special controls should apply to the manufacture of premium denim.[14] "There's a big gulf between designers and dyers," he said. "[Dyeing] is really quite crude, [but] it's a necessary evil."

Mercer is not alone. The half dozen or so industry experts who would speak to me said the same thing: that dye chemicals were inherently toxic, that developing countries avoid wastewater treatment when no one is looking, that environmental safety and health controls are abysmal or nonexistent. A handful of dyes used for jeans and other apparel are, according to the Department of Health and Human Resources, either "known" or "reasonably anticipated" to be human carcinogens. These are generally no longer produced in the United States, though this is not to say they are not manufactured and used in many other countries around the world for the clothing we buy daily. The link between textile workers and certain cancers, like bladder or nasal cancer, has long been known. Epidemiologists recognized the connection

*Slowly, however, treatments like stonewashing are being replaced by more environmentally friendly enzyme washes.

as far back as 1920. Benzidine, perhaps the worst offender, was one of the first chemicals to be linked to an occupation and increased risk of cancer. It is categorized as one of those amines that Harry Mercer warns about, and while it is not made in the United States, at least nine suppliers shipped it to U.S. companies as recently as 2003. Curiously, though, the most current data on the amount imported comes from 1980 (nearly 9,000 pounds). Benzidine also carries a potential long-term risk for those who live near former dye or waste disposal sites. While the dyes remain legal to import into the United States, one report I found warns, ". . . microbial degradation of these dyes may release free benzidine into the environment."

Such substances put textile and dye workers at considerably higher risk of cancers. Of these, the overwhelming majority of workers are women. Cancer rates, along with infertility or menstrual dysfunction among those in the textile trades, are increasing,[15] reports claim. Bladder cancer is the fifth most common form of cancer, with more than 55,000 new cases in the United States alone each year.[16] A quarter of working women report exposure to one or more harmful substances (accidentally inhaled or from contact with skin). Certain heavy metals like mercury and lead can travel through the placenta of a pregnant woman, and chemical workers report unusually high instances of spontaneous abortions. Even irregular shift work appears to be potentially damaging to a woman's fertility (and in many countries it is her fertility, rather than her factory paycheck, that brings value to her).[17]

Of course, record keeping in developing countries is fairly abysmal, and death by distinctive diseases in countries where childbirth and broken limbs are routinely life-threatening are rarely singled out, on paper or otherwise. Still, occupational hazard regulation is more than a signal of social progress and a strong economy; it is a symbol of governmental commitment to the health and well-being of its citizens.

These issues, at least for the United States, go beyond the obvious environmental and social responsibility arguments.

Greece recently refused the sale of certain U.S. textiles because they did not have the Oeko-Tex seal.[18] Without the standards that the rest of the world employs, our producers cannot always sell to foreign—particularly European—markets. One industry group in the United States had spent more than two years trying to research all the chemicals used in textiles to try to determine how manufacturing might need to make changes. I was told there were more than forty thousand chemicals in use for textiles and apparel, according to the REACH list. The group had intended to compile a chemical report for its members to make clear what they'd need to train their dye factories across the world, but even they found the information on chemicals incomprehensible. They were months late with their report and still couldn't wade their way through the dense information they'd managed to find. They were worried, and all the United States had done so far, they claimed, was accuse Europe of overly strict measures. But if U.S. corporations (and government, frankly) continue to fail to make strict environmental controls a priority in their manufacturing plants across the globe, they are unquestionably going to find themselves facing the prospect of more closed doors.

IX

HOW THE WEST WAS WON

THE ORIGINS OF DENIM HAVE LONG BEEN THE CAUSE of debate. For centuries it was believed that denim was invented in Nîmes, France, and used as far back as the fifteenth century for sailcloth. Some people even swear that Columbus outfitted his ships with denim sails. Though he did bring cotton from India back to Europe, even Columbus (perhaps the most geographically challenged explorer of his day to reach international fame) was not so inept a sailor as to use fabric that sags and grows heavy when wet. More likely, he used a waxed canvas. In any case, the real origins of the textile are wholly ambiguous.

What is known about denim is roughly as clear as the process of converting thermophotovoltaic light into electricity. And even that is probably less hotly contested. Jeans can refer to garments, technically speaking, that are made both from denim and from other fabrics, so that the correct term for what we recognize and wear today is actually denim jeans. Jeans as a term was first used to describe the vestments worn by Genoese sailors. These pants

weren't, of course, made from denim, as that would be overly con-
venient for the history books. Instead, they came from a fustian,
or a blend of cotton and wool or linen dubbed "Jene Fustyan" in
the sixteenth century. Fustian was imported into England as far
back as 1500.

Despite French claims for the invention of denim, at least one
curator at the Paris Musée de la Mode et du Costume, Pascale
Gorguet-Ballesteros, calls this merely "patriotic myth." Gorguet-
Ballesteros believes that the word denim, as it refers to an all-
cotton textile, can be traced to England in the 1700s. Serge de
Nîmes, the fabric, was a twill of wool and silk (though I found
sources claiming that both "serge" and "nîmes" were names for
blended fabric woven in France, which hardly helps here). What
was made in England, Gorguet-Ballesteros claims, was a similar
twill, though made entirely from cotton. She believes denim came
about as a result of the dramatic rise in demand for American cotton, particularly in England in the eighteenth century. Fabrics
needed differentiation as more and more types were developed or
imported, and serge de nîmes soon evolved into the anglicized
"denim" in part for the purposes of categorization, and in part
because the English may have believed such etymology would lend
sophistication to their product.[1] The French working class did
have an all-cotton fabric that we would recognize as denim today,
but since the word did not exist, she believes it was likely to have
been called by another name.

In the mid-1800s, Levi Strauss, a native of Bavaria whose given
name was Loeb,* developed rugged-wear pants that he dubbed
"waist overalls" for fortune seekers during the gold rush. They
were made mostly from brown canvas fabric called cotton duck,
of the sort used for tents; the indigo dye of today's blue jeans
came later.

---

*It's hard for me to envision this in an advertising campaign: "Loeb 501s."
Would Russians in 1985 have clamored so passionately for a pair of Loeb's?

At the same time, New England mills churned out the fustian fabric worn by Genoese sailors and dubbed it "jean." Jean was a lighter, uniformly colored form of denim that fell out of favor sometime in the nineteenth century, along with the term "jean." The word wouldn't resurface until the mid-twentieth century for reasons that confound historians, while the fabric itself seems never to have returned. Denim was both stronger and more expensive than jean material, and even then it was woven with one natural or white thread and one colored. Both jean and denim were made in American mills as far back as the 1700s.

Though Strauss is often credited with inventing denim jeans, the real inventor likely worked a century earlier and will remain forever unknown. While he may not have invented denim jeans, he was the visionary who pulled a number of disparate elements together to create what is arguably the most symbolically powerful article of clothing in modern history. In 1872, Levi Strauss received a letter from a Nevada tailor named Jacob Davis, who'd come up with a strategy of using rivets to reinforce jeans at their stress points—namely, the pockets and the bottom of the button fly. Most of these rivets are still in use today. The fly rivet, however, quickly lost favor, as rumor has it that a camping cowboy found his delicate nether parts nearly branded when the rivets heated up in front of the fire. Also more common nowadays on the back pockets is a quarter inch of thick thread known as a bar tack reinforcing the stress points. Davis didn't have enough money to patent his rivet idea, so Strauss fronted the cash. They received their patent for an Improvement in Fastening Pocket Openings in 1873, and the two enjoyed the profits until the patent expired and other manufacturers replicated the invention. Their partnership changed the course of fashion.

Strauss's trademarks emerged slowly. The Two Horse Brand patch advertised two horses attempting to pull apart a pair of Levi's. Undoubtedly, such a feat would be easy in real life for a couple of hulking stallions, but the marketing strategy worked nonetheless. The famous 501s, which denoted a batch number, came in 1890. Copper rivets had been in use for nearly two decades by then, and the telltale *M*, referred to as the Arcuate logo, in orange thread and meant to symbolize a bird in flight, had been sewn on the back pocket almost from the jeans' very beginning. The red tab came in 1936.

The very early Levi's had elements that we wouldn't recognize on jeans today. Like the zipper, belt loops were a fairly late addition. Items nixed for the sake of modernity include the single back pocket (it's double or nothing these days), a cinching belt at the waist in back, suspender buttons, and that curiously placed fly rivet. It is likely urban legend that the crotch rivet branded many an unsuspecting cowboy; regardless, it was unceremoniously removed in the early twentieth century. In 2006, the fly rivet seems to be making a comeback, as I've spotted it on several brands—I personally am very excited to see it return. Cowboys and campfires are perhaps a rare enough partnership nowadays that designers have either forgotten the rivets' inauspicious origins, or they're playing games with our delicates.

The real evolution of jeans both as a symbol and as a style began during World War II. The grainy black-and-white photographs by Walker Evans of Depression-era families, unsmiling, with haunted eyes and uniforms of stained jeans, seemed to suggest something uniquely American, the will to believe in your own strength and dignity against overwhelming circumstances. Everything about the photos, from the faces to the clothing to the ragged decks and dusty window frames, suggests endurance, and the power of humanity. Levi Strauss's gold rush jeans meant something similar. They'd been created at a time when industry was burgeoning and prosperity didn't need to mean anything other than a tin pan and a lot of luck. So when the photos of stoic families surviving inside their crumbling homes, beside their empty cupboards, and in their torn jeans hit mass media magazines like *Life* and *Look*, everyone could relate. One writer called these people "the foot soldiers in the war on poverty" and claimed, "The enduring spirit, tenacity, and strength of these people were mirrored in the simple strength and dignity of denim."[2]

When World War II ended, it marked the first time jeans were worn for leisure. During the war, denim had been deemed essential to the war effort and rationing had changed the look of them.[3] Levi's had no longer been able to use copper rivets to reinforce pockets, and the Arcuate logo was deemed an unnecessary use of thread. Jeans themselves had been slimmed down to avoid using excess fabric. During the American occupation of Japan, soldiers wore jeans in their off-duty hours—the Japanese dubbed them G-pans—and denim began its long association with relaxation, modernity, and American wealth. Because they were rare, jeans in Japan could cost upwards of nearly half a month's salary in the immediate postwar period.[4] Around Tokyo, secondhand markets for soldier's cast-off jeans thrived. Like cars, jeans had become mass-produced, and they suggested almost endless economic possibility and industry. In the *New Yorker*, they were called "the classic of mass production" by Janet Malcolm.

By now, Lee and Wrangler, along with a handful of other smaller brands, like Pay Day, Tuff Nut, Hercules, Buckhide, Union Made, Big Ben, and Carhart, were established manufacturers (Lee introduced the zipper fly in 1926). And Hollywood made them acceptable not only for cowboys and soldiers but for women as well after a 1939 movie called *The Women* showed women lined up and waiting for divorces in Reno, clad in blue jeans. Heartthrobs like Marlon Brando, Gary Cooper, and James Dean had started wearing jeans in all their pictures. It was perhaps the first realization of the power of a star vehicle to sell an idea or a product. (Brando and Dean weren't saving Darfur, but these were the days when people didn't expect their celebrities to go save the world on their behalf.) Throughout the 1960s, jeans came to symbolize the counterculture, the Leary-Hopper-Ginsberg set. Those who wore them were connected to one another politically and philosophically. Jeans had been banned from schools early on, but when antiwar protestors, particularly recently returned Vietnam veterans clad in jeans, threw their medals to the ground, the context in which they'd voiced their anger came to mean as much as the words themselves. Jeans and long hair identified where one's loyalties lay. If the establishment couldn't control the social behavior of those at odds with their policies, it could at least shape a symbolic message: Do not listen to what is said, those in power subtly urged their constituents, look at who is saying it.

Arguably, the establishment failed on all counts. The Vietnam conflict ended in American defeat and shame, and jeans moved from the lower to the middle classes. By the late 70s, jeans were respectably ubiquitous. High-end fashion houses began to embrace denim. Advertisements for cigarettes, airlines, cameras, diamonds, and liquor began to feature jeans. The Italians are often credited with bringing a couture sensibility to jeans with their introduction of Fiorucci's Buffalo 70 jeans in the 1970s. Buffalo 70s were skinny and blue-black and came with a hefty price tag if you could find them. They were also enormously successful, and other well-respected designers followed, including Gloria Vanderbilt and Calvin Klein.[5] With no history of jeans as work wear and the desire to replicate the postwar look of now vintage jeans, the Japanese began to invent new methods of treatment, finishing, and washing, eventually earning them the worldwide reputation they now enjoy as premier denim innovators.[6] And yet they still covet the post–World War II-era vintage look; more than two thousand tons of vintage and contemporary American jeans are shipped annually to Japan.[7]

Through most of the twentieth century, jeans came in one basic look: blue, five pocket, straight leg. Levi's hadn't changed much in over a century. Suddenly, beginning in the late 70s, and continuing even more today, there are thousands of looks and styles. And price tags to match. These days denim is found in the most unlikely of places: on living room furniture, in government offices, in posh urban night clubs, and even on car upholstery. It is found on rap stars, soap stars, farmers, accountants, and factory workers. The Smithsonian in Washington, DC, has hung it as a particular American heirloom. Republicans and Democrats wear it. Babies and grandparents. In New York Paris Hilton wears it, and so does my Aunt Barbara, who lives in Pittsburgh.*

But denim is also found in the high-tech testing laboratories of scientists around the world.

*My Aunt Barb neither receives nor seeks sponsorship, though in my personal view she would be far more deserving than your average heiress.

X

A SOCIETY OF THE MIND
AND OTHER
ATMOSPHERIC CONTAMINANTS

RESEARCH TRIANGLE PARK IS A BUCOLIC LITTLE TRAPE-
zoid of a town tucked between Raleigh-Durham and Chapel Hill,
North Carolina, where it would not be inaccurate to say that a
whole lot and absolutely nothing occur concurrently at any given
time. Though nearly forty thousand people might be inside its
borders every single day, you are unlikely to see them. There are no
restaurants in Research Triangle Park, no shops or bars or gas stations, or even any residential buildings of any sort. The post office,
the sole public building apart from a hotel or two and a couple of
drive-up banks, will offer a critical mass of humanity that rarely
goes above the single digits. The day I was there the six people
ahead of me were sending packages to Canada, India, Tokyo, and
China, and the clerks were nearly breaking out in a sweat. Except
at rush hour, there is rarely any traffic at all on the super-smooth,
two-lane roads. I never saw a police car, an ambulance, or a truck

at any time during the several drives I took around town. It was as if the whole town didn't exist, except on paper.

Which is appropriate, in a way, since it is a place of ideas.

What really happens in Research Triangle Park, or RTP, as it is known to locals, is, in a word, everything. It is perhaps the most research-intensive town on the planet. The streets have names like Development and Silicon Drives. Nestled inside large swaths of forest sit one corporation after another: IBM, GlaxoSmithKline, Nortel, Burt's Bees, Sigma X, Eli Lilly, Verizon, Cisco, DuPont, MCI, Lockheed Martin.* The USDA Forest Service and the EPA are also here, as is the National Humanities Center and the National Toxicology Program. But none of these is a headquarters. Indeed, perhaps the single most important requirement for tenancy in RTP is that somewhere inside each building there must be research and development happening. In fact, this R & D must be the single galvanizing activity going on inside. The idea, one local scientist told me, was to build a "society of the mind." So if you're looking for a concentration of product development and consumer testing, this is probably your place.

I was in RTP visiting a lesser-known entity: the American Association of Textile Chemists and Colorists (AATCC), or A-squared, as it is called by enthusiasts. These people keep your clothes from fading in the sun, from staining via perspiration-under-duress, from sudden and random combustion, from unwanted bugs and ticks and all manner of invisible bacteria. They keep lying on your living room carpet from being an act of passive suicide and your jeans from disintegrating under extended exposure to exhaust fumes. These people, and forgive the cliché, are unsung heroes.

I had been invited by the AATCC to attend their annual con-

---

*RTP has building codes that state only 50 percent of a corporation's land holdings can be developed, including parking lots. So the place, in the fall, is as tranquil and beautiful as any arboretum.

ference in RTP, where testing labs, manufacturers, textile professors, students, and all manner of industry professionals gather to
determine what sort of tests our clothes endure before they
become our clothes. These tests range from the standard ones for
wrinkles and flammability to those for microbes and moths, only
the lexicon involved is far more interesting. "Dimensional
change," for example, is a lyrical way of saying shrinking or
expanding or otherwise morphing into a shape other than what
the designer had initially envisioned. "Wrinkle recovery" carries
such poignancy, as if an article of clothing has emerged from a long
and senseless illness, that you will likely not even be disappointed
to learn that it is merely about the ability of a garment to keep
itself from needing a good iron. Despite the fact that "fugitive
color" might suggest a nefarious hue on the lam, it actually refers
to fading. Likewise, "atmospheric contaminants," in this context,
are not intergalactic bacilli from the troposphere but rather
exhaust fumes — a necessary test given the amount of time a garment will sit in inventory in some warehouse with trucks moving
in and out daily.

The first session I attended was International Testing Methods. Because the word *international* was used, I figured this might
have some relevance to my research. I'd asked, upon registration,
what sessions the secretary, whom I'd been in e-mail contact with,
thought might be most interesting for a book on jeans; she offered
me a bemused look but didn't say anything. In this session, when
the first sentence I heard was, "Japan says they've run out of testing material," I began to understand why. Then someone asked
who the project leader on "whiteness" was. This is how my notes
from the first thirty minutes read: "A new method for staining proposed by the Japanese in '98 — I propose that it is dropped." "The
U.S. developed a crop meter cloth with correct whiteness. It's a
murky issue." "Sweden is pushing colorfastness to upholstery. The
ball is in China's court."

The AATCC's mission, along with another group called the

American Society of Testing and Materials (ASTM), is to develop a base of comparison for garments and other household items; they don't decide the standard of quality—that's left up to the manufacturers—they simply offer up a measurement of it. While all manufacturers and brands the world over must adhere to a certain range of standards, some fall on the lower end of this spectrum, while others are higher. This explains why the sheets you buy from an inexpensive retailer like Family Dollar might not have the same softness or longevity as those you buy from Calvin Klein. They adhere to different measurements of quality. In essence, setting international standards also means a brand in Japan can buy cotton from Mexico and Turkey and have it made into cloth in France and North Carolina and sewn into a garment in China and Bangladesh and sell it on store shelves in Tokyo and Madrid and have the consistency and quality be exactly the same for each garment in every country. This means not only the fabric itself, but how consumers are instructed to care for it and what is listed on the label. Even the label icons—how Americans understand the symbol for dryers versus the British versus the Japanese—are hotly debated.

THE AATCC BEGAN IN 1921 IN PART BECAUSE OF GLO-bal changes brought on by World War I. Prior to America's involvement in the war, most of the world's synthetic dyes came from Germany. The mid-nineteenth century had marked the beginning of the study of organic chemistry, and a young British scientist named William Perkin had embarked on what was ultimately both a medical failure and history's most significant advance for the fashion industry. Perkin was not a fashion guy; he was a scientist in the Einstein-test tube-lab coat kind of way. He'd been charged with synthesizing a quinine-based treatment for malaria, a disease that remains today the world's biggest killer.

Though he was never able to solve this devastating public health issue, in 1856 he did present us with mauve dye.*

For that, he was eventually knighted by the royal family.

Prior to Perkins's dramatic chemical detour, dye had come mainly from roots, bark, and flowers, which rendered color choice somewhat limited, and supply unstable and inconsistent. Spice merchants and apothecaries included natural dyestuffs among their wares. I even came across one dye recipe from sixteenth-century Venice that called for: water, white vinegar, human urine, live lime, ashes of oak, and a yellowish mineral called orpiment. Apparently urine from, say, small forest animals was deemed sub-par. The dyer was instructed to boil all the ingredients together and then put them through "dog-tongue shaped felt."[1] (This recipe, of course, predates Gene Simmons). Dog tongues aside, however, most dyes were extracted from their wild elements and then soaked in water-based solutions to mine the color; for many such crops, including indigo, vast quantities of plants were required for tiny amounts of dye. In the nineteenth century, demand for dyes increased as cloth production—due in no small measure to the increasing efficiency with which cotton was grown and processed—increased production to meet growing market demands each decade.[2] By 1920, natural dyes constituted less than 10 percent of the worldwide market.[3]

In the mid- to late-nineteenth century, Germany was widely considered the world leader in organic chemistry. The Germans held a monopoly over the synthetic dye trade and by World War I accounted for more than 75 percent of global production.[4] Given German expertise, most American textile manufacturers did not bother to acquire the training or knowledge to make dye. When the war broke out, the United States and its allies blocked German-made products, and American companies were forced to produce their own dyes—which, for a while, were substandard and led

*For those who enjoy celebrations, you may take a moment to belatedly celebrate the 2006 150th anniversary of synthetic dye.

to what the handful of industry professionals who keep track of this sort of history call the "dyes crisis." During the crisis one U.S.-based factory owned by the German company Bayer had been seized by the U.S. government at the start of World War I and proclaimed "enemy territory."[5] Finally, in the 1920s, America had established its own dye industry.

The AATCC was created as a response to manufacturers' outcry against inferior dyes and consumer demands for better products. Disputes that erupted in the industry could not be resolved without a set of acceptable standards. One of the AATCC's first standardized tests was devised to assess the fading of textiles when exposed to light using a machine developed solely for this purpose called the Fade-Ometer. The first incarnation of this machine is charmingly anachronistic and makes Will Robinson's *Lost in Space* robot look avant-garde.* An enormous metal hulk, it resembles a rocket with the tip cut-off and a microwave oven plopped on top. Though updated—slightly—the Fade-Ometer is still in use today.

- -

RETAILERS LIKE THE GAP, NORDSTROM, TARGET, NIKE, Talbot, Sears, and JCPenny had representatives at the AATCC conference, and a handful of international testing companies—including Intertek, where Mehman works—were present as well. The idea behind the conference is to revise and update test methods, particularly in light of new fabrics being developed. For a retailer to sell jeans anywhere in the United States, their products must comply with the range of AATCC and ASTM test standards. Today, there are more than 1,000 different tests for clothing and household items—the U.S. military alone has more than 600 developed by AATCC. Though it's difficult to conceive of this industry, its members are responsible for keeping lead out of our

*For the trivia buffs among you, the robot's name was Gunther.

houses, snaps on our children's pajamas secure, and bacteria from migrating to the crotch of our pantyhose.

The government has a multitude of standards that manufacturers must meet before most items will ever hit store shelves. Children's clothes, for example, must be washed fifty times before they're even put through certain tests—for example, for flammability. The AATCC headquarters in RTP has a lab that resembles something like an oversized laundry room with machinery. This lab serves as ground zero for the development of new testing methods, or tweaking of old ones. Manufacturers have their own labs as well, but each is structured according to the AATCC's standards. In addition to the Fade-Ometer, there is the Laundrometer, the Crockmeter, the Gas Fading Test Chamber, the Ozoniter, and the Weather-Ometer, which basically re-creates weather inside a tiny box. Instructions carved onto a plastic plaque and glued to its front remind the operator to turn on the gadget's water and air-conditioning before use. It is, perhaps, the coolest invention I know short of those that send people to space. Mostly, it re-creates sunshine and humidity to see how various fabrics hold up, but I also like to think that sometimes the lab techs re-create tiny monsoons inside there, or even the occasional twister.

The tests, though, play a large part in actually saving lives. We owe the safety of our clothing, at least in part, to the military. As methods of warfare grew more sophisticated—World War II was the first significant military engagement in which cavalry did not play a significant role—so having a soldier's uniform not add to his already colossal burden of death and injury also needed to become more sophisticated. Soldiers needed uniforms that could adapt and function in a variety of climates, from tropical to arctic, and uniforms that would be flame retardant. The more advanced weaponry and ammunition got, the more advanced uniforms needed to be. The military also wanted to find a way to standardize the dyeing of uniforms; up until that point, khaki could mean a variety of greens, browns, and grays. The committee formed to investigate this was called the Olive Drab Committee, inspired no doubt by the color the army was after. Perhaps they wanted to avoid any potential design confusion that might arise from the popular olive of the day used on many American families' couches and carpets.

Other military-related tests involved sulfur-dyed fabrics, mildewproofness* of garments, and water repellency. As technologies were able to make more and better forms of synthetic fabrics, new tests had to be formulated. To determine static electricity in nylon, most notably nylon slips, a woman, presumably in some sort of lab setting, dressed only in skivvies and a slip, rubbed her rear against a piece of nylon sailcloth a certain number of times, and then wandered across the room. In this way, static charges were measured, and the testers—mostly male back then—went home whistling.

- -

ON MY FINAL DAY IN RESEARCH TRIANGLE PARK, I sat in the lab, beside the rain tester, as a panel of scientists described microbes—particularly those found in sweat and urine. "It's not the liquid that smells," one of the panelists had told me the night before, referring to sweat and urine, "it's the bacteria." Today, he was regaling the audience—standing room only—with tales of the new bacteria he and his colleagues had been replicating in his lab. Fake sweat and urine were tough bacteria, he conceded, to dispose of. "But you ought to *see* what we've got growing in there!" he said to one woman in the front row. He laughed uproariously at this and bounced a couple of times in his seat. She laughed, too, and promised to pay a visit soon.

Several weeks after the AATCC conference, I went to a lab in

---

*Mildewproofness is not my word. Someone else, fifty years ago, decided that in the absence of a suitable word, multiple ones could just be chucked together.

New Jersey to try to destroy some denim myself. Since most people in the world never get such an opportunity, I was understandably elated. A woman named Karen who used to run the lab at AATCC invited me, and she knew the various tests so well she could recite the number code and testing requirements for pretty much all 1,000 or so—at least it seemed so to me.

Inside her lab, where I was delighted to discover that people actually wore white coats, eight or ten employees were busy testing various types of fabric on a dozen or so machines. We kicked someone off their real work so that I could do some fake testing on one of the machines. Karen had prepared a handful of denim swatches for me that were uniform in size and weight. In order for there to be international replication in tests, exactitude at every turn is mandatory. If one of those swatches had been a sixteenth of an inch shorter than the others, it would have been tossed out (except for my purposes, of course). This particular machine was used to measure tensile strength in denim—some higher-quality cotton is stronger than others. Sizing, a kind of chemical strengthening, makes a difference as well.

She walked me through a labyrinth of testing rooms. One had several dozen washing machines, each with a large silver intergalactic arm that ran the length of the room, disappearing into the ceiling in what seemed to be an exact replica of a 1950s horror movie set. It was called the wash/dry room, and colorfastness was one of the main tests. Another was for water resistance, which has certain duty fees according to customs regulations that differ from country to country. Fabric undergoes simulated tests for rain, humidity, and, of course, human sweat and urine. The rain tester gauges the absorption rate of water, as when, for instance, you're wearing jeans in a downpour and the water begins crawling up your legs as if your pants had suddenly morphed into denim straws. In Karen's world this is called wicking.

Formaldehyde is used to make cotton wrinkle resistant. Karen and her colleagues test to make sure it's used in acceptable ways and at acceptable levels. Air permeability, wind resistance, and stiffness are all tested, too. The Crockmeter checks colorfastness, or how long before indigo dye will leave a bluish haze on white fabric.

I also subjected a denim swatch to something called an Elemendorf machine. It was another way of gauging strength, basically, but rather than judge the tensile strength it gauges the amount of force, in pounds, that denim can withstand. As another white-coated lab technician prepared the machine, a woman to our left hunched over a table looking through a microscope. She was not looking at molecular structure, as I'd thought; instead, she was engaged in what has to be one of American's top ten worst jobs ever. She was a thread counter. She was actually counting threads. Thread. Counter. If an Egyptian sheet claims to be three hundred count, it would have likely passed by her, or another thread counter, for verification. An 80/20 cotton/linen blend should have eight hundred threads of cotton and two hundred threads of linen in the *one thousand* yarns the thread counter is required to count *five* or *six* times. Just looking at her hunched-over back made my eyes feel fizzy. For lace, Karen told me, thread counters have to sample from every repeat in the pattern.

I couldn't watch her without weeping, so I turned back to the Elemendorf. Denim is typically supposed to withstand seven to ten pounds of force before it tears. Just for kicks—and these are the kinds of kicks textile lab technicians in New Jersey find pleasure in—the technician set it at thirty pounds. "Ah," he said, a little gleefully. "Two point four." Karen explained, as if I was simpleminded, that this was too much weight for the fabric.* At fifteen pounds, the result was three point seven. My stomach began to hurt.

Next, Karen led me to what she called the flammability exclusion test—or what I called the fire room. She was not, however, foolish enough to allow me free rein in there, as she had in the

---

*Admittedly "two point four" meant about as much to me as a calculator might have meant to the thread counter.

other labs. Or any rein at all, for that matter. She walked me to a large silver casketlike box with a glass window in front that had black smudges all over the inside of it. "After we wash it and bang it around," she said, referring to the denim being tested, "we burn it up." I was dismayed to learn that she referred to the people who worked in this lab as *technicians*, as if they were on equal footing with the thread counter and the Elemendorf operator. These people were in a whole other class. I called them Fire Starters.

For the fire test (I mean, flammability exclusion test) the fabric swatches are put in an oven to take out moisture, and then, to drive home the point, they are subjected to the desiccator, which takes out any seditious remaining water and is akin to letting your underwear hang from a saguaro cactus for a hundred or so years. It's done under what Karen called a worst-case scenario. (You have no pores *and* you've been camping in Joshua Tree for ten years in the same pair of jeans.) Once the sample is aflame in the silver box, the time it took to burn and the surface charring combined give the Fire Starters their results.

No matter how you tell the story of the testing labs, though, there is a tinge of American history and human frailty in each test. For each lead button, each pH balance, each charred sample, someone, somewhere on one very unlucky occasion endured something that went on to inspire a quiet group of scientists in a quiet little suburban town doing surprisingly important work.

XI

THE ARTISAN OF
UNBEARABLE SHOPPING

Première Vision, held in a suburb of Paris near Charles de Gaulle airport, was one in what seemed like an entire village of five shows. Laid out like an enormous fan, it took over an hour to walk one way. The area was bigger than some American neighborhoods and had, in addition to the vendors like Legler, gourmet restaurants, cafés, art installations, chocolatiers, Häagen-Dazs ice cream stands, and large areas of beanbag chairs for those who succumbed to the show's sheer velocity. Thirty thousand people would visit here.

There were thousands of mobile phones in use at the show, and their tinny speaker sounds filled the air, along with the rasp of metal hangers moved across metal racks, and the drone of conversation swallowed by soaring ceilings. During the setup, Pascal and several colleagues had hung samples from the new geographically grouped collection: Africa, Europe, Japan, South America, United States. Someone asked if Africa should be next to Europe. "Why not?" Pascal said. "It's a free world." This cracked him up a little.

Monica, a co-worker, arranged beer, wine, chocolate, salami, cheese, espresso, and water to give away from a temporary Formica countertop and bar. Overhead, one of the fluorescent lights flickered on and off and Pascal grooved for a second. "Discothèque," he laughed. When they'd finished, Monica locked the door to the booth, and Pascal took a moment to stand on his tiptoes and peer over the door. "It is a beautiful booth," he proclaimed.

Legler's booth occupied a far corner section called "casual-wear," and when I arrived, it was so busy that half a dozen people were milling around the entrance waiting until there was room to wander inside. But this, I was told over and over, was quieter than in years past. Pascal told me that when they were setting up the previous year's show there was a bomb scare toward the end of the day and the whole building complex had to be evacuated. What baffled him wasn't that there had been a bomb scare but that so many of the other exhibitors hadn't taken it as an opportunity to flee their tiny booths and explore Paris. People just stayed there, in nearby hotels or even just hovering on the sidewalks that ribbon the area. He'd sort of shrugged and gone into the city center, content with a few quiet hours of exploration that he'd normally never allow himself.

For Pascal, trade shows like Première Vision represented the start of a new collection. There was no past or present in this world, only a total fixation on the future. By the time PV rolls around, Pascal's customers had already chosen most of what they wanted for their designs and needed to purchase only smaller amounts of fabric to fill out their collections. This focus on the future is a little like putting your house on the market before you've even moved your stuff in and tried the place out. In the world of apparel—high-fashion or everyday garments—the future encroaches more and more, demanding bigger sacrifices from the present. Pascal's new lines each season are already old to him before the fabric even hits store shelves in the form of apparel.

At PV, booths specialized in the tiniest minutiae of clothing:

zippers, buttons, lace, beads, rivets, even hangers. There were more than seven hundred exhibitors, many of whose booths took up what seemed like half a city block. Some booths had gotten extravagant, with hardwood floors, handmade furniture, and artistically rendered displays. One booth had built a mock sailboat and pontoons, and benches offered seating where the deck would have been. There were draperies, dyes, upholstery, and accessories. Legler's booth was, by comparison, smaller and not showy at all.

When I finally made my way into the booth on the opening day, Pascal was engaged by customers from Alexander McQueen. He placed both hands on the table's edge in front of him and, for a split second, stretched his back upwards like a cat, then stood up straight again. His hands were clean today, but very often they were tinged with blue from touching denim all day; he once told me that he accidentally ate a lot of indigo by forgetting to wash his hands. Metal frames held jeans samples from the collection. Running the length of the metal frames were tall tables where customers met with Legler sales or design staff, and beyond the tables, a series of pale Formica desks. Roughly one hundred color and variation styles were on display, the sample jeans held in place by whimsical clothes pegs a foot long with Legler's eagle logo painted on them. The pegs were clipped to the frames, which stood in rows that took up half the space. At one end of the booth the food counter held the Parmesan tire, red wine, cappuccino, croissants, mini-sandwiches, and chocolates. In the official PremièreVision guidebook, Ariana was still listed as Legler's contact.

What PV was really about, though, was the same thing Cotton Incorporated's presentations in Milan were about: creating a fantastical world within a world. A place neither real nor unreal. The elements, pulled from our shared history and experience and desire, all added up to something slightly more romantic, more hip, more color-saturated, and more enchanting than everyday life. It was the essence not only of fashion but of fiction and art and culture and, of course, consumerism. It was ultimately what compelled us to buy things we don't actually need; things we hope will make our everyday world just one small move closer to fantasy.

At PV, the concept of real and unreal juxtaposed against each other was everywhere, all of it out of balance and disproportionate. Enormous painted pots with faux moss cascading down the sides à la Lewis Carroll hold thick-stemmed irises three feet tall. The pots stood higher than my rib cage so the plants towered over me like trees; I was a miniature in someone's living room garden. It was both absurd and delightful, which was probably the point. In one area, where much of the world's fashion press had small displays in half a dozen languages, a multitiered seating area was draped in actual rectangles of sod, as if we were all sitting in our own backyard. By the middle of the second day, the edges of the sod were ragged and muddy tracks had formed around the area. Stylish men with shaggy hair and Razr phones strode purposefully and seriously through the hallways while licking popsicle sticks of Häagen-Dazs.

Part of Pascal's job was shopping. One afternoon during the show he took the train to central Paris to conduct, as he called it, "research" around the pricey area of Louvre-Rivoli. As we exited the Metro, a rock video was being filmed and Isabella Rossellini walked regally by with her family. Pascal, being Italian, found this titillating. Many people, including myself, have commented on the extraordinariness of having to shop for a living. It's like playing baseball for a living, or singing on a massive stage before tens of thousands of fans, or flying to the moon, or hunting dinosaurs—all things that are theoretically fun until someone demands that you do them, indeed, *pays* you to do them—and suddenly they can become very unfun.

Pascal looks at a pair of jeans, touches them—rubs them ferociously to see how well the dye is set. He studies hems and inseams and weaves, rivets and buttons and belt loops. He can do this in two, maybe three, seconds. I had had visions of us wandering hidden stores, Pascal the fabric sage instructing me on what was beautiful, what was quality, what would transform me so that walking down the street would be an experience beyond walking down the street. I suppose I'd envisioned it happening under the same psychological imperative under which much shopping around the world happens: the desire to make ourselves a better us than we imagine we already are. An us we imagine we aren't quite yet. But no.

Shopping for Pascal was purely utilitarian. He was not that rare man who loved to shop. He was that rare man who shopped to work. He scuttled sharply around racks and other shoppers and displays, lingering only rarely, before he zipped off somewhere else. His moves were so strident that several times I lost him and after a while realized he was patiently waiting for me outside in the Paris winter. The shopping lover and the shopping worker. It's not often I find myself the weak link in an activity that doesn't require much physicality. He zigzagged around tiny streets, crossing to one side, then the other. Once, he told me he made maps of certain stores in Tokyo, Paris, New York. No roads. Only shops. Maps of malls and stores not to be missed. There were three denim stores around Louvre-Rivoli—an area as familiar as his own home. "It's like my own hand," he said—and the managers greeted him like family. They showed him their prized jeans. One manager from a Japanese store called Cabane de Zucca showed Pascal a new indigo chambray. "This is poplin, eighty/eighty. For top," he said. He was wearing a knit cap, chambray shirt, and dark denim jeans.

Pascal said, "Crazy."

The manager plucked another pair of jeans off the rack. Cut timber lined the walls of the store and the floor was made of slate. Bare tree branches had balls of denim like flower buds hanging from them and the entire store smelled like cedar and incense. "For a left, it's fantastic," Pascal said. Usually, he said cryptically, a "left" is soapy and soft. Strangely, I knew what he meant: the fabric didn't hold up. It wasn't stiff like denim should be in pants.

The manager led Pascal to the back of the store and pulled a pair of purplish dark blue jeans out. "This," he said, "is the Pope of denim! The best denim in Paris!" It was dyed by hand and dipped twenty-four times. It was made from ultra-high-quality Zimbabwean cotton that has long, *V*-shaped fibers.

"If you want to buy a fantastic jean, you buy this," Pascal said, fingering the jeans. He was clearly awed. They looked like plain old jeans to me, and when I asked what was special about them, Pascal, who seemed almost bewitched by their beauty, said, "Everything."

We walked out of the store and into the waning twilight of a cobbled street. He told me that everyone in the industry went to this particular store to "make research" because they were the real "artisans" of denim. The jeans had had an asking price of 850 euros, or nearly a thousand dollars.

"If they were three hundred fifty euros, I would have bought them," he said.

"For yourself?" I asked.

"No!" he stopped walking for a second. "For Legler. I *never* buy jeans!"

He told me that very few pairs cost more than about twenty dollars to make, even for premium denim. In some rare cases, it might go to fifty dollars, but short of having precious gems sewn into the pattern, even the finest pair of five-hundred-dollar Bergdorf Goodman jeans cost only fractionally more to make than your average Levi's. This doesn't take into account marketing, advertising, or a buyer's overhead. Or, of course, a company like Edun that tried to pay its factory workers much more than the minimum wage.

Tokyo is probably Pascal's favorite place in the world to shop—not because of geography or culture or logistics, but simply because Japan offers the world's most interesting and innovative denim. He'll buy a dozen or more garments in a day that are interesting to him or provide inspiration to him in some way for his own designs. He once had his Visa card frozen until he could prove that he was spending money at women's stores all over Tokyo legitimately. "It's very strange to be in a young girl's shop with thirteen-year-old Japanese girls," he said. And not just looking, but feeling and studying. "They all look at me and I'm not only looking at trends, I'm actually purchasing clothes. I'm a Western man all alone and I'm buying Japanese skirts made for young girls. *Everybody* looks at you; *everybody* notices you!"

- -

AT THE END OF ARIANA'S LAST DAY, BEFORE THE MILAN and Paris shows, Pascal has sat quietly in Legler's conference room with blank scraps of paper and sample garments he'd purchased at shops around the world, thinking about designs for the next collection. This was his own personal creative moment, when his team was not yet working to make his visions evolve and his customers were just beginning their own production cycle with fabric they'd received from what was now his previous collection. Somewhere else in the world, someone like Ganira was picking bolls for what would result from Pascal's work today. In this moment, he was alone with his ideas and inspiration. "If the world has five hundred denim suppliers there are probably five trendsetters," Pascal said. "The rest are waiting. We try to stay out of this circle; we try to be the guys developing. You stay just a little bit ahead."

Pascal's mobile rang once again. After Ariana had left, one by one the rest of the department had quietly wandered out until just Pascal was left. We sat talking about corruption in Italy in the 1990s. The Berlin wall coming down had changed everything for Italy, Pascal believed, along with a massive push to end graft and corruption in what the country called the "clean hands" operation. It was a moment of hope for Italians all over the country. But then recession came, and the disastrous euro, and global terrorism. "People are not happy," Pascal said. "There are so many problems . . . and in general, [we] have no hope. Terrorism, Israel, Palestine — these are the problems." He picked up his phone and looked at the caller's number. "In the end we live . . ." He pressed a button on his phone and greeted the caller. In seconds, he was up and looking through fabric samples in a drawer. When he finished with the call, he did not return to his thought, just left the sentence there, drifting, full of a hundred conclusions. Or just one. "In the end, we live."

PART THREE

XII

IN THE LIVING WE LOSE CONTROL

ON MAY I, 2002, A TRUCK TUCKED INSIDE A CONVOY of eight vehicles carried three garment workers to a small demonstration in the Cambodian capital of Phnom Penh. May Day honors the laborer. It's a day when international workers' rights are celebrated in Cambodia and elsewhere. All three in the truck were women; all three were union leaders in their factory. The demonstration was about holiday pay owed to a number of workers, and the three women were on their way to lend their voice to the cause. None of them ever made it.

Such a demonstration is a miracle in Cambodia. The country is categorized, like much of Africa, as an LDC, or least developing country. The per capita income is just under $400 a year. The average salaries of government employees or civil servants like teachers and police officers is $25–$30 a month. The government is notoriously, almost shamelessly, corrupt and seeming to get more so. The educational and legal systems are barely functioning. Health problems like AIDS, diabetes, and malaria are endemic. To have workers aware of even some of their rights, to have them represented in unions, and to have them willingly go out and advocate for change is a tiny picture of what has been a monumental and audacious transformation in the country over the past decade. There is a reason for all this change. Cambodia, as it turns out, is one big massive laboratory.

During the Clinton administration the United States signed a bilateral trade agreement with Cambodia. The agreement established Cambodia as a country that would enjoy an ever-growing portion of the textile quota to U.S. markets on a single major condition: the country had to agree to eradicate sweatshops in their garment industry. The better they did each year with labor rights, the greater share of the quota they could get. This required the country to admit there was a problem in the first place, which was no small step. Sweatshops are the world's ugly nonsecret; everyone knows they're ubiquitous, but no country throws up its hands and admits foul play. Under the agreement Cambodia was to rewrite its labor laws, welcome union formation, and allow the International Labour Organization (ILO) to monitor factories and publish their findings.

Such agreements weren't exactly what the founding fathers envisioned for global trade. The United States had historically engaged in trade protectionism for its own exports. One of the ways this was manifested was to give Congress sole discretion over tariff reductions on imports. This practice meant constituents could take up their economic woes with their congressional representatives, particularly if foreign imports appeared to threaten their livelihoods. It's difficult to believe, but sometimes businesses weren't entirely honest about just how threatened their livelihoods were. A number of them perceived any competition at all to be a threat and so made every attempt to quash it using political capital they'd *earned*, so to speak. Sometimes these same people also offered their congressional representatives trinkets and things; thank-you gifts like large bundles of cash or fat T-bone steaks. The practice led to political corruption (which does tend to be where these sorts of sweetheart deals end up). In 1934, Congress passed something called the Reciprocal Trade Agreement Act. The act was meant to root out corruption by allowing the president—in this case, Franklin Delano Roosevelt—to establish tariff reductions through his own office in the form of bilateral trade agreements with individual countries. Within ten years, nearly three dozen such agreements had been negotiated, bringing the average tariff down by 44 percent.[1] After World War II, dozens more followed. The practice evolved throughout the decades and over changing administrations.

With a country like Cambodia, the trade deal was a risky endeavor. For starters, the garment industry there was less than five years old. Launching the program would almost inevitably increase production costs, and costs were already high since Cambodia made no raw materials of its own—fabric, thread, buttons, or zippers. Everything had to be imported. In a country where the prime minister's nephew opened fire into a crowd in late 2003 and served no jail time, trying to convince an entire industry from management down to the workers to abide by a new set of rules was no small task. Basically, the challenge in a country like Cambodia with no rule of law lies with convincing one segment of society in one industrial sector to believe in, to embrace, to help establish rule of law in this small arena. Even with the increased quota access, the accord couldn't be extended beyond January 1, 2005, when the Multi-Fibre Agreement expired and countries around the world started competing against one another. The end of the MFA was especially worrying for Cambodia, since its neighbor, of course, is China.* Finally, there was the prospect that the experiment wouldn't result in increased consumer or multina-

---

*Geography matters here. If you're making garments in Mexico or Honduras, you have a slight edge given proximity to the States, which not only means accessible markets but cheaper transportation costs—and, of course, the need to maintain stability in the region, which keeps Central and South American on the radar in some ways more than a country like Laos or Cambodia.

tional buyer demand. Cambodia could do everything the agreement asked of them and still there was no guarantee brands would come. Or stay.

Cambodia was desperate for industry. It was only two decades past a devastating civil war and subsequent genocide that killed nearly a quarter of the population and the vast majority of educated professionals.* It is probably not possible to overstate the effect this has on the future of a country. The fact that Cambodia today is still around and not folded into one of the neighboring countries like Thailand or Vietnam is probably a minor miracle in itself.

A market like the United States could change the destiny of a country like Cambodia. The risks were obvious, but the opportunity was too good to pass up. Cambodia could never have done away with sweatshops on its own. Even if the political will was there—and that was highly debatable—it would cost far too much to put into practice and manufacturers would likely close up shop and relocate elsewhere. Even if they stayed, there'd be very little incentive to get them to change their ways. But money, in the form of quota access to the highly lucrative American market—that's what you might call meta-incentive.

There was an equally significant incentive to make Cambodia a model of decent working conditions and progressive labor standards. Sweatshops had plagued the industry ever since the sewing of apparel had moved from family rooms to factories in the nineteenth century. A century later, companies like the Gap and Nike found out just how much publicity could hurt when a series of investigative articles about abhorrent labor conditions in some of their factories led to boycotts and deep market losses. Nobody had really tried anything like what was being proposed in Cambodia. Brands had established codes of conduct and a small monitor-

---

*It is now commonly accepted that what happened in Cambodia was crimes against humanity, as opposed to genocide. There is a legal difference between the two, though it's far afield from this book's topic.

ing system for their contracted factories abroad, but that was a little like having a corrupt mayor's office check itself for bribes. Even if the brand had the best of intentions toward every single seamstress, no one from the outside was likely to see them as unbiased. Nike could hire Jesus himself and the critics wouldn't assume him nonpartisan.

The experiment worked.

The ILO moved in and began monitoring in 2001. Multinational buyers almost all do some level of monitoring around the world themselves, but it is often criticized as ineffectual; problems aren't fixed, codes of conduct aren't enforced, auditors are paid off. The ILO, as an independent group, is seen as both unbiased and trustworthy, a status hard to earn in Cambodia. By 2001, the Cambodian government had created a set of progressive labor laws—based on those in France—where workers got overtime pay, annual bonuses, eighteen vacation days plus sick leave, maternity leave, more than a dozen federal holidays, health clinics and day care on site, unions and collective bargaining, the right to organize, and a minimum wage of $50 a month for a 48-hour, six-day work week.* The brands came en masse. And other countries took note. Around the world, people began to watch Cambodia, to monitor whether or not its newfound market strategy could sustain itself. Economists and developmental organizations, multinational buyers and factory owners all looked at what Cambodia was doing. Garments now compose more than 85 percent of the country's exports. The work of the ILO was pivotal; trade negotiators for the United States and Cambodia used their reports when they renewed the agreement each year. Cambodia is the only country in the world where a respected body like the ILO publishes reports four times a year with factory names and the improvements they need to make. Clothes, it is safe to say, have saved this

---

*It bears mentioning here that the labor laws only apply to the garment industry and not to others. So construction workers, for example, neither abide by the same laws nor enjoy the same rights.

country. In 1995, there were 20 factories in Cambodia. By 2003, there were 255 and a quarter of a million workers, most of them women. This included two women named Nat Ouk and Sary Muong, who were riding in the truck inside the convoy on May 1, 2002.

Surrounding the convoy, hundreds of workers marched on foot, striking for their pay. They could do this now. Strike. Speak out. Sary, who goes by the nickname Ry, had been recovering from surgery to remove a benign tumor from one of her breasts. To pay for the series of operations she needed, she'd had to sell three of her cows for a mere $250 each. She could have gotten double for them if she'd waited for a better price, but the surgeon wouldn't operate unless she showed him she had the money to pay. It had taken her years to save up enough to buy the cows. The surgery cost four hundred dollars. She wished she'd kept one of the cows.

Suddenly, a line of men emerged from the crowd and stood between the truck and the car in front. The men curved themselves to form a semicircle around the truck and forced it to either run them over or stop. The driver put the vehicle in park and fled. He may have been part of their gang—or not. In Cambodia, it was impossible to tell. Someone with you today could be bought and turn against you tomorrow. This is one of the issues overlooked in the sweatshop debate. A country could write good labor laws, a foreign brand could demand excellent working conditions, managers could have their employees' best interests at heart, and still the forces of poverty—violence, jealousy, greed—could win. The garment workers, though poor, when juxtaposed against the rest of the country weren't doing too badly. The lawmakers, the foreign investors, the managers . . . they could control things inside the eye of the storm, but they couldn't control the storm itself.

The men flung open the passenger door of the truck. One by one, they pulled each woman out. Nat was first. She is a tiny willow of a woman, no more than seventy-five pounds. They tugged, she pulled. She managed to wrest herself from their grasp. Perhaps her thinness caused them to handle her lightly, afraid she might snap in two. She ran a few steps, then stopped and turned around. She didn't want to leave her friends.

Ry was next, thrown to the ground by the men. She remembers the white hot sun of the day, and steam rising off the pavement. She remembers blood on her forearms and acute pain in her breast. She doesn't remember how many men there were or how she went from the seat of the truck to the pavement, the concrete seeming to billow up and over her. She rolled, covered her face with her hands, lying on her back, a beetle. She was sure she was about to die.

Nat was torn between fleeing for her own safety and staying to help Ry. Just a few years ago she'd have run for sure, but working in the factories had changed her, toughened her up. And the unions had taught her to speak her mind. She realized, in that moment, that it wasn't death that terrified her, it was disappearing. She stayed. Later, she would say this: "We all die; I wasn't afraid of dying. In living we lose control."

Ry remembers the feeling of someone standing over her, the blossom of a shadow, many men, and nothing more. But Nat remembers their warning: "You are allowed to work," one of them said to her, "so do your job." The instructions were simple. They were not to demonstrate ever again.

The entire incident lasted only seconds. The men were quickly enveloped by the crowd and disappeared. Neither Nat nor Ry would be able to recognize them again. Ry returned to the hospital and had her stitches redone, her forearms cleaned. The rest of her cow money dwindled to nothing. And though they hadn't been seriously hurt, the fear set in immediately. After that day, they quit their positions as union representatives. Nothing more happened. No one at their factory ever brought it up, the incident was never reported—the police tend to help the highest bidder in a country with no rule of law—and Nat and Ry could hardly report on men whose faces they couldn't describe. The factory that precipitated the May Day protest closed down and the management disappeared.

Intimidation is one of the biggest challenges the International Labour Organization contends with in Cambodia. In theory, there is a hotline for workers to call to report incidents, but none of the factory workers I met ever reported anything (I have met dozens, but in light of the country's current 310,000, I don't want that fact taken from its context). What would it have done, Nat and Ry wondered later. At the end of the day, the two women needed their jobs; their families had come to depend on them for income. Both had younger siblings they were supporting. Ry had a young daughter being cared for by her parents in the countryside. Nat's father had died, leaving her to provide for her mother. If you were going to complain, they agreed, your case had to be wholly winnable and wholly untraceable, and almost nothing in Cambodia is this sure.

I met Nat and Ry almost two years to the day of the 2002 incident. It still spooked them. Neither had returned to union leadership, though they still belonged to a union and often gave younger girls advice on their rights. They'd both been working at a factory called United Eternity for years—Nat for nine and Ry for eight. It is in Chak Angre, one of the city's three main factory areas on the outskirts of Phnom Penh. It was the season of the mango rains, a time when the sky opens up briefly each day, not only signaling the short mango season but reminding the country that the real monsoons are not far behind. April and May are punishingly hot to begin with, and the rains only make it worse, creating a thick layer of damp heat across the land. The water can rise so fast in Phnom Penh that curbs disappear in minutes, eclipsed by opaque, muddy water. Lakes bloom on dirt roads in furious seconds and intersections that were passable only minutes before become impenetrable. The first days of the rains bring an unadulterated joy to the country: the unbearable heat of the season will soon subside, farmers can plant rice crops again, and the levels of the Mekong River rise to change the course of the Sap River, where they intersect in Phnom Penh, bringing hordes of fish into waiting nets.

A century ago, the area had a series of small channels, akin to the tiny waterways of the Mekong Delta. Cambodia has long been in a state of semipermanent drought, and the canals have been replaced by dozens of garment factories built on the cheap mostly over the last ten years, though some of the buildings have been around many decades. I'd heard from the local district commune office that United Eternity's building had apparently been used to make mosquito nets when the Khmer Rouge were in power. Luen Thai Garment, Kings Lane, Sei Lei Fung Woolen Knitting, Top World, Eternity Apparel, Supertex Cambodian Sportswear, Ospinter Garment, Kintai Garments, M & V International Manufacturing—the factory names belie the clients, who are household names both here and in the west: Anne Klein, Gap, Ann Taylor, Levi's, Marks & Spencer, Adidas, Puma, Nike, Disney, Sears, and others.

In Chak Angre, thousands of workers stream from behind steel gates at set times: 11:00 A.M., 4:00 P.M., 10:00 P.M. Highway Two cuts through the middle of these gates and its normal traffic flow slows and soon stops when the workers emerge, trucks and motorcycles and pedestrians commingling in a traffic jam that even the police get lost in. In loose, pajamalike bottoms and wildprint polyester shirts, some wearing smocks and plastic ID cards tied with shoelaces and looped around their necks, the workers are largely women, and their sudden appearance on a street normally much quieter is akin to a sudden and furious human monsoon.

Nat and Ry came with the lunchtime wave. Both thirty, they'd been best friends for nearly a decade. Ry is short and round, with curlicue bangs of wavy black hair and a ponytail. Her freckled face is thick and pudgy, with round, close-set eyes, spaces between her teeth, and a near-constant expression of delight. She is outspoken, looks directly at you when she speaks, and is prone to a kind of giggling that incorporates her entire body from the waist up. The very first words she spoke to me, through my translator, Sophea, were: "Do you know any markets in the United States we could sell clothes to?"

Nat, on the other hand, is taller and painfully thin, with sharp angles and a hesitant laugh—all indications of the severe malnutrition she endured as a child. She is a supervisor in the factory. A missing incisor in Nat's mouth proves, jokes Ry, that she talks too much. Ry dissolves into giggling when she repeats this joke and Nat smiles placidly.

Outside the factories, vendors have set up stalls or laid out blankets selling hair clips, makeup and perfume, combs and brushes, wigs and baby items. Fruit sellers and food stalls, produce and meat markets, lotus and jasmine flowers in buckets, fried crickets in woven baskets, inner tubes and bike tires hanging from hooks, baseball caps on hat stands, folded pajama sets wrapped in plastic, and key makers behind wooden block desks. None of the vendors who line the street like sentries work in the garment factories, but everyone survives off them. Estimates vary, but conservatively more than a million people live indirectly off the garment industries, out of a population of thirteen million.

The day I met Nat and Ry, Sophea and I escaped the rain under an enormous blue tarp covering a sidewalk restaurant. Rickety wooden tables were empty and reached just below my kneecaps. I settled myself onto a wooden stool several sizes too small for its task and smiled at a group of young girls who stared, giggling at me. They were workers at the stall, serving up bowls of food from massive steaming pots, clearing and washing flowered porcelain dishes full of chips and cracks, collecting the ten cents or so that each meal cost. I felt the uncomfortably sticky heat under my poncho that comes from too much warmth and not enough rain to cool the air. The ground under the tarp was steaming. Remorque motos—tiny motorcycles with wooden flatbeds hitched behind them that taxi as many as 50 workers home after their shifts— were lined up and waiting, their drivers hidden under thin pink and yellow ponchos. Soggy garbage piles and puddles ran over curbs. The street was relatively quiet, with vendors quietly chatting away, some with their children swarming around their ankles. They were one another's closest friends and confidants, their relationships born out of sixteen-hour days of sitting and serving and selling. They were here day after day, week after week, month after month, never far ahead of where they'd started economically, but not as worse off as they'd been before the textile centers had come.

The restaurant was owned—if such a thing can be owned at all—by a woman named Rath and her husband. It is probably more accurate to say they owned a set of rickety wooden tables and enormous pots, and had staked out their claim to this patch of sidewalk. Rath sells breakfast, lunch, and dinner to workers. Rice with pork, salted fish with carrots and morning glory, a green spinach-type vegetable sometimes grown in sewage around Phnom Penh. They fed six hundred workers a day, rising at 4:00 A.M. to begin their cooking. "I am like a mother," Rath said to me. Feeding, cooking, cleaning. She carried a blue Pan Am shoulder bag, vinyl, circa 1976, full of money (Cambodian riel, 4,000 to the U.S. dollar) and a long ledger account. Her husband said food costs were always rising, but he couldn't raise prices or he'd lose his business. "I am a frog in a well," he said. Stuck. Surrounded. No way out. It's a common adage in Cambodia.

Workers suddenly filled the tables surrounding me. They ate quickly, using forks and soup spoons—the latter in place of knives, which Cambodians tend not to utilize unless they're of the machete variety. (In that case, they're used for all sorts of things, from cutting grass—cleavers are preferred for edging—to chopping ice blocks.) Nat and Ry sat at my table and offered me a small bowl of food. Ry pushed pork fat on me, which I recognized as one of those unfortunate cultural signs of esteem and so I chewed on it haltingly. Later, I recognized the same tendency in myself when we went out to a fast food joint in town called Lucky Burger and I pushed French fries on them. They ate dried fish and rice for three hundred riel, or about eight cents.

I smiled. They smiled. And then Ry asked her question about U.S. markets and whether I could help them out. Just having wandered around in a Gap or a Wal-Mart seemed to put me in as good as position as they imagined I'd need to nail a few orders for them. They sewed jeans, cords, and khakis but they often never know for whom. Wal-Mart was the current buyer. At least the name was familiar to them. They clearly couldn't grasp the scale or complexity of the system in America, any more than I understood how a pair of pants was actually made. At the time, I still thought: one woman, one pair of pants sewn. But it wasn't like this at all. As many as sixty pairs of hands touch jeans in the manufacturing process. Every element is a separate job, done at a separate station, from the pockets, to the tags, to the labels, hems, and seams. Long lines of machines, each responsible for a step of the process, make up what is called the sewing line. Typically, two side-by-side lines complete mirror halves of a pair of pants, and when the legs reach the front of the line, they're sewn together. Keeping sewing lines balanced is a constant issue for factories.

During my first conversation with Ry, it took me a long time to understand what her job was. "Luf. Luf, it's the luf," Sophea said. Luf?

"Luf," she said again, exasperated, and drew it on a scrap of paper she'd pulled from her bag.

Loops. She'd meant belt loops. Five to a pair of jeans. Ry's entire job, eight or more hours a day, six days a week, was belt loops. Actually, not even belt loops, but *one end* of belt loops. Pairs of partially finished jeans piled up in a plastic basket beside her, and she attached five separate rectangles of denim with half an inch of excess cloth to a waistband. When she finished her basket, it moved up one step to the woman in front of her, who sewed the top part of the belt loop. This process of incremental steps included everything from the inner and outer seams, to the designer pockets, to the rivets and zippers and buttonholes. This is the irony not just of jeans but of manufacturing generally. The volume of global production is staggering, but the individual steps are both incremental and integral to the success of the entire endeavor.

After each pair of jeans is stitched together, quality control takes over. QC, as it's called, tends to happen in stages as well: as the sewing is completed, after the pants are ironed, or tagged, or packaged. Nat worked QC in the sewing department, so if a seam was buckled, or the pockets were lopsided, or the bar tacks didn't measure exactly half an inch (or whatever the design dictates), Nat was often the one to send them back to be resewn. There was, of course, a small attrition rate of those jeans too screwed up to be fixed. These were handled in a variety of ways, sold in outlet stores or whisked out back doors of factories and sold to locals, or simply given back to the brand as mistakes. Ry's joke about Nat's tooth was a common quip among workers: The QC girls never stop talking— pointing out mistakes, demanding alterations. Alongside QC stations are often AATCC test standards with samples showing acceptable and unacceptable wrinkle recovery, or button strength or dye crocking. Nat had never heard of the scientists at AATCC, of course, but she used their research daily in her job.

Nat and Ry may not have known much about the global market of apparel, but they knew all about the quota system. They had a better grasp of how international trade worked than most people I met. They knew the baseball hats worn by remorque moto drivers had come from America, and the baguettes sold warm from the baskets affixed to bicycles had come from the French. And though they weren't sure of the particulars, they knew that in eight months, on January 1, 2005, things were likely to change for them. When I asked how, Ry smiled benignly and pushed her empty bowl away. For the first time, I noticed that every finger on her right hand apart from her thumb was missing. "That's when the U.S. won't give us orders anymore," she said.

XIII

THE GHOSTS IN THE TREES

I NEVER VISITED THE INSIDE OF UNITED ETERNITY, not because it was necessarily off-limits, but because I never wanted to put Nat and Ry in a position where they'd have to lie or pretend, or where they'd feel fear of possible repercussions after I'd left. I wasn't sure whether they ever talked about me to their co-workers, but I suspect they did. A white woman hanging around Chak Angre was news. Ry's landlord saw me coming and going, as did Nat's neighbors. There is a saying in Cambodia that whispers travel faster than words spoken aloud, and I knew my presence was noted. Sophea had told me once that Cambodians were greatly honored by visits from Westerners and such visits would hold them in high standing among their peers. Passing along news of my visits would be customary, so I usually met Nat and Ry at their homes, or far away from their factory, in tea shops or restaurants. Twice, they came to my house in Phnom Penh, after I'd known them for several years.

In some ways, they were easy to get to know, and in other ways very hard. They took great pains to meet with me when I wanted, but their schedules were sporadic. They worked six days a week and in the beginning, in 2004, overtime was daily. They worked from 7:00 a.m. to 7:00 or 8:00 or 9:00 P.M. back then, Monday through Friday, and 7:00 A.M. to 5 or 6 P.M. on Saturday. Sundays were the only days we could meet. They spoke no English and in fact had no interest in learning—I once offered to pay for lessons, but they told me they would prefer sewing lessons in how to make fancy dresses. Tailor shops with glass cases holding mannequins in all manner of lavish dresses were ubiquitous in Phnom Penh. No one wears their own dress to attend a wedding; they rent a frou-frou cupcakey thing from one of these tailors. But I doubted they could earn more with a tailor shop than they could in the factory.

I spoke little Khmer, and though I took lessons, Nat and Ry typically just laughed when I spoke to them in their language. Instead, I brought Sophea. Sophea was a spunky young woman who was on her way to becoming the country's third female PhD candidate before she married and gave birth to a son (she vows she'll return to it someday). Sophea stayed in touch with Nat and Ry even when I wasn't around, and then she'd e-mail me updates about them: illnesses, accidents, marriages, births, and even when they were frustrated with their managers, or their work, or if they'd participated in a strike. Nat lived in the city with her mother, but Ry's family was far away in the countryside. I visited them with her four or five times.

Ry came from a village two and a half hours northeast of Phnom Penh in the province of Kampong Cham. In 1995, she was forced into an arranged marriage with a man whom she did not love and who abused her. Her family allowed her to divorce him after a year. By then, she had a green-eyed daughter named Pov. Ry and Pov moved back in with Ry's family. At night, termites and woodworms nibbled their way through the walls. Her father was a farmer, mostly rice, but he also grew carrots, cucumbers, and long beans, which are basically green beans except they grow to be half a meter long and they tumble down vines like graceful waves of hair. It's a delicate agricultural dance: not enough water and the rice won't grow, too much and the vegetables won't grow, Ry taught me. Farm work was drudgery, but farm work in the face of drought or floods was terrifying. They worried at night, each of them: Ry and her parents and some of her siblings and her grandmother, all sharing a single space in a thatched-roof hut, all sharing a single fear.

Ry had learned to sew from a woman in her village and she knew garment factories had opened in the city and were looking for employees. Villagers told her she was crazy to go, she'd never be hired. Not with her fingers the way they were; she'd never keep up. If she left, they said, she would be a ruined girl; the scandal of her divorce had already brought shame on the family and now she was going to go to the city? Alone? Where she would have no family, no protection, no monitoring of her life and her time and her activities? The factories were brutal. The rumor was they worked you sixteen hours a day. They raped women and locked them up and the city was dark and dangerous and thugs were always on the prowl, looking to steal from you. Looking to steal you.

But Ry felt she had no choice.

All the factory girls feel they have no choice. They live inside two opposing forces: to care for their families and to keep themselves pure. Pure means something different in Cambodia than it does in the west. Virginity, yes, but it also means you don't go out with men, you don't go out with other girls on your own, you don't leave the confines of your own family. In Cambodia today, girls can very rarely do both and so survival dictates choice. The girls like Ry who left a decade or so ago were castigated, shunned by their villages and even sometimes by the families they'd left home to support.

When girls first began to leave the countryside to work in urban factories, families were left with a sort of resigned shame. The rest of the village looked down on girls like Ry. Far from bringing a sense of empowerment, it seemed to humble families, turn them inward. The girls found themselves avoiding people they'd grown up around when they went home to visit. Boys leaving home did not carry this same stigma; boys leaving home was expected, even encouraged, but boys were also not expected to forgo whatever desires they may have envisioned for their own lives to support their immediate families.* Girls, as in much of the world, were held to a different standard. There is a saying in Khmer for the ubiquitous gossip spread by villagers once a girl leaves home. It translates roughly to: The teeth and tongue cannot help but touch inside the mouth. Another is: Stacked plates in a basket cannot help their rattle. They both mean the same thing: People cannot help but gossip. For the first few years when Ry made the two-and-a-half-hour trek home, usually once a month after payday, she would avoid going out to the market if she could (which is basically the only place a girl can go out alone). She only saw her daughter and her family and tended to stay, as she does now, only a day or two. Sometimes just a few hours.

But two things happened gradually that have begun to bring the villagers of Cambodia around. First, more and more girls began to leave, and families began to see how you could let a child go but not lose her to the world. Their girls left, but they came back home, too. And, second, people began to see what a factory paycheck meant. More and more girls went, an attrition of girls, and more families learned that factories may have claimed their daughters for a time, but their daughters returned with money, with gifts, with food. They returned different than they left. Strong. Powerful in their own ways. They didn't want to marry. They wanted to earn money, have things, make friends. In incremental steps, they wanted control of their lives. In exchange, they offered their families survival.

For Ry, work in the factories has offered an entirely different setting for her family. They now own five expensive cows (she's

---

*This is not to say that they don't contribute once they begin earning a wage, and this is also not to suggest that all Khmer families are like this. Certainly, the educated urban population is more progressive than those in the countryside.

managed to replace the ones she sold to have her surgery). A new, large wooden house on stilts replaced the thatched-roof hut, and the family has enough money to grow their crops. Last year, Ry paid to have a pool-sized fish pond built on their property— though she's not yet figured out how to keep the neighbors out of it at night. Neighbors, she said, are sometimes closer than one's relatives; if you are hurt or need help immediately, your neighbors are often closest to you. Even when you know they're stealing your fish, you keep quiet. Two years ago, she paid to have a well dug, but there was no water; she'll try again next year. The family's money comes not just from Ry but from pooling her salary with their farming income. Pov is in school and, in addition to her regular subjects, is studying English.* Ry's younger brother graduates from high school this year. Her grandmother has her own small house now and most often she can afford the medicine she needs. The changes are lottery-worthy. Garment workers, in a country like this, are the rising middle class.

Except for one thing. These women don't yet necessarily recognize their newfound economic strength in a way that transfers power from their bosses, from the men in their families—fathers and brothers and husbands—to them. That takes education. Their daughters will have it. And they'll know it.

Ry is the eldest of her siblings and understands that this means she bears responsibility for their upbringing. In Khmer culture, it is the daughter who helps provide, the daughter who pays to send her brother to school. In the 1980s, after the Vietnamese invaded what was then Democratic Kampuchea and freed the Khmer people from life under the Khmer Rouge, a deforestation program began whereby large swaths of trees were cut down and essentially given to the Vietnamese with the cooperation of the newly installed Hun Sen government. (What trees remain, Hun Sen

---

*This is tenuous in Cambodia, however. One in nine students leaves grade school, and one in four leaves high school. More than half of Cambodia's children don't go to school at all.

appears content to let China come in and take.) Families were obligated to send one member, most commonly the father, for several weeks each year to work in the lumber corps. The program was so wildly unpopular that it ended after only a few years, but not before thousands of people from an already grieving and decimated populace died from malaria, dengue, and other diseases endemic to Cambodia's forests. The assignment was terrifying for a host of reasons. The Khmer Rouge had fled to the forests when the Vietnamese came, and from there they launched occasional attacks even up until the mid-1990s. The forests were also full of other dangers: landmines and malarial mosquitoes and spirits. Rural Khmer today still believe that ghosts live among the treetops. Ry's father was too sick to go to the forests. Families were occasionally allowed to substitute another family member for the father if he had a legitimate reason not to go. So when she was fourteen, Ry went.

It terrified her, being in the mountains, away from her family. But when she spoke of her experience, she didn't appear troubled by the memory. It had become a sign of her strength, like being the first factory girl in her village. Ry was an unusual woman in Cambodia, strong from a young age, and given remarkable freedoms. She carried water for the adults in the camp because she was too small to cut down trees herself. One afternoon, a firefight broke out between a Khmer Rouge faction and a squad of government soldiers. Petrified, Ry lost her footing and tumbled down into a gully, where she lay trying to control her breathing. A man from the camp saw her and made his way quietly down into the gully and lay beside her, speaking comforting words to calm her down. They stayed there the whole rest of the day and night, and in the morning, he helped her back up. She was grateful to that man still today. Afterwards, she convinced two others to flee the camp with her and the three of them walked for two days with no food or water, until Ry made it back to her family's home. The villagers knew, even then, that Ry was a remarkably determined girl.

The first factory she applied to work in told her she'd never find a job with her fingers the way they were; everyone seemed convinced she'd never keep up. Her fingers were a birth defect and she'd long ago learned to adapt. She could handle utensils and small tools as well as anyone. She persisted, and eventually she made her way to United Eternity, where Nat worked, and when they too refused she asked them to give her a sewing test to gauge her speed. They did. It wasn't exactly an Olympic moment. She wasn't as speedy as many others, they determined, but she could hold her own.

At first, Ry hated the work. She was lonely and she worked twelve-, fourteen-, sixteen-hour days. Sometimes, she wasn't paid for overtime. Other times, if she was sick, or needed time off to take care of personal matters, the factory threatened to fire her. Once, they tried, but Nat stood up for her and begged them not to fire her. Nat was a supervisor and had earned the respect of management.

In 2000, after the bilateral agreement came to be, everything changed. Fans appeared on the factory floor. They were given time cards and their hours were noted. They were given classes on their rights, on what they could expect from management, on what they could ask for and how. HIV/AIDS was openly discussed for the first time. They learned about unions, child labor, women's rights, overtime compensation, collective bargaining, and striking. They were paid for holidays and maternity leave—not always, but much of the time, which was progress of a sort. To hear from outsiders and from leaders in their own country that they had permission to seek what they were owed was a minor revolution. Before, if they complained, they were told to look for work somewhere else if they didn't like things, or they were fired, or mocked, or ignored. Generally, they just kept quiet. But now they learned there was a higher power, a higher law than the factory manager. Ry earned more and more, up from the $50.00 a month minimum wage to around $80.00 a month.

THE WORKERS IN CAMBODIA ARE NOT THE ONLY BENE-
ficiaries of the country's grand experiment. The ILO, in addition
to monitoring, also offers potential buyers an extraordinary
glimpse into the inner workings of the country's factories. The
program, called Better Factories Cambodia, allows buyers to view
online reports about individual factories—where they fall short,
where they've shown improvement, where they excel, and basic
information about their capacity and their cut-and-sew specializa-
tions. Unfortunately, at this stage it may not be replicable, at least
not at a cost consumers are willing to accept. Still, in late 2006, the
ILO announced that it would partner with the International
Finance Corporation, which is the private-sector branch of the
World Bank, in a global attempt to improve working conditions in
factories. The partnership, Better Work Program, is based in part
on Better Factories Cambodia. Part of the success of the Cambodian program has been the ability of the ILO to convince factory
owners that good working conditions lead to increased productivity and thus increased profit—something that speaks to all business managers.

Back before the ending of the quotas, the United States and
Cambodia and several other donors and brands shared the cost of
the ILO program. In 2005, those costs began to be covered by just
a handful of big brands, including the Gap, Disney, Levi's, and
Sears, along with the United States Agency for International
Development (USAID), the World Bank, and others. It's a temporary fix, though. The contract for the ILO is set to expire in 2008,
after which Cambodia is expected to take over fully. Many in the
industry have doubts about Cambodia's ability to run the program
at an acceptable level of transparency. There is a saying in Cambodia about corruption: If you can't go in the front door, go in the
back. What is often viewed as corruption by the West is simply
seen as the methods for conducting business in Cambodia. However it's defined, this could prove the program's undoing. Corruption is so notorious in the country that many nongovernmental

organizations tally annual bribery or other related costs in a line item marked "professional fees." In addition, charitable donor organizations or aid groups must continually be found or the program will end. Who would shoulder the bill and how the program would run are not easy questions when you're talking about thirty million-plus workers in sixty different countries making clothes for thousands of brands and living under governments plagued by corruption. How many among us would be willing to shell out $15 or $20 instead of $7 for one of H&M's disposable T-shirts?*

Monitoring comes in two ways: spot checks and in-depth analysis. Spot checks are brief and basically visual: Do workers have adequate ventilation and lighting? How are the bathrooms? Do workers use protective gear, like metal gloves with band knives, which slice through dozens of layers of cloth at once? Are there protective masks for chemical use? Auditors performing spot checks look for fire extinguishers and fire exits on each floor, and determine whether there are enough toilets for the size of the factory and fresh drinking water for employees. They check the number of beds in the health clinics and look at the expiration dates on medicine. Even a perfunctory walk around the factory can tell them if there is day care, if labor laws are posted, if a doctor or nurse is on site, and if all the employees have ID cards.

The analysis, on the other hand, takes several days to complete and follows a checklist of 500 items. These include things like talking to the employees—often off site on weekends—about whether they're getting overtime pay, sick time, vacation time. Whether there are any children employed or if they work unacceptably long days. Do they attend union meetings? What is the turnover rate? Is the minimum wage posted, and what do the company books record about all this? It is commonly known that fac-

---

*If you readers *are* willing and I have judged you wrong, then by all means, write to your local legislator *and* to your favorite brands and let them know! It may be news to the industry. Trust me.

tories around the world often keep two sets of books, only one of which goes to a monitoring team, of course. Rumors abound in China that some markets even supposedly sell software to help factories learn to keep dual sets of records (no word on whether this software is pirated, of course).

The truth is, however, that almost no factory is in full compliance in Cambodia. Clinics are a big point of contention, for example. The law requires one bed for every fifty workers. It's fine for smaller factories. But a factory with five thousand or more employees would find themselves running a hospital. Day care is a similar hot button. Workers are required to get three months' maternity leave, and then two thirty-minute breaks a day for breastfeeding. Most factories do not provide, for example, day-care facilities—not only because of the expense, but because few working mothers would put their child in such a facility when extended family is available. Where family loyalty is paramount, children are left with grandparents or other extended family, so a day-care center is culturally mystifying in much of Asia. Even the ILO admits some of the labor laws need fine-tuning.

The best factory I've seen is a small affair that makes men's shirts for Marks & Spencer run by a cheerful Irishman named Adrian Ross. The floors were clean enough to dance barefoot on, and there was a method in place to account for every broken needle, every unused piece of cloth, every mistakenly sewn garment. Sometimes, just for fun, Ross throws spontaneous picnics for employees and their families. His remains the only factory I have ever visited with no advance warning. I called, and fifteen minutes later we were drinking tea in his office, where one enormous wall looked to the factory floor—not down onto but level with the factory floor. Even the best factories I've visited in Asia required days or weeks of e-mails, letters, phone calls until finally permission was grudgingly granted after I'd made promises not to give factory names or other details that would enable identification. Adrian Ross, whose factory is called New Island, maintains an open-door policy. Outside his window, the women were laughing and chatting away, occasionally waving to him. He's proud of what he's done and loves to bring people around to see it. Also, and this is probably the most telling detail, the factory has zero turnover.

RY LIVES IN A SINGLE ROOM SEVERAL MINUTES' WALK from her factory. Cambodia tends not to have the enormous factory compounds with workers' dormitories like China, the Philippines, Indonesia, and other countries have, though there is talk of building them in a special zone near Cambodia's only port, Sihanoukville. It worries some people. In other countries, such areas, often called EPZs, or export processing zones, often operate outside the laws of the country they inhabit. There is no real consensus on whose laws apply or how they are to be enforced. Conditions are terrible and often the most egregious abuses, like forced labor and child labor, happen behind the gates of the EPZs.

Ry's room was a dismal affair: a ten-by-ten square, far down a dirt alleyway paved with broken ceramic pots and brick shards—a poor man's asphalt to combat the slick mud of the rainy season. Her landlord, a carpenter by trade, was outside making a table, pounding a metal chisel with a wooden mallet to create a groove in the wood. We walked past a shrine with burning incense and an offering of bananas, into what looked like a wooden barn—dirt floors, a doorless hallway with padlocked doors lining the walkways, eight rooms in all, with four on each side. Many workers live three or four to a room, but Ry lives alone, or sometimes with her sister, who also works in a factory. She pays $15 a month, a break from the landlord, who usually charges $20. Her room is a single wooden platform built into three walls that rise to just under six feet. If I stand, I must bend over to keep my head from hitting the girders. A corrugated asbestos roof keeps most of the rain out, though water sometimes leaks through three nail holes onto Ry while she sleeps. Along three of the walls are nails with clothes hanging from them, and a small woven mat is rolled up and stuck between the boards—the bed. One small shelf built high into a wall holds a fraying cloth suitcase, and below it is a single square-foot wooden table with a hot plate. I notice one pot and spices for cooking, salt and pepper, fish sauce in a discarded water bottle, soy sauce, hot sauce. Like most Khmers, Ry boils water for drinking. She keeps it in her landlord's refrigerator. Down the hall is a shared bathroom. Ry has a single window, roughly a foot wide, covered by a wooden board that she can prop open with a stick. No air moves, and the mosquitoes are oppressive. She laughs every time I slap at one—most Khmers have become immune, and in any case, there are so many that it's like trying to sweep the street with a toothbrush. The room is a far cry from her family's breezy home in the country, where air whispers through the house she built for them. We sit cross-legged and barefoot on her platform/bed/couch. Red and white cigarette posters for Gauloises line the walls, covering holes. Her landlord's mallet pounds away, and the faint smell of fish sauce and oil wafts into the room. "When I'm rich," she tells me, "I will buy a fan."

The truth is, though, that Ry could afford better. Even at $70 or $80 a month in salary, she could find a nicer room, except that $40 or so of her salary each month goes to her family in the country. This is the conundrum of every textile worker I've ever met. They are, to a one, daughters working for the betterment of their families at their own expense. A friend who has lived in Cambodia for eight years said to me, "If you're the eldest daughter, you are basically sacrificed for the family and you understand that. You expect it." Every female worker I ever met had the following in common: they were sending brothers and occasionally younger sisters to school on their salaries, they lived in hovels just like Ry's if they weren't living with their families, they sent more than half their salaries home each month, they weren't married and most didn't ever expect to be married, and whatever they may have wanted for themselves—if they dared to want—was unlikely to materialize given what they were expected to provide.

They were also symbolic of that middle class that Cambodia has not had in decades. Even with the responsibilities they bore for their families, they had a freedom now they would otherwise never know. When Ry meets me in Phnom Penh, she wears coral lipstick and garish tops, fabric with gold thread woven through it or fancy lace collars. When she goes home to see her family, she often changes into a sarong, and wears no makeup. For all her talk of loving the countryside and wishing to farm again one day, Ry has become a fussy dresser, wearing fancy ponytail holders with sequins. In Phnom Penh, she can buy little items she wants, eat what and when she wants, and even go on walks with friends without having to be accompanied by family members. These maybe aren't the freedoms that will ultimately change society, but they are freedoms that matter each day in her own life. "In my family now, if a man came to ask to marry me," Ry says, "my family would ask me." In other words, no forced marriage. All over Cambodia, I heard a similar refrain, across all industry sectors and socioeconomic communities. "I think they've seen the aftermath and they've learned," Ry says. "[Our parents] don't want us to blame them. We feel strong now because we support ourselves. I feel like we have more freedom now because we can make decisions ourselves, about going out, about things in the house, about shopping."

These days Cambodia may not be a factory worker's panacea, but it is hardly the worst offender when it comes to women's rights. Women often don't learn to drive cars here, but they do tend to work—a few in government positions—and the wealthier families educate both their girls and their boys. If poor girls are uneducated it is most often a matter of money rather than of a chosen patriarchy. For the garment workers, life tends to be a single trajectory. Meeting them made me think of my own family. My great-grandmother was a maid in Ireland; my grandmother had a third-grade education, my father a bachelor's degree; I have a master's. Today's garment workers are likely to give both sons and daughters high school educations—and maybe their granddaughters will attend university and their great-granddaughters graduate school. Nat and Ry talk about how they've changed, how bringing in the paycheck gives them a different status in their families, how they feel independent in a way they've never felt before. With thoughts of working on the farm again one day and living in her parents' home receding, Ry cannot imagine being unable to take walks along the river with Nat or control whatever limited free time she may have. "I feel there is a big part of my life my family doesn't understand now," Ry says. This makes her a little sad, and also a little happy.

One day, Ry takes me out to her village in Kampong Cham. Nat, who has become a goddaughter to Ry's mother, comes along. We share a taxi from Phnom Penh and take a single long road all the way there, turning off into what is basically an oversized dirt median between rice fields. There is no marker, no identification that this can be used, in fact, as a road. The car lurches and crashes through craters in the mud, the driver grimacing and clenching the steering wheel just to keep us from diving into the bordering rice paddies. A disembodied scarecrow with no head is propped up in one of the paddies. It takes us fifteen minutes to go the last quarter mile. I suggest walking, but the girls laugh. "You won't get nauseated," Ry informs me, helpfully, "if you pull on the driver's ear."

I am fond of the driver, Mr. Heng. He ferries us often in rainy season or trips to the airport, and he talks jovially in broken English about his four wonderful children. But I really think pulling on his ear is beyond the boundaries of my casual acquaintance with him.

A plastic garbage bag in the trunk is filled with airy baguettes for Ry's family. She has also brought a pot of curry, a massive bag of plastic spools from the factory that her family will use for kindling, and Ry's hot plate because, she says, "It's easier to bring the kitchen with us." More bags contain sardines, canned milk, vanilla wafer cookies, fruit, sugar, and drinkable yogurt. Normally, Ry spends 5,000 riel, or $1.25, to take a shared minibus home, but today I have hired Mr. Heng and six of us have situated ourselves into his white Toyota Camry. In addition to Nat and Ry, another friend has come, and Sophea.

Ry tells me she feels she is being watched by her manager for mistakes. She is certain that every time there is a walk-out or a strike or a dispute, her bosses think she is behind it. Even when the factories nearby have problems, she thinks the boss might worry about a labor epidemic—a problem in one place leading to problems in other places. Twelve workers were allegedly dismissed at a factory next door earlier in the week, and small demonstrations took place all week; for two days she didn't work because of protests, and she claims her employer owes her for those two days and only wants to pay for one. When this was announced, she went to the assistant manager to discuss the issue. "Of us all, I quarrel with him the most," she says. But the fact is, under the labor law, the employers are not always required to pay workers when they strike.*

As a one-time union leader, Ry should know this; the fact that she doesn't is emblematic of the uphill climb that the ILO and others must make regarding the educating of workers. It is undeniably important for workers to recognize exploitation; it is equally important for them to recognize when that word is not an appropriate descriptor. It is always fairly easy to tell when workers have been coached by NGOs because they almost always describe themselves, very early on in a conversation, as "exploited." Once I went with an NGO to a meeting of factory workers on a Sunday afternoon. (The NGO was once the local branch of Oxfam Hong Kong, but Oxfam has since severed ties with the group, who are

---

*Workers are required to go through a series of steps before striking. If they skip ahead, straight to striking, they are not entitled to pay. For more on this, see the next chapter.

still active in Cambodia.) The two NGO representatives talked to the twenty-five or so workers present about health issues, and after the meeting, the workers gathered for a photo to be included in the group's regular newsletter to its donors. An NGO representative—a young Cambodian woman—reminded the workers not to smile. "Remember," she said, "you are victims."

Factory management, of course, is equally guilty of this, or perhaps even more so. Workers are regularly told how to answer the questions of factory monitors. When I met Nat and Ry, they were the first workers who seemed to me to have been uncoached by either side. They neither praised their factory nor denounced it. Occasionally, Ry would lapse into some vague complaint about the factory, but usually she relented when I'd ask for further details. Nat believed that one of the best signs of a decent environment was whether workers talked and laughed together at their stations. In United Eternity, she said, they had this camaraderie most of the time.

Ry says the factory doesn't follow labor laws and it depresses her, but when I press for details, she is vague. I ask again and finally she says: "They don't have day care for us." Of course, neither Nat nor Ry has need of day care, and when I ask them, they can only think of one fellow worker who has a baby, but they are still aware that the law requires it. Child labor, though, is something else. Ry says that to the best of her knowledge, there is no one underage working in the factory, but even if there were, she says, "If I tell ILO, the child will lose her job and the family cannot survive. So we close our ears and our eyes. We try to protect younger workers, but they sometimes lie to us even. They need the job." Familial law rather than labor law rules supreme here.

Nat says a factory boss would hide any girls under eighteen in the bathroom when the monitors come, anyway. In most cases, monitors do not just show up at factories without warning; this is perhaps the most common industry complaint about monitoring in general, and it does render it less effective than it should be. The ILO says all of its visits are unannounced. Nat and Ry say there is no child labor at their factory, but they say it's not uncommon in other factories. (Though I believe them, the fact is that everyone knows what the worst labor conditions are in the industry—from the management down to the cleaners—and all claim these things happen at other factories, never their own.)

Ry's family pours from the house to greet us, and Ry immediately begins to unload the substantial foodstuffs she has brought. Red hibiscus and bougainvillea surround the house. Pov hovers around her mother's hips, holding onto Ry's purple slacks (minutes later, Ry dons a sarong to cook and serve food) and then letting her hand drop. She is a stunning child. Her hair hangs down to the middle of her back, and her eyes are a luminescent hazel; it is almost difficult to look away from them. She seems to carry within her both a profound shyness and a sense of strength. She doesn't turn away, but she doesn't talk much either. Ry told me once that there is a saying in Khmer that translates roughly to: When we love, we love very much; when we hate, we hate very much. She thinks her daughter embodies this intensity.

We walk up a wooden flight of stairs to the main house. Spaces between the floorboards make sweeping easier, though the dirt falls to the ground below, where the outdoor kitchen is set up. Mats cover much of the wood floor, and one enormous red and green gecko sits lazily on a post. (Massive geckos are rare and considered a good omen.) Chickens run free and a few attempt to peck at my shins. The men in Ry's family wander slowly in. Her father, her uncle, a cousin. They have weather-beaten faces and sinewy, thin torsos, edges like pummeled copper. The father, Mok Kong, tells me he is proud of Ry and the work she's doing, proud of the money she brings to the family. Then he tells me his Khmer Rouge survival story. Every Khmer over the age of thirty has one. During the Khmer Rouge regime a cousin saw his name on a list— a register of upcoming executions—and the cousin simply erased his name. A tiny, secret gesture, and it saved his life. There are many stories like this, stories of luck and fate and timing. Mok

Kong doesn't know why he was on the list in the first place. Hardly anyone ever knew.

Ry's mother, Mok Porm, sits sideways, like the rest of the family, on the floor. Sophea leans over and gives me a cultural readjustment about the way I am sitting, with my legs straight out and the bottoms of my feet facing Ry's parents. It is disrespectful to point your feet at someone, she tells me, so I fold up my legs and sit like Ry's mother. I want to tell Sophea that this position is disrespectful of the physical limitations of my own pliability, but I keep quiet. Behind Ry's mother are the house's two other small rooms. One tiny wall shelf holds two shrines with old milk cans used to burn incense. A little girl's rainbow umbrella sits in one corner and a single cabinet along one wall holds plates, bowls, fake plastic flowers, and a single metal bowl from the Pol Pot era. Pov lays with her head in her grandmother's lap, her celestial eyes opening and closing slowly with a fever she's had for several days. When Ry and her husband split, her father says he felt like there were "fires" everywhere and the family needed to bring peace into their lives. They bought a book on dharma, translated from Pali, the language of the monks, to Khmer. Now he and Ry's mother chant together almost every day. Mok Porm describes their motivation during that time somewhat differently. "Because we have a daughter and she carries more sadness than the men," she tells me. "I do not have words to describe the fighting."

Ry begins to bring the food up the stairs. Smoke billows into the house from the cooking below, but no one seems to pay it any mind. We eat curry with rice and beans, and morning glory, and bread. Ry's grandmother has painstakingly made her way over to the house and climbed the stairs with the help of Ry's aunt. She has the shaved head of a widow, and she wears a pair of oversized glasses that have been broken and taped together and sit cockeyed and enormous on her small face. It is both comical and endearing. "I always try to tell my daughter and granddaughters to study hard," she says. Her voice quavers as if she is divulging a fact of great emotional weight. Minutes later, I understand why. "I love intellectual people." She says she was the only one in the whole village to have all her children go to school when they were young. This may explain why Ry's father's name was on the list. "I have three children left," she tells me. The Khmer Rouge took her house and two of her sons. She begins to weep and shake, holding her hands in a prayer position and raising them up and down. Most of her teeth are gone and her mouth caves in on itself as she tells more and more of the story. "They didn't allow me to cry. Now, all I can do is cry."

Ry looks up at the wooden rafters, bored, as the story is recounted. Later, she tells me her grandmother has never been "right." In the industrialized world, we would say she has endured post-traumatic stress disorder for nearly three decades. Here it afflicts a quarter of the country and hardly anyone has ever heard of it. "When they wanted to kill someone they ordered him to go to a meeting," she says, recounting the death of one of her sons. "They killed him and put him in the river and I saw him. I don't know the reason they killed him. They used to listen under our houses to us talk, but I didn't care if I starved so long as my children lived." She spends most of the rest of the afternoon crying quietly, moaning, while her family continues conversing and eating around her. Nothing can be done for her illness. Her husband died of cancer in 1976 and there were no doctors to consult at the time, no medicine to ease his pain. "I could not even get coconut juice for him," she says. She pulls a small shard of mirror from her sarong and pops it in her mouth, gums it absently, and her crying begins to ease. I try not to look, silently hoping her mouth is subjected only to the smooth sides. Luckily, she doesn't swallow, but after a while pulls it from her mouth and pops it back into her sarong. Some people have security blankets; others I suppose have broken glass.

Ry gives her mother money to get medicine for Pov. The chickens wandering around below have begun to coo and make weird chicken noises that I've never heard. Ry fusses with her daughter's sleeve, buttoning and unbuttoning the cuff. Pov has on a batik shirt and green, polka-dotted pants; her elders dress in sarongs and print tops. Pov says she is always happy to see her mom, but she stopped crying each time her mother left long ago. "Now," she says, flopping her body into her mother's lap, "I just miss her." Ry uses these words to describe Pov: smart, clever, brave. "I ask her for one word and she gives me three," Ry smiles.

We slowly wander out of the house and down to the car to drive back to the city. We want to beat the darkness and the rain, if we can. Ry packs up a bag of cucumbers and long beans for me to take home, then, laughing, offers me a cow. Just before we pile in the car, she decides not to return to the city for a couple of days, to stay with Pov and make sure she recovers. If she is fired, she says, she will look for another job. If not, she has decided it's been long enough; she will run again in the next election to be a union representative. She claims she has shed her fear from the 2002 demonstration. We leave her with her family and start back on the bumpy track as she waves behind us. I don't understand how she could decide, without a moment's notice, not to show up for work for a few days. Her daughter is ill, but she didn't seem dangerously so to me. She was up and walking around and helping with the food. I don't see Ry again for five months.

NAT OUK'S IDENTIFICATION CARD SHOWS THAT SHE is United Eternity employee #1099. She has worked at this factory nearly a decade and watched its ownership change hands multiple times. The vast majority of factories in Cambodia are owned by Chinese, Malaysians, Singaporeans, and others. The first time I meet Nat alone, she wears a gray, button-down shirt and beige pants that hang off her tiny frame. She has her hair back in a pony-tail and keeps her eyes trained toward the metal folding table at a tiny café where we have tea. Behind us, groups of men watch a kickboxing game on television. Nat fiddles with a toothpick as we talk.

She was born at the tail end of the Pol Pot regime. No one in their immediate area expected her to survive as an infant. Her mother was so malnourished that her body never produced milk. Nat says she stayed alive on sugar water and watered-down coconut milk. She was extremely malnourished. Even after the Vietnamese invaded and ended the Khmer Rouge reign, she was too weak to go to school, too weak even to walk. "I started school when I was ten," she says. "And I started walking when I was twelve or thirteen." The effects of this stunted development are still visible today in the hesitancy of her walk, the frailty of her legs.

When Nat was in seventh grade, her father got sick. She describes his illness as "bones beginning to grow through the skin of his feet." I couldn't understand what she meant by this, but it's likely that he, like many aging Khmers, simply had something like undiagnosed diabetes. She worked odd jobs for the next few years, selling cakes along the street (she carried them in a basket atop her head), working construction (not uncommon for women here), and selling lottery tickets. She earned next to nothing. Her mother, too, went to work selling homemade cakes in front of nearby factories. Nat finally got a factory job in 1994, when the manufacturers began to move in. "I was so scared of people at first," she says. "I used to be the most gentle in my family, but [the factory] treated me so bad. The boss sent me to work in the washing group, right in front of the toilets. I tried to hurry, the smell was so bad." Nat believes her boss wanted to fire her and had simply given her the worst job in the factory to get her to quit. Instead, she worked hard and fast and the employees around her began to call her "thick-faced," a Khmer saying that basically means you can take what the world dishes out to you. She was finally moved to a sewing line and became, she says, "absolutely different from before." She worked hard and stood up for herself, but in 1995 there were no labor laws and no benefits like sick days.

If you got sick, she says, you got fired, which is what happened to her.

United Eternity hired her after that, though it went by a different name at the time, and she says she learned to be "brave." She adds, "I was never afraid of being fired again because of my skill. If the boss says something to me, I respond immediately." She laughs at the incongruity of it, how the factories have unwittingly made her strong. Even today, an outing of women for tea is anathema to traditional Khmer culture and Nat doesn't have free time of her own, like Ry, because she lives with her mother. She'll sometimes lie to her family about the hours she works, so she and Ry can steal a late Saturday afternoon stroll along the riverside in downtown Phnom Penh. "In Khmer we say that a mean teacher makes a tricky student," she laughs. "So this is me." The tiny deception of a daughter to her mother.

Over and over I heard a refrain similar to Nat's: My father got sick and I had to work.

It took me a long time to understand how a single broken leg, how a flu, how a respiratory infection could so debilitate an entire family. How? I kept asking. Ten years later, why do you still have to work in the factory? I thought the workers weren't telling me the whole story, or perhaps something was lost in the translation. One day, I finally got it. In Cambodia, a broken leg is life-threatening. If it is set at all, it will likely be set wrong. Often, the only medical care a villager receives, even for a broken bone, is a local salve from a village elder who may or may not practice a whacked-out form of black magic and who may or may not have rudimentary medical training. A broken leg in someone malnourished, with no money for treatment and no knowledge of calcium, vitamins, protein, and no money to come to the city for hospital care does not heal in ten or twelve weeks. Most often, it does not heal at all.

One visiting doctor from the States told me that most doctors are paid only thirty or forty dollars a month, so they basically have to make money other ways and their offices aren't even staffed half the time. By this measure, garment factories are a better professional option. Medical treatment is pay as you go here, so if a family has no money, a family gets no treatment at all, not even from a traditional healer. If you have undiagnosed diabetes, for example, and you get a cut on your foot, it could put you over the edge. It could kill you. A sick relative means one less person to go out and earn a dollar that day. A sick father, who is often the main wage earner, is even more financially draining.

Nat's father died of emphysema in 2003. Her mother has an irregular heartbeat that keeps her housebound and bedridden most days. On her good days, she still prepares and sells jellied cakes made from coconut, squash, sweet potato, and sugar palm. Her mother is sixty and Nat wishes she could stop working altogether, but the factory work doesn't pay enough for that. She figures she could support the whole family—her mother and six siblings—on three hundred dollars a month, though four hundred would be easier. She makes around one hundred. Her salary is higher than Ry's because she is a supervisor.

Nat says she still has regular anxiety attacks; the 2002 incident in the truck terrified her. "I believe life is over for me now," Nat says. "I don't blame anyone, because my parents didn't force me to stop studying. But I felt I wanted my siblings to not have as difficult a life as me. I think of them going to the best university. Time is over for me. What I have to do now is help [my brothers and sisters]. They are like trees that need my help to grow."

One afternoon, we go to Nat's house. She lives with her mother and younger siblings in a small, three-room house a kilometer from the factory. She has four brothers and two sisters, but her eldest brother and sister are married and living elsewhere in Phnom Penh, which makes Nat, at thirty, the eldest child still at home. We walk down a small alleyway like Ry's and we pass Nat's brother and his wife stationed behind a tiny glass case that holds lottery cards, cigarettes, candy, gum, and an assortment of nails, screws, nuts, and padlocks, all selling for pennies. Nat's neighbors peer out at us from behind walls and glassless windows. Dengue fever is reaching record levels in Phnom Penh, and no one even has screens on their windows. Nat smiles shyly at her neighbors as we wander past. On the main road behind us, moto horns bleat and scads of factory workers all begin to make their way home. As we walk, I see a confidence in Nat, the unhurried swagger of a familiar route. "Maybe our parents are beginning to see the modern world," she says, skirting a puddle. "We've been earning money since we were thirteen or fourteen, but our freedom is only coming now. Maybe they knew I'd had enough experience and I didn't make any trouble. They trusted me not to disgrace the family."

Nat's living room is bare. We sit on reed mats, opened for our arrival, on a red and white cement tiled floor. Mold creeps up the concrete walls in corners. Nat's smile disappears once we are in her home; she carries a perpetual heaviness with her. I imagine her as a quiet superhero in a way, standing up in spite of her frail physicality, the world throwing lightning bolts at her that she easily deflects. I imagine she'd say of course she can overpower the lightning, but she needn't be hopeful about it, or happy, or pretend that it'll end someday. Where Ry is flighty and jovial, more brash and outspoken, Nat is thoughtful and steadfast, sad and fearless.

Outside, the sun has nearly set and Nat's living room gets darker and darker, but no one turns on a light. Electricity is prohibitively expensive in Cambodia.* Neighbors peer in the open doorway every few minutes, then wander away. Nat says she is bored working in the factory. "Sometimes I am awake all night," Nat says. "I cannot find a word to describe my worry."

Phom Un, Nat's mother, shuffles into the living room with her irregular heartbeat and her shy grin and plunks herself down on the mats with us. She is a tiny woman with gray curly hair and tiny eyes like seeds and wears a purple print sarong. I fear using the word adorable to describe her, but it's true. She is *adorable*. The sort of plump, grandmotherly woman with fleshy cheeks and

---

*I have a small, four-room apartment in Phnom Penh and the electric bills run about US$200 a month, or 25¢ per kilowatt. In the United States, the average is about 10¢ per kilowatt.

cherubic mouth that makes you want to sit at her feet and listen to her century-old wisdom. Someone lights an oil lamp. Nat, employee #1099, gets up and clips her ID card to a wall calendar bearing the legend A Stroll Through Kyoto. It is two years old and shows the pristine, orderly beauty of a Japanese garden. When Nat talks about her parents, she often tells the story of how they met. Her father, riding his bike in the dark, very fast, crashed into Phom Un, who was also riding her bike. As she fell, the contents of her bag spilled onto the dirt road. She quickly gathered them as best she could and rode off without a word. It would have been improper for her as a single girl to speak to a man, even though that man had just plowed into her accidentally and was inquiring as to her overall physical injuries. In her bag, however, she had had pictures of herself, and she failed to retrieve them all from the ground. Nat's father found the photo and, in the style of Hollywood movies and German fairy tales, went searching for the woman in the photo. He eventually found her through her uncle and the two were married shortly afterwards. To Nat, it was a tale of true love.

"When Nat was born, I was sick with fever," Phom Un tells me. "We had no medicine, no food to eat. One night they came to take my husband, but he was sick with malaria and fainted often. His sickness saved him," she rubs her fingertips, slowly, one by one. I can smell rice cooking, and the super-sweet smell of longan, or lychee fruit. "We are so lucky to have lived." The mat beneath us is yellow, blue, and red. A single fan in the corner remains off, though it's sweltering. Mosquitoes nip at my ankles and arms. Before the war, Phom Un had a small stall that sold produce, fruit, spices, and shampoo. Her family was sent to dig irrigation channels when the Khmer Rouge came, and many people got malaria. "It wasn't prison, but it was like prison," she says. She remembers the very day the regime ended. "We saw the Vietnamese come; they moved from east to west and in the dawn we saw figures and heard shooting." She says sometimes at night, now, she doesn't sleep.

Phom Un is happy Nat is working, happy she's contributing to the family, and she thinks the factories have helped Nat, too. "Before she began to work at the factory, she was not as smart, as clever. She didn't even know how to cook rice, and she was always sick," Phom Un says. A pipe running up the height of the wall hisses. "Sometimes I look at her and she is so different now."

Nat nods and smiles as her mother speaks. "[Before], I was afraid of people," she says.

"I don't mean to sound proud, but I wonder how she got so smart," Phom Un says, earnestly. "At home she talks back [to me]. She stands up for herself!" Phom Un and Nat laugh together. We sip tepid tea from chipped cups, listen as the traffic begins to subside, the horns going quiet for the night. "You know, when she was a child," Phom Un says, taking a moment to study her daughter, "her grandfather used to joke that if she died, he would not be able to bury her. The ground was too hard [to swallow her frail] body." Nat just smiles and looks at the floor.

- -

WHEN WE FINISH AT NAT'S HOUSE, SOPHEA PULLS ME aside on the street for a cultural readjustment. She brings up Ry's and Nat's homes. To me, they're a step above squalor (actually, Ry's room isn't even a step above), but by Khmer standards, they are perfectly acceptable—perhaps even a little grand, especially Ry's family's out in the countryside. What Sophea wants me to know is that both families would never talk about how good they had it now, even if their lives were perfect, even if they were millionaires. "It is not in our tradition," she said, "to make a show of ourselves. It is our custom to talk about the struggle of life, to be humble."

It is a monumentally important point when you're talking about garment workers. No one would be so naïve as to call them well off, but what looked to me like humble circumstances might simply be a recipe formed of my own cultural interpretation and their modest propensity to talk about the negatives in their lives: premature deaths, sick relatives, wars and Pol Pot and lack of medicine. This shouldn't be taken to mean they don't deserve higher wages; it simply means that cultural clues are often more complicated than mere conversation allows for. Indeed, even wealthy government ministers and private businessmen in Cambodia—men driving around in Mercedes and Land Rovers—talk about the difficulties of life, the cloying exhaustion of existence.

IN OCTOBER OF 2004, NAT AND RY AND I MEET AGAIN at Phnom Penh's only mall, an air-conditioned, gleaming box of a building, with stores that sell suitcases and cosmetics and sports clothes. It is famous among Khmers as the only place in the entire country with an escalator. When it was first built, many people were terrified of the moving stairs and came just to look at them. Indeed, Nat and Ry tell me they have never ridden the escalator. It is ten feet from where we're sitting and I tell them I'll take them on it, but they are afraid. Nat is wearing a T-shirt with sequins that spell out the word *beautiful* in English. She can't read it. Ry wears a gray shirt with lace printed onto the fabric. Nothing I say can induces them to ride the escalator.

Nat's brother has had a motorcycle accident with a policeman and has been jailed until his family can round up enough money to fix the policeman's bike and pay for his hospital bill. The police officer's family has asked for fifteen hundred U.S. dollars; it is now up to Nat's family to negotiate.

Ry is doing, in fact, less well. Out of seven hundred employees at her factory, only fifty are working. Nat is one of them. Ry is not. Instead, Ry is being paid ten dollars a month to wait. The factory owners claim this is the first time in seven or eight years that the factory has closed, and they believe the cause is the coming end of the quotas, but it's also not uncommon to have a slowdown at this time of year, between December and March. The Christmas rush generally happens between July and September, and factories tend to get fewer orders in late fall and early winter (or, in Cambodia's seasons, late rainy season and early cool). What's different this year is that the slowdown carries such portent; fear within the industry, from top to bottom, is palpable.

Ry says she doesn't know which country will save them. They *expect* to be saved, by someone, *anyone*, but they don't trust their own government to change anything significantly. In the aftermath of the Khmer Rouge period, thousands of nongovernmental organizations and aid workers have flocked to Cambodia to build health, economic, human rights, and other programs. The sheer number of organizations operating here has caused more than one person I know to begin calling Cambodia a "beggar country." It's a much easier place to be an aid worker than, say, sub-Saharan Africa. Phnom Penh has great restaurants, decent spas, cheap labor, and nice places to live. But Ry's expectation of being "saved" is likely a direct result of the massive NGO influx throughout the 1990s.

"I heard a rumor," she tells me, "that at the end of the year, the factory will change [management]. We're not sure what buyers will come, or what countries we'll export to." Ry says the last time Cambodians trusted their government was under the rule of King Sihanouk in the 1950s and 1960s. (He abdicated his throne in 2005 to his son, Prince Sihamoni.) They compare their current government to a mother who calls her child stupid, blaming the government for the people's lack of development because it fails to have faith in the competence of its own citizens. "How can that child do anything, become anything?" Ry asks.

One of Ry's brothers has stopped studying to help bring in some income, and her daughter has stopped her English classes. The family's crops were dismal this year because of drought, and they had very little to sell. Indeed, even now at break time, the streets and stalls of Chak Angre aren't as flooded as before. Rath has not even had to break out her extra tables. Ry's landlord, the furniture maker, died suddenly a few weeks earlier and his wife has subsequently raised the rent to $17 a month. "I used to think we would spend this year and save the next, after we had everything we needed," Ry tells me. I know this paradox. Having all you "need" is a continual cycle. Ry will never win. There will always be drought, or family accidents, or failed businesses.

Her family wants her to come home, she says. "My mother says I should be at home," she says, "but if I was at home, my mother could not survive." This is the conundrum of her life. Yes, her salary helps her family survive, but there is also a tiny corner of her heart that just simply likes the life she has created for herself. Ry isn't yet looking for work at another factory, but says she will if too much time passes. The factory told her there would be work in the future, but she doesn't know whether or not to trust this. She is dipping into savings just to pay her rent at the moment, and hoping that every day she will get a call back. "My mother feels a daughter should not be away. Sometimes my family is strict, and they say that Phnom Penh is really far." Half of Ry, of course, silently disagrees.

Still, they have not forced her to return, and I suspect that they are as hopeful as she that the factory will have more orders soon. Their hope pays off; by the end of April, Ry is back at work.

XIV

THE LONG ARM OF THE NON-LAW

A MAN WITH A PINK DRESS SHIRT, GRAY SLACKS, AND Nike sports socks sits thumbing through a book called *Labour Law*, while a wall unit hums before him, chilling the air. He is an attorney, called today to defend a garment factory whose workers have filed a series of complaints against their employer. Next to him is one of the managers of the factory. Across the table from the two of them, five union representatives, in faded shirts and rubber flip-flops, wait for him to speak. They wear nervous smiles. They represent a group of workers who recently went on strike and now they have brought the case here, to what is called the Arbitration Council, where they are hoping for a settlement in their favor. The two sides sit on the edges of four oversized glossy tables pushed together into the middle of an otherwise small plain white room, which creates a curious honey-colored landscape; the ratio of tables to humans is almost equal. Three arbitrators sit in a single row a step above the feuding parties at the front of the room.*

---

*I am not allowed to name any of the arbitrators by name, or the feuding parties, or the attorney, or even the factory.

The room is airy, tiled with shiny flooring reminiscent of a public bathroom; one wall is a series of windows, beyond which a brand-new parliament building is under construction just beside the shore, where the Mekong and Sap Rivers meet. It is being built in the Khmer style, with whimsical horns at the roof corners, rounded roof tiles like fish scales, and earthy colors like burnt sienna and ocher. Behind the arbitrators hang pictures of the retired King Sihanouk and his wife, Queen Monineath, along with their son, King Sihamoni. There is also a Khmer national flag with its red background, and three temple spires of Angkor Wat—modeled after lotus flowers—in the foreground; two blue stripes border the top and bottom of the flag. The field of tables supports a single box of tissues in the middle, covered with a decorative Khmer-print fitted cloth. Tissue boxes are always elegantly dressed in Cambodia.

The Arbitration Council is new for Cambodia. Established in 2003, it can be defined as somewhere between a court of law and a group of very pleasant people who help you work out your problems, your frustrations, and sometimes just your anger or confusion. For free. The ragtag group brought together in this room are engaged in an operation that could bode well for developing countries around the world. Between the nightmare of the developing-country sweatshop of horrors and the dream of the fairly well-established labor system in a country like the United States or Great Britain, there lives a world of nuance. People mistakenly think that creating good ventilation and making sure everyone is paid for overtime solves the problems. But these are merely the beginning. Eradicating sweatshops opens its own Pandora's box. One of the biggest problems in Cambodia, in fact, comes from the labor laws themselves. Like the Bible, they're open to much interpretation. People from the factory management to the unions to the employees to the monitors often understand them very differently, if they understand them at all. Take Article 67, for example. It says:

> The labor contract signed with one consent for a specific
> duration cannot be for a period longer than two years. It

can be renewed one or more times, as long as the renewal
does not surpass the maximum duration of two years.

Does this mean renewed up to two years *each time*? Or is two
years the maximum so you could have, say, four six-month contracts?

How about Article 166, which says:

The length of paid leave as stated above is increased
according to the seniority of workers at the rate of one day
per three years of service.

One factory gave its workers an extra day every three years
then stopped, whereas workers wanted that extra day for every
subsequent year after three.

THE LAWS READ WELL, UNTIL YOU FIND YOURSELF HAV-
ing to interpret them. The Arbitration Council was established to
do just this. As a consequence it is as important to the success of
the Cambodia fair labor movement as contracts from buyers, and
by all accounts, it has begun to accomplish the impossible in the
country—that is, to be universally recognized and revered as
incorruptible.* The Arbitration Council has been credited, since
its inception, with single-handedly diminishing the number of
strikes in the country. I was also told that it's the only functioning
body of its type in the developing world.

The key to this incorruptibility has to do with the arbitration

*The United States Agency for International Development called the
Arbitration Council Cambodia's "only quasi-judicial body never accused of
corruption."

process, and its subsequent transparency. Court proceedings in Cambodia are never public, and even a judge's ruling, assuming it has a logical rationale (and that is often a *very* big assumption), usually fails to offer any insight into his reasoning or lack thereof. Some rulings are actually just a single sentence long, maybe a paragraph. We take for granted open court documents in the United States, where precedent from a previous trial often dictates future trial outcomes. No such concept exists in Cambodia. Courts take months to hear a case, if they hear it at all. Often, lawyers and judges siphon off high-profile cases or rich clients and leave others to languish. Nimmith Men, the executive director of the Arbitration Council Foundation, calls what they do "helping out the courts." He says before the advent of the council, people didn't know what to do with disputes; there was no alternative process. All of this, it's important to note here, is free. The legal system in Cambodia is widely perceived to be wholly purchasable. The beauty of the Arbitration Council is that it takes away the incentive for bribery; why would someone pay for a certain outcome if he could simply reject a ruling for free?

Once a case is brought to the council, it has fifteen days to hold a hearing on the issue (in the States, a similar arbitration process between unions and employers can take six months). Three arbitrators are chosen: one from the worker's side, one from the factory side, and one from the Ministry of Labour.

At the beginning of a hearing, the parties are asked whether they want a binding or a nonbinding award. Binding means they must accept whatever the arbitrators rule and parties must implement the arbitrators' ruling. Admittedly, roughly a quarter of cases have parties who operate in defiance of the rulings and will eventually need to be dealt with by the Cambodian court system and/or government. In a binding award, strikes and worker walkouts aren't allowed. Most often unions bring complaints against a factory and not vice versa, and they almost always choose to have an award binding. Employers, surprisingly, also often agree to a binding award. They seem to recognize that a nonbinding award could cause further problems in the future for them. They also probably feel confident they'll win their case. On the face of it, a factory with resources—money and attorneys—against a group of union reps with limited experience and education and no resources seems wholly unbalanced. But the Arbitration Council rights that imbalance.

The arbitrators conduct a hearing and issue an award within fifteen days of receiving the case. If the feuding parties chose a nonbinding award at their initial hearing, either side has eight days to object to the ruling. If no one objects, it becomes binding. If one party objects, workers then have the right to strike legally and the parties may try again to negotiate a settlement or turn to the Cambodian courts. Everyone recognizes that possibility as a profoundly undesirable outcome, since both employees on strike and the Cambodian judicial system will always be very costly; the Arbitration Council believes it may be a strong economic disincentive for choosing nonbinding. Since its inception, the council has successfully resolved around 70 percent of the disputes that have come before it.

"What we're doing is building a body of jurisprudence that says what the rules are," Michael Lerner, a lawyer from California who has been an advisor to the Arbitration Council since 2004, says. "In the courts, there is corruption, conflict of interests, unclear decision-making. The Arbitration Council, in its small domain, is fair. The 'why' is key to us here."

The day I visited, the union reps and factory manager and his lawyer sat politely across from each other. I happened to know that this particular factory made clothes for Gap. The fact that I knew this and no one else in the room (or even the Arbitration Council at large) did was a telling detail. In the States, we envision a direct link between the Gap and all its factories in fifty countries around the world, but here that link is irrelevant to the proceedings. One season the factory may have Gap orders, the next season Ann Taylor. Often a third party contracts with factories for specific buyers. Gap has its own monitors who visit factories fairly regularly, but the company may not be informed of a case like this unless a serious violation has occurred. From the Arbitration Council's standpoint, what matters is the issue at hand and the subsequent solution. We tend to think of the world as an increasingly connected place, and this is not wrong, but ten thousand miles away is still ten thousand miles away. It is a sign of progress, at least in Cambodia, that local labor issues can now often be worked out judiciously and quickly by local offices and local mediators without involving buyers.

Consider this factory, for example. It is one in a number of factories in Asia owned by a company out of Hong Kong. It has Khmer workers and its Chinese management interacts mainly with the parent corporation in Hong Kong, not with the buyer in San Francisco. The orders come from the Gap in San Francisco to the contractor in Hong Kong, who then hires local factories in the region. So here, in this little room of tables inside one of Phnom Penh's only substantial office buildings—and by substantial I mean four stories—a group of seven people have gathered to hash out their differences. In these cases, the brand never comes up. The arbitrators don't even know whether the factory makes shirts or socks or underwear or Superman costumes and they don't care. Helping workers and management cooperate is what matters. At the end of the day, the Gap is as relevant to a hearing like this as a hot dog vendor in the East Village is to a polar expedition.

THE ARBITRATORS, TWO MEN AND ONE WOMAN,* BEGIN by thanking everyone for coming and giving the overall structure of the arbitration process, particularly the concept of nonbinding. "We want to encourage you," the council says, "to come to an agreement yourselves, between the union and the factory. This is an opportunity to exchange information here."

*She was once a factory monitor for Nike.

The union is asked to name their grievance. The leader begins, slowly at first. "The manager speaks to them using 'bad words,' " he says. And, "several workers have asked to visit sick family members and been denied."

Quickly, the list gets longer and longer, with small annoyances given the same weight as larger complaints. Some of the issues include:

- When workers go to the toilet, they are asked for identification cards
- The entrance to the factory is smaller now and workers have to wait to come inside.
- Sometimes the manager knocks on the door when workers are in the bathroom and he yells at them.
- Workers are not allowed to use their mobile phones anymore
- The radio has been turned off

To my surprise, the lawyer of the factory thanks them when they have finished. "There is a new president and a new manager," he tells them, making no attempt to disavow the complaints, "and we are trying to make it better." (The factory manager present at the proceedings is a representative, but he is not the manager in question in the case.)

The union leaders, as it turns out, had compiled a full fourteen pages of complaints by the workers and that list had been whittled down to the six or so brought today. The arbitrators press the union on specifics. Were workers not allowed to take vacation days to visit sick relatives? Were the factory doors too small for workers to get in and out of safely in case of a fire? Was bathroom usage monitored? Had the offending manager verbally threatened anyone?

Some of the complaints, though insubstantial, seem valid to me. Why couldn't they use their phones, listen to the radio, or use the bathroom in peace?

The factory manager and his lawyer sit and listen intently as the arbitrators pull more and more information from the unions. Several of these issues, it became clear, aren't really issues at all. What seems more the point is simply resistance to change, like taking time off for sick days. Workers are supposed to go to the human resources office for permission to take vacation time, and in several cases, they simply went to the managers. Since the management is new they haven't made the new rules clear enough to the workers. Compounding this, the managers are also all Chinese and tend to speak little or no Khmer, so they've had trouble explaining changes to the staff. This is common in Cambodia; as I noted earlier, few factories are Khmer owned or managed, with the overwhelming majority coming from China, Singapore, Malaysia, or other nearby countries. The Taiwanese-owned factories were the fastest growing in Cambodia in 2005. The workers had a name for Chinese managers who came to Phnom Penh and ordered them around and didn't speak Khmer. They called them Raw Chinese. (Nat and Ry say they have never worked for a Khmer manager.) Communication problems are rampant. In fact, this is true around the world. Chinese managers are as common in Honduras, Mexico, the Caribbean, and Africa as they are in Southeast Asia.*

When the arbitrators finally turn to the factory representatives, they offer up what seem like reasonable explanations for a number of the minor grievances. The doors were replaced because the previous ones had been corrugated, rusty tin. They promise to have someone come look at expanding them. The radio is not banned but rather is played only between 9:00 A.M. and 10:00 A.M. and again between 1:00 P.M. and 3:00 P.M. The owners feel that is a compromise for those who may not want to listen to it all day. Likewise, mobile phone usage is an issue of occupational safety; workers are entitled to use them, but only when they are not at

*Numerous garment workers I've interviewed often perceive conversing in Mandarin or Cantonese as "yelling." It is often simply a case of not understanding a foreign language, particularly a tonal foreign language.

their work stations or around machines. Doors to the factory were now to be kept closed in order to keep air-conditioning costs down. The issue of bathrooms, they say, is simply a matter of numbers. They had forty bathrooms in total and thought ID cards would make their usage equitable (personally, I would think "equitable" is probably not the best approach to biological necessity). The only grievance they deny outright is any monitoring of bathroom usage. They don't address the issue of the manager yet.

The arbitrators ask the union if they are requesting that the factory build more bathrooms. But the unions do not answer directly. Instead, they say, simply, "The workers are unhappy."

One of their biggest demands arises only fifteen minutes into the proceedings. They want the company to pay them for a two-and-a-half-day strike from several weeks earlier. The company has refused. From the standpoint of the workers, unacceptable conditions led to the strike so the company ought to be obligated to pay. They are asking for five dollars for each employee. From the viewpoint of the firm, the workers went on strike illegally without going through the steps outlined in the labor law.*

Forty-five minutes into the proceedings, the arbitrators have managed to whittle down the list of complaints to just two: payment for the days the workers went on strike and the dismissal of the mean manager.

In the case of the manager, the factory lawyer concedes that his client has received complaints and the head office in Hong Kong has issued the manager a warning. The unions ask the arbitrators to force the factory to fire him altogether, but this is a losing battle for them. The Arbitration Council's Web site lists every case that's ever been brought before them and many dozens of cases about disliked management have been lodged. "No one will ever win that kind of case," Michael Lerner told me earlier in the day. "That's a contract between a factory and its management staff

---

*One of the more common complaints I hear about unions in Cambodia is that they encourage their workers to strike first rather than as a last resort.

and it's frankly not appropriate for a third party to determine the outcome of a contractual agreement." Only in cases where there was clear harassment or physical threat would a group of arbitrators make this call, he said. Indeed, in the case I hear, the union is asked about direct harassment or physical threat from this manager and both are denied.

Midway through the morning, the session adjourns for fifteen minutes and the arbitrators go into a back room to discuss what they've heard. Outside the arbitration room in a waiting area, the groups mill around, sitting on black vinyl couches and drinking cups of bottled water. There is seemingly no animosity between them; they talk a little, and then the lawyer disappears to the hallway to call Hong Kong. I try to imagine legal proceedings in the States where both accused and accuser break for a chat and a drink together. This might be both a strength and a downfall—everyone is polite and respectful, never causing another to "lose face." But everyone is also failing to engage in direct negotiations because of this and so you get great "face" but you never get what anyone actually thinks.

Cases about strikes and payments for lost days are brought before the council regularly, but the factories often have the law on their side. Article 319 of the labor law says the " right to strike . . . [is] guaranteed." But it also says striking can only be "exercised when all peaceful methods of settling the dispute with the employer have already been tried out." Peaceful methods include having the Arbitration Council hear a case. In this instance, the employees went on strike first, so while a misinterpretation is understandable, they don't have the law on their side. Why the factory doesn't just outright refuse to deal with them is testimony both to the council's insistence that every case be approached fairly and evenhandedly and to the plain truth that strikes, whether legal or not, are the most useful tool to get your voice heard. What this has meant, in real terms, is that factories understand that outright refusal, even in the face of complaints where they are clearly in the right, does not produce an effective work-force. While they may not lose money this time around, it will likely mean bigger problems further down the line. Michael Lerner told me about one case that came to the council from a group of workers who'd learned their factory had fired a number of other employees and given them substantial severance pay. "They were demanding the factory fire them," he told me, "and give them the same severance pay. And then hire them back."

Cases don't have to make perfect sense (or in the latter case, any sense at all, really). The goal is to create a functioning system of open dialogue and compromise in a region with no history of this kind of debate. Eventually, Lerner believes cases like the one above, and even the one before the council today—workers demanding payment for an illegal strike—would evolve into the sort of gritty, real-issue disputes of a more established system. Hopefully, with jurisprudence people will slowly begin not only to understand the rules but to resolve issues, even in the gray areas, themselves.

When the arbitrators finish talking, they call only the factory rep and his lawyer into the room this time and ask what they are willing to compromise on. For the first time that day, I see a glimpse of how the factory really feels about being there.

The lawyer nods, smiles, and then announces: "If workers protest, we will shut the factory down." The room is quiet for a minute and the arbitrators' faces show little response. They encourage the lawyer to continue. "We do not want to pay for the protest days and we are not required under the labor law. We cannot afford compensation and we are afraid it sets a precedent."

This is also a common problem. Where workers strike frequently, factories cross their collective arms and simply threaten to leave if the workers don't fall in line.

First, the head arbitrator tells them that pulling out of the factory is "complicated. Please," he says in an even tone, "do not just leave. You must try to make workers happy. The new management seems stricter [than the old] and it's a change for employees." Then, something a little amazing happens. The arbitrator shifts gears and compliments the company and their experience; he thanks them for taking all these issues seriously even though the law might be with them in this instance. "Workers must understand the changes," he says. "We've seen these salary demands before. Can you give any concession on this?"

"Maybe if we could have the council's recommendations?" asks the attorney.

"We can't give you advice," one of them says, "but we encourage you to try to solve problems as they arise, rather than waiting until [they pile up]." The factory manager nods, laughing in a genial manner that suggests he would take that advice to heart.

By the end of it, the lawyer promises to go into the hall and call Hong Kong again.

Next, the union is called in. The council assures them, as they did with the factory reps, that whatever is said in the room will not be passed on to the other party and they should speak freely. The union thanks them.

"Do you think the protest helped solve your problem?" asks the female arbitrator. "Was there a strategy to the protest?"

Of course, everyone knows the answer already; if the strike had solved their problem, they wouldn't all be sitting in this office today. But it is a telling moment anyway. What she is really offering is advice on a context for striking; the hope that they will begin to understand striking as one of many tools at their disposal rather than the only tool. The idea that there is a natural progression or escalation of issues leading to a strike is one of the bigger challenges facing the industry in Cambodia, and in moments like this the point hits home.

The union leader doesn't quite answer the question but begins with the same unyielding, worst-case-scenario angle as the factory reps. "If we don't get five dollars," he says, "then productivity will be lower and they will protest again."

"If you carry on with more protests," says an arbitrator, "you'll lose money. Workers lose money and management loses workers." Michael Lerner told me that in the beginning, it often happened that both parties would disagree when they were facing each other, but then later they'd both call and agree to the terms of their own accord.

The union leader thinks about this for a moment, then offers what he believes is a compromise: "If the company gives five dollars, then workers won't protest again. Or, if they dismiss the manager, they won't ask for five dollars. If they can't dismiss the manager, then they want five dollars."

Basically, his idea is to go for one of the two. I probably don't have to say that these two demands didn't exactly seem analogous. It was akin to, say, my losing a seat on a ticketed flight and asking for a small parcel of land in South Dakota instead.

The council reiterates that it is not up to them to say who should or shouldn't be dismissed; then they encourage the union representatives to be "open-minded" and think of concessions. One reminds them that their strike had not followed legal procedure, but the union leader doesn't seem to feel this was a particular problem. "Relations must be softened," an arbitrator says, using a phrase that seemed particularly fitting today, with the lack of heated discussion and table pounding that I was expecting (though I was assured those kinds of sessions happen often as well).

Finally, the union seems to understand that they simply won't get anywhere on the issue of the manager's dismissal.

"Okay," they say, "If not five dollars, how about four?"

It is unlikely they will get any money for the strike, given that such a ruling would go against the labor law. But what is important for the Arbitration Council is that each party begin to witness the process of debate and compromise. When both groups are called back into the room, the factory manager is the first to speak.

He says, "We have all lost."

It isn't exactly a clear compromise yet, but acknowledging this is almost surely the day's greatest gain. One week later, the Arbitration Council finds in favor of the factory, ruling that the workers' demands for compensation are not in accordance with the law. The workers objected to the ruling by going on strike. The manager in question eventually quit and the workers dropped their demands.

XV

THREE MEN AND A
FOREIGN POLICY

IN JULY 2005, THREE MEN BOARDED A PLANE IN PHNOM
Penh, Cambodia, bound for Washington, DC. They were hoping
to meet with President Bush or, if not him, at least a member of
his administration or a staffer—anyone, really, who could get his
ear for a minute. They also planned to meet with senators and
members of Congress and whoever else who would give them a
few minutes—perhaps Senate staffers.

The team was made up of Cham Prasidh, the Cambodian minister of commerce (first class flyer, diplomatic passport), Van
Souieng, the head of the Garment Manufacturers' Association of
Cambodia, or GMAC (first class flyer, nondiplomatic passport),
and Ken Loo, the secretary general of GMAC (business class flyer,
nondiplomatic passport, Singaporean turned Cambodian resident
as a result of falling in love and marrying a Cambodian). This was
the second lobbying trip for the three of them, and they got on the
plane with high hopes and great trepidation in equal measure.
Their timing was less than perfect. The U.S.-Central America Free

Trade Agreement, which was supposed to have been voted on by the time of their trip, hadn't been, and everyone in Washington was focused on it. The president, for his part, was also busy trying to get everyone to acknowledge his wisdom in appointing John Roberts to the Supreme Court.

Six months had passed since January 1 and the ending of the quota system. Things were tense. In the first three months, Cambodia saw its contracts plummet. Multiple factories closed and more than ten thousand garment workers lost their jobs.

Historically, it had always been a slow period, the post-Christmas wane. Ry has been among those laid off and then rehired. Given that the slowdown coincided with the demise of the quotas, however, it seemed more portentous than it otherwise might have. But then the United States instituted its "safeguards" on China, which basically meant the country couldn't export more than a set volume in a variety of categories—the Quota System Lite was really what it amounted to. It was a measure meant to ease the potential deluge of business that China likely would have received after January 1, 2005. It also gave countries like Cambodia a little breathing room. The safeguards, according to WTO rules, will expire at the end of 2008; they are a temporary measure. Still, after the safeguards were established, Cambodia's exports began to grow again—albeit slower when compared to previous years—and most of the workers who'd lost jobs, like Ry, got them back, along with several thousand new hires.

So Minister Cham, Van Souieng, and Ken Loo came to lobby for something called the Trade Act of 2005. It was basically a bill put to Congress that would give Cambodia, and a group of other least developing countries in the region, duty-free status for a period of ten years. The Cambodians had begun to look at the Trade Act as their salvation. Without it, they believed they were sunk as soon as 2009 rolled around. "You have to understand," Ken said, "even a fifteen percent drop for us means a loss of forty thousand jobs. Jordan is fifty cents cheaper than us. With the Trade Act, we'd be twenty-five cents cheaper than that." Given that garments are nearly 90 percent of the country's exports and in Cambodia nearly a quarter of a million job seekers come on the market each year, such a loss could be socially and economically cataclysmic (more than half the population is under twenty-five). When you add economic forces like growing layoffs to vast increases in unemployment within a country's majority demographic, the result often looks a lot like social chaos. Given Cambodia's recent bloody history, this is an almost Pavlovian fear.

The genius of the Trade Act was that it didn't pertain to Cambodia alone but rather a group of countries with economies as precarious as Cambodia's, or even more so. The group included Afghanistan, a tactical addition given U.S. interest in making Afghanistan work socially, economically, and politically. It also included Sri Lanka, Bangladesh, Nepal, Laos, East Timor, Yemen, Samoa, Maldives, Kiribati, Tuvalu, Solomon Islands, Bhutan, and Vanuatu. The way the Cambodians saw it, they were simply asking the United States to give them what thirty-five other LDCs around the world had been given. They pointed to policies like AGOA—the African Growth and Opportunity Act—and the Caribbean Basin Initiative as evidence of tax-free status granted by the United States to exports from African, Caribbean, and Latin American LDCs. The Cambodians believed that their country and the Asian Pacific Rim had simply been left out, the subjects of a foreign policy oversight.

A few days before the three men left, GMAC hosted a group of twenty-five potential investors from Singapore. They wanted to prove that the country was still a viable place to make a profit even in the post-quota world, that buyers weren't going to just pull up roots and leave. Most buyers claim they have no plans to leave Cambodia, though many of their corporate Web sites also espouse the logic of consolidating some production. Whereas before a multinational corporation may have had forty different countries involved in production operations around the world, it is reasonable to think that number will diminish over time. It's a lot easier to manage bigger operations logistically in twenty countries than forty. The Singaporeans were attractive to GMAC not simply as garment factory investors but because at least half of them represented diverse businesses related to the industry, like fabric weavers and shipping suppliers. Cambodia needed desperately to diversify.

Much of the Singaporean fact-finding visit involved scoping potential land for building opportunities and touring existing factories. They'd also been to Vietnam on this trip, and Van Souieng and Ken Loo wanted to do everything they could to persuade them that Cambodia was the better choice. Ken thinks they've been somewhat protected by Vietnam not yet gaining admittance into the WTO—a status that changed at the end of 2006 and which petrifies Cambodia. After China, Vietnam is one of the garment industry's heaviest hitters. One afternoon, the interested parties all met at GMAC's headquarters, where Ken basically offered them a pitch on the country. Tropical fruit and bottles of water sat on three big trays in the middle of the table, but otherwise the room was stark. Outside, noodle vendors and other merchants pushed carts along Jawaharlal Nehru Boulevard, one of the city's main thoroughfares, while Land Rovers and Lexus SUVs whizzed around. The Singaporeans seemed cautiously friendly. "Cambodia has a good reputation with many international buyers, especially the big buyers that are concerned with their corporate image, corporate social responsibilities," Ken told them. "Gap has been our single biggest buyer."

Really, it's the only thing Cambodia has to sell: social responsibility. Otherwise, it's a relatively expensive endeavor to set up shop here. Transportation costs are high and Cambodia doesn't have any of the raw materials needed to make clothing efficiently—buttons, rivets, zippers, cotton, packaging. Nothing. This is one of the reasons why the minimum wage is relatively low, because the cost of manufacturing is relatively high. Of course, the single biggest monetary funnel is probably corruption—not that real numbers are available. Along with the disappearance of the quota system, it is the most significant threat to new foreign investment in the garment industry. Ken insisted to the Singaporeans that many of the country's biggest brands have "indicated their intention to increase sourcing from Cambodia." He named Levi's, H&M, Nike, Adidas, Reebok, and Disney. A year later he told me Levi's had cut their "basics" line from Cambodia, resulting in about a 25 percent drop in business from Levi's for the country. Disney had come only on a trial basis, which Ken saw as a promise not quite kept. These brands were the names I'd grown up with, the names that embodied my personal retail culture, and yet hearing them in this context, they sounded foreign, like disembodied voices.

But Ken was also honest with the Singaporeans about certain on the-ground realities. "Of course, Cambodia is not a panacea for production," he said. "We have our own internal problems, and these are the problems faced by all developing economies in the world, namely corruption [and] bureaucracy." He was frank, and he insisted that GMAC was working steadily to get the government to address the most egregious issues.

He also told them about the unions. At the moment, there were more than eight hundred, but Ken said new ones appeared so often, practically daily, that there was a comic element to the issue. Far more unions than factories existed in the country because by law you only needed three people to form a union. Factories could have multiple unions and workers could belong to as many as they wanted provided they paid the dues. As a result, the rate at which unions formed and disbanded and reformed was ridiculously fast. Still, those in the industry knew the serious unions. What this meant was that occasionally you had one group of workers within a certain union protesting while another worked away at their posts. It made negotiations unwieldy, which was one of the more compelling reasons for the Arbitration Council. I waited to hear one of the Singaporeans ask about Chea Vichea, but no one did.

Chea Vichea was the wildly popular leader of the country's biggest union. He was aligned with the Sam Rainsy party, the only significant political opposition party in Cambodia. Unions here, like the media, openly ally themselves with one of the country's political parties, either the ruling CPP or the Funcinpec—which was disbanded in 2006—or the Sam Rainsy party, most often. Vichea was a handsome, well-spoken Khmer whom some saw as a modern-day Cambodian Che or Massoud (of course, people who made this comparison forgot how violent the latter two were). Vichea fought for workers' rights and had made relatively significant headway.

In early 2004 Chea was shot in broad daylight on a Sunday morning at a newspaper stand, along a busy road in Phnom Penh. I ride a motorcycle past this intersection almost daily—it is a block from the Independence Monument, the city's best-known landmark. Kids fly kites in lush green parks there every spring, and couples play badminton each evening. In New York City, it would be the equivalent of getting gunned down at Columbus Circle. Fifteen thousand people attended his funeral in what remains one of the saddest days in Cambodia's post–Khmer Rouge history. People still talk about him today; garment workers across the country continue to mourn him and no one—not even his brother, Chea Mony, who took over the union after his death—has emerged to fill his shoes.

Less than a week after his murder two men were arrested, tried, and almost immediately sentenced to long prison terms. None of the evidence against them has ever been made public, nor have any of the court proceedings. These men could not have appeared less likely perpetrators, and no one believes honestly in their guilt even today. Both were rural peasants with no history of violence and no connection to the garment industry. Both had sound alibis far outside the city. One was actually at a large gathering of villagers. In newspaper pictures following their arrest they appear dazed, void of emotion, and wholly confused. With the murder unsolved (many have accused the prime minister or his minions of ordering the hit) and two innocent men behind bars, the episode is a stain on the hard work of the country and makes the lobbying efforts of Minister Cham, Van Souieng, and Ken Loo all that much harder. Chea Vichea, as it is believed of so many ghosts in Cambodia, will also come back to haunt them.

KEN GAVE THE SINGAPOREANS WHAT HE HOPED WOULD be the deal maker: the Trade Act of 2005. They would not have to pay the average 17 percent in export taxes to the United States, Ken told them; the Trade Act would eliminate those costs. It would offer the Singaporeans a win-win investment opportunity— a socially responsible sourcing country with no duty paid to the world's biggest market. The bill clearly resonated with the Singaporeans, and they encouraged Ken to talk more about it. He said he'd be going himself the next week to lobby for the bill, along with the minister and Van Souieng. He said the lobbying firm they'd hired—Sandler, Travis & Rosenberg—was one of the biggest and most successful in Washington and that they were practically assured success. Not only were they approaching the bill in what Ken believed was the only "logical" way—that fourteen LDCs in the region had been left out—but they'd included Afghanistan for obvious reasons, and Sri Lanka, because the tsunami in December 2004 had earned it the world's sympathy.

Ken also talked about support they already had within the U.S. government. Barack Obama supported it, he said, calling him "the leader of the young generation of politicians in the U.S." And they hoped for Hillary Clinton, who, in his view, "represents a lot of the female voice" in America. It was bipartisan—the liberal Senator Dianne Feinstein *and* the conservative Senator Rick Santorum!— and already a series of cosponsors had signed on and they all expected more.*

The Singaporeans asked for more details about the bill. They said the way Congress voted would sway their decision about investing in Cambodia.

*A version of this chapter aired on public radio's *This American Life* in December 2005. During the editing of the piece, when we got to this part, Ira Glass, the show's host, said to me on the phone: "Okay, let's play a game. Name two parliamentary politicians in *any* country *anywhere*." The point of course, was that when you're the little David up against Goliath, you have to know *everything* about Goliath and Goliath doesn't even know you exist.

Of course, the bill hadn't yet even made it to the floor.

And what Ken and Van Souieng didn't tell the Singaporeans was that if the bill didn't pass soon, by the end of 2005 or the beginning of 2006, they believed it might be too late anyway. For the bill's effects to be felt at the factory level, they thought it would take a year or more, and from their vantage point they had only until the end of 2008, when the safeguards on China would be lifted. "Factories need to make a corporate decision a year to a year and a half in advance," Ken told me later. "If we don't get the bill until 2007 or 2008, it might be too late. Factories might already be gone."

WHEN KEN AND VAN SOUIENG TALKED ABOUT THE BILL in the meeting, it all sounded so promising. Buyers kept pledging to stay, and the Cambodian government was making some effort to streamline the bureaucracy and stanch some of the corruption in the industry, they said. But in private, and on the streets, the view was much grimmer. Van Souieng's brother, Van Voren, ran a factory that made Levi's jeans on the outskirts of the city. It was a relatively small factory of seven hundred workers, and though Van Souieng was the owner, his duties at GMAC kept him away much of the time. Van Voren said it would only take two months without orders to force his factory to shut down. In that same amount of time, he said, you could be up and running in another country. All you had to do was rent a space, ship your machines, and hire some workers. This is one of the reasons why garment factory work has always been so unstable, the proverbial "race to the bottom," as economists and activists call it—chasing the low-wage populations around the world. Van Voren said if the Trade Act didn't pass, the industry in Cambodia could die about that fast, too.

To hear Voren tell it, business was bad. First, there were all the costs of the inputs: the zippers, the buttons, the thread, the rivets and fabric. Then there was the expense of transport—the country's only port was more than three hours away, compared to some of China's "supply chain cities" like Guangzhou and Shenzhen, which were both practically seaside. He said a recent study found that the cost of electricity in Cambodia was the same as in downtown Tokyo. And there was the cost of labor compliance, the very thing that made Cambodia viable in the first place, which was huge. "It's actually very worrying," Voren said, "Our costs [are] actually very high. Just to give you an example. The cost of electricity that I'm paying every month is about six thousand dollars. Now, if I do not bother about compliance, I will switch off the lights and my workers can sew in the dimmer light. I can save maybe twenty percent. That's a lot of money. And you're just talking about electricity. How about drinking water? If I don't give my workers proper drinking water, I can save six hundred dollars every month. But of course . . . it's not right."

Voren's factory had a reputation for some of the best conditions around. He believed in fair labor laws, that they would eventually transform society—and the country—by turning peasant farmers into an educated middle class. But doing the right thing, not dimming the lights or taking away drinking water, meant Voren was only scratching by.

"I can say that seventy percent of the factories here are struggling," Voren said. His own factory made eighty to a hundred pairs of jeans an hour. "I don't think any of us are making money. I think it's just to maintain the workforce here. I know a lot of factories are not doing well. They may close down any day. If I can plan three months ahead with orders, I consider myself very safe. The situation is very bad right now. The situation is that I cannot even plan for more than two weeks."

One morning, I went to a local hotel called the Cambodiana to meet Van Souieng for coffee. When I arrived he was furiously text messaging, arranging to sell a factory's assets—mostly sewing machines—after the owner skipped town and blew off paying nearly a thousand workers. Van Souieng was fuming, trying to cover as much as he could of the lost wages. "I feel I have a duty to do it," he told me, "because that factory that closed is a bad one. It is like a thief running away." His English is accented with French, evidence of the Parisian education he received from age fourteen on. Van Voren, on the other hand, who spent much of his life in Singapore, has British intonations.

"It happens in all capitalist countries," Van Souieng said. "Even in the States. But in America, citizens have money to survive for a few weeks, a few months. But in Cambodia, they cannot survive without their wages for over seven days, ten days, so they're hungry. They're hungry."

Van Souieng and Van Voren come from a powerful family. Van Souieng has the kind of money where he's imported about eighteen horses from France (they're used by one of the local expat schools), and he's driven around town in a green Mercedes. He could be doing anything, but he happens to believe in what Cambodia is trying to accomplish. He and Ken are the face of an industry forced to operate in a new way now that the quotas have been lifted. He considers it his duty to try to save the industry in Cambodia; he'd been given a life of privilege and survival—neither of which was common in a generation who'd grown up knowing mostly war and bloodshed. He'd studied business and lived more years outside Cambodia than in—not only in France but in Hong Kong. He felt it was important to return, to help his country. To do this, his days were crammed with meetings, like the one with the Singaporeans, from dawn until dinner nearly every day.

After the meeting, Van Souieng took the Singaporeans on a tour to see some land on the outskirts of town earmarked for new factories—provided the investment is there. The group expressed concern about the state of the roads and some of the infrastructure, but overall they seemed positive about the prospect. Later in the afternoon, Van and Ken returned to GMAC for a meeting with half a dozen leaders from the industry's biggest unions. They wanted to make sure they had the unions' support for the Trade Act—nothing can be taken for granted when it comes to union/factory relationships in Cambodia. Van started by telling them Cambodia was 30 to 35 percent more expensive for buyers than China, 25 percent more expensive than Bangladesh, and 6 percent more expensive than Vietnam.

It seemed like overkill and maybe a little patronizing, since everyone in the room established immediately that they supported the bill. Later, when I went to see Chea Mony, whose absence from the meeting had been glaring, I found out why Van and Ken had taken this precaution.

Chea Mony had taken over the Free Trade Union almost immediately after the murder of his brother. He claimed to represent sixty thousand workers, and while the number probably isn't that high, his union is still the biggest in the country. I visited him one afternoon in his dingy, cramped offices, where there was a single computer for the entire staff and none of the fans had front covers. I had once asked Van about Chea Vichea, but the issue was still so sensitive that he refused to talk about it. When I arrived Mony was half lying across his desk, looking exhausted and disinterested. He had the same good looks of his brother, but none of the charisma. Pictures of Chea Vichea were dotted around the office and it remains the only professional building I've been in without pictures of the king and queen. When I asked him about the Trade Act, I learned why it was so important to Ken and Van to have the support of the other unions. Mony believed the United States should vote no to the bill.

"I hope it's going to be difficult for the United States to make this decision," he said, "because we lost the person who was trying to protect the worker. I hope they don't give anything to Cambodia, because if they do, it would create [more] corruption. The killing would never stop." He believed that offering a reward to a country with no rule of law and no real political will to curb corruption only gave the message that change was not necessary. He hoped the United States wouldn't pass the Trade Act. It would be a hard economic lesson, he conceded, but without it, he believed his country would never know justice.*

In early 2006, Chea Mony was diagnosed with tuberculosis. By the spring of that year he'd stepped down from leading the union.

IN JULY, MINISTER CHAM, VAN SOUIENG, AND KEN FLEW to Washington. For two days, they lobbied any member of Congress who would see them—which turned out to be eight. Most of the people they saw seemed sympathetic, and three of them signed on to the bill. But it was hard for the Cambodians not to be a little disappointed. The trip had been planned months in advance and they had banked on the fact that CAFTA would be resolved by then. It wasn't. The Senate had voted on it, but the House hadn't. "They were all obsessed with CAFTA," Ken said. "When we asked them if they were ready to sign onto the bill, they said, 'Not at this moment. This bill is not going to move unless we defeat CAFTA. Or unless we get CAFTA approved.' So that was a bit . . . disheartening."

They didn't meet with President Bush either. Or any of his staff. Senator Clinton neither met with them nor signed on to the bill. Two previous trips they'd taken had gone about the same, and the bill had only twenty-five sponsors—well short of the seventy they wanted. "Every single person we speak to tells us, 'Impossible.' When we speak to the U.S. administration, when we speak to

---

*Their concerns about corruption are probably worse now. China has recently become Cambodia's largest donor country, praised by Prime Minister Hun Sen for their "no strings attached" approach to aid. No need to stem the corruption, the problems of infrastructure, or the human rights violations—all things that Western donor money is typically tied to.

the U.S. Embassy [in Phnom Penh], they said, quote, 'No chance in hell. You're not going to get it,' " Ken said. "But still we commit our resources, we commit our time for this cause."

In Cambodia, the garment industry is front page news every single day. Factories open or close, workers strike or factories hold lockouts, new brands come in or leave. And while this bill means everything to the Cambodians, the sad fact is that Americans don't even know any of this is happening. "Actually, when I go," said Minister Cham, "I have the feeling that I'm going like a beggar. But I need to go, despite my feeling like a beggar, because behind me I have two million and a half people who are counting on this Trade Act to survive."

One might assume that the one natural ally Cambodia might have in this bill would be the stateside labor unions, who are always trying to get the United States to include workers' rights overseas in its trade bills. But in fact, the most vocal opponent of the Trade Act *is* a labor union, and the most dramatic moment of the Cambodians' trip came when the minister was speaking at the Carnegie Endowment for International Peace and Mark Levinson, the chief economist for UNITE (formerly the Union of Needle-trades, Textiles and Industrial Employees), the textile union, stood to argue with him. Levinson said that since the U.S. bilateral trade deal with Cambodia had ended, workers' conditions had gotten progressively worse. "What we hear from workers in Cambodia is that since that link ended, there's backsliding. The situation is deteriorating in Cambodia because the experiment that was a success is now over," Levinson said.

Chea Mony had told me the same thing. He swore that if I had two weeks, he could take me around and show me underground sweatshops that had cropped up since the ending of the quota system. When I told him that, in fact, I had two weeks—more than two weeks, since I lived in Phnom Penh—he waved it away. Clearly, he'd thought I'd flown in just briefly for this story. I pressed him, but he wouldn't allow me to pin him down to a day. While I can't verify the existence of underground sweatshops, the government did openly threaten workers through official statements after January 1, 2005, that if they caused trouble by striking too much, the international buyers would pull out. Michael Lerner said during the first two months of the year, grievances dropped off sharply at the Arbitration Council—they only had two—but around March, when it became clear that buyers wouldn't flee en masse, things picked up a little.

In Mark Levinson's view there's no real incentive for the country to maintain labor compliance when it will only make manufacturing more expensive. Workers were regularly threatened and even small demonstrations were often broken up by the police. But when Levinson brought this up, it utterly galled Minister Cham. He believes established democracies like America don't have realistic expectations of young democracies like Cambodia. A new country isn't going to solve all the corruption and civil rights abuses all at once, and without help like this trade bill it would just make the problems harder to solve, not easier. "You have to understand the context in which we are living," the minister said. "You know the history of Cambodia, but you have not known everything. We have gone through six successive political regimes in Cambodia in thirty years. People of my age, they saluted six different national flags of Cambodia. How many have you saluted so far? Only one.

"And through this type of conflict, genocide and everything, we come out and try to find peace first. We are all new. Six years ago, there was almost no union in Cambodia. There [were] not unions in factories because there [were] no factories in Cambodia. We are all young. The workers are young; the unions are young. The factory managers are new. And we have a system that is also new. We are open to democratization, but we need a kind of transition period where people mature in learning the laws and abiding to the law."

In Cambodia, Cham Prasidh is usually lumped in with the rest of the corrupt politicos. He's got a brand-new SUV and an enormous office, and his children study at American universities. He's a workaholic; sometimes I get e-mails from him well after midnight. And he's come back from unimaginable tragedy. He lost most of his family during the Khmer Rouge regime—his parents, his grandparents, one of his sisters. Later, I spoke with people who'd heard him offer up what they saw as this stump speech, about saluting different flags and about the genocide and about a young democracy. They seemed to think that his saying it more than once somehow made it untrue. But what's happening in Cambodia is beyond people like Minister Cham Prasidh and even Van and Ken. The thing that's happening in Cambodia is an opportunity that extends far beyond the borders of a single country, the actions of a single politician, and the work of a single buyer. Its failure won't just mean economic upheaval for one tiny Southeast Asian country and one tiny group of global garment workers; it will mean someone can do nearly everything right and they still won't prevail in the end. If Cambodia fails, it will be for a lot of reasons. Corruption, greed, economic instability and trade gone a little berserk, and fierce competition. But mostly it will be because we have allowed it to fail.

AFTER THE MINISTER'S SPEECH, MARK LEVINSON WENT out into the hall with Van and Ken and told them he didn't believe the Cambodians would maintain decent working conditions. Levinson said he had no faith in the Cambodian government and called them "useless." But Van said the issue wasn't about the government (no one seemed to argue on behalf of the government, even those who work within it, like Minister Cham). If factories don't comply, Van pointed out, they'll lose their orders from Gap, Nike, Sears, Levi's—the ones who care about labor conditions. Levinson said the only way he'd support the bill would be if all the participating countries beyond Cambodia also pledged to have fair labor conditions in exchange for the trade access. But it would be difficult to force sovereign nations to have specific labor laws. Even if the other countries adopted Cambodia's labor model, it would take such a long time and so much money that their industries would die out in the interim. The ILO claims that what they've managed to do in Cambodia, while hugely successful, took a combination of political will from multiple countries, the cooperation of governmental and nongovernmental agencies, and many millions of dollars. And when you ask the ILO if such a program can be replicated in other places, they don't necessary deny the possibility, but they never come right out and say what you want to hear: yes. Ros Harvey, the former director of Cambodia's ILO program Better Factories (she has since moved on to ILO's headquarters in Geneva), said they learned four important lessons: 1) trade incentives work; 2) a tripartite approach including employers, unions, and governments is necessary; 3) a national approach with governmental support is needed; and 4) staff the program from the local community.

Just before they walked away, Levinson asked Van and Ken one final question. "Who do you think killed Chea Vichea?"

They quickly recounted myriad theories: random violence, a love triangle, bad luck, a local vendetta. All of them were pretty hollow sounding.

BEFORE THEY LEFT WASHINGTON, VAN AND KEN TOOK A walk through a series of chain stores in Georgetown: Abercrombie & Fitch, Gap and Baby Gap, and a handful of others. They did this on every lobbying trip—in search of Cambodian labels. At Adidas they didn't have any luck. The same scenario was repeated at Gap Kids and Abercrombie & Fitch. Cambodia didn't seem to be anywhere. "China," Van read. "China, Vietnam . . . we cannot compete with China." Then Ken spotted some familiar shirts on a table. "I know the whole table is made in Cambodia," he said. But when they checked the label, it was a different story. Sri Lanka. One sweatshirt they found with a Cambodian label was selling for fifty dollars. Cambodia would get roughly ten dollars of that. Jeans cost about six or seven dollars to make in Cambodia, and the average manufacturing profit was about thirteen cents per dollar. If someone somewhere is willing to take twelve or eleven or even three cents' profit per dollar, you can be sure that there will be a buyer willing to go there.

Most of what Ken and Van found were simple T-shirts or sweatshirts, none of the more complex garments with ornamental stitching that command higher prices—the kinds of things that China, Vietnam, and Thailand make. Van said they should go to Old Navy. Lots of Old Navy is made in Cambodia.

In the car, driving through the wide paved streets of Washington, DC, Van mused about the possibility of Cambodia becoming its own brand, with a symbol and everything, sort of like the organic cotton movement. He pictured a world in which kindly Americans sought out Cambodian-made clothes like they do with products not tested on animals. But then he admits that even he doesn't look at labels much when he shops.

All in all, it was hard not to be discouraged by the trip. Ken was getting worried about the end of the year deadline. Cambodia was still a small player in the industry, and the way he and Van saw it, their fate was now in the hands of the U.S. Congress. They scheduled another trip for the fall, but it was canceled at the last minute because of Hurricanes Katrina and Rita. Another was then scheduled for January 2006, but it, too, was canceled. Finally, in July 2006, they returned, but this time the war in Lebanon monopolized the attention of Congress. "Lobbying is just so subjective," Ken said. "There are no milestones for lobbying. It's all or it's nothing. You know you're making progress, but it doesn't mean anything until the day the bill is passed. We just have to be patient, I suppose. Although, time is critical . . . [and] it's running out."

By the fall of 2006, well past Ken Loo's deadline, Van's factory, run by Voren, had closed for three months from lack of orders, and the bill had been referred to the finance committee. By the beginning of 2007, GMAC was no longer working with the Washington lobbying firm, and the minister, Van, and Ken had not returned to lobby. Ken said GMAC had paid $350,000 in 2004 and 2005 for the lobbyists. Still, he had hope the bill would move of its own volition and eventually get passed. At the moment, it was essentially stuck. Not passing, but not entirely gone either.

XVI

A VILLAGE WITH NO DAUGHTERS

IN THE KHMER LANGUAGE, PAST AND PRESENT TENSE are not commonly used. There are two linguistic ways to set a moment in time. The first is to add a verb to present tense. The second, more common way is to add a word to the beginning or end of a sentence: yesterday, tomorrow, later, earlier. In this way, time is manageable and life seems always about this single present moment. Nat and Ry have both survived the post-quota fallout. United Eternity shut down for a little while and neither of them worked. Then Nat was rehired, but Ry wasn't. After several weeks, Ry was hired at another factory down the street as a supervisor, and now her salary is about $90 a month, depending on overtime, which is rare for either of them these days. Ry bought a small, two-room house on a little plot of land outside Chak Angre that she shares with three other girls. She wants her daughter to move to Phnom Penh and live with her so that she can get an education in the city, which Ry believes is better than anything offered in Kampong Cham.

Ry has become that thing her parents feared—a city woman.

Cambodia has always had a significant separation between rural and urban. Village life is seen as pure, uncomplicated, untainted. During the Khmer Rouge regime, an agrarian utopia with everyone working the land was the goal; there would be no urban center, no elitism. No crime, no sinister underbelly. Even today, if you ask city people to describe their ideal life, most often they describe a life among the fields pushing a hoe. They'll say these things even if they don't own a farm, or if they've never worked on a farm, or even visited one. Ry says these things, too, but then everything else in her life points entirely away from the rural life she once had. "I think every family has a girl who left," Ry says about Cambodia's villages. "Now there are no daughters at home."

In the first year after the ending of the quotas, exports from Cambodia rose by nearly 27 percent, surprising everyone. There was still trepidation about what would happen when the stopgaps on China were lifted after 2008 and when the effects of Vietnam joining the WTO in early 2007 would be felt, but in the meantime, Cambodia was enjoying its success. The downside was that wages—when adjusted for inflation—had fallen by 6 percent and Cambodia had had to lower its prices to compete; on average, they'd lost 4-1/2 percent per garment. Nat had put on some much-needed weight. Her mother had stopped selling cakes because of her ill health. Ry's grandmother was alive, but she'd stopped taking medicine for her "hypertension," and she spent long afternoons wailing and gumming her mirror shards. Aid money in the country continued to pour in, particularly from China. Inflation was high and the workers had all noticed an increase in the prices of everyday things. Nat said meals had doubled in price, and gas prices were high—around $6 a gallon and rising. They ate a little less meat and took fewer moto rides to walk by the river.

In Cambodia, there is a color of clothing that corresponds with each day of the week and for certain ceremonies. White is the color of funerals, of death. Red is the color for Sundays. Ry was often dressed in red when I saw her, though Nat, having been born and raised in the city, didn't follow these sorts of traditions.

One afternoon we meet at a hamburger place at a busy inter-section in Phnom Penh. This particular place once had an ad cam-paign that I cherished, a picture of a giant burger in the foreground with a faded-out photo of Angkor Wat, the ancient temple complex and the sole reason most tourists come to Cam-bodia, in the background. The message was simple: Come for the burgers, stay for one of the wonders of the world.

Nat, Ry, Sophea, and I are discussing notions of death in Cam-bodia. As so often happens in Cambodia, the conversation quickly turns to ghosts. The second floor of Tuol Sleng Genocide Museum, which is closed to visitors, is said to be crowded with them.* Ghosts only come to those who are alone, the Khmer believe, and it is partly for this reason that they live communally and that they don't understand the Western need for solitude. Khmers believe that sometimes animals can channel ghosts, that the spirits of the dead still walking the earth can howl through dogs. Sophea tells us about her aunt, who cleans at one of the gar-ment factories at night. "There is a girl," Sophea says earnestly, "who sings a lullaby." Sophea says this girl sits in the rafters swing-ing her legs and that she has long hair. "My aunt sees her almost every night." I have to admit, no matter how much I claim I don't share their beliefs, stories like this from people I know freak me out.

"I was afraid of the ghosts when I was small," Nat says, "but not now." Her mother wouldn't let her play in the dark when she was young. "She said it was because of the mosquitoes," Nat smiles. "But I know it was because of the ghosts." She tells me that all Cambodian children fear the ghosts, so when they are old enough—nine or ten—they will wash the body of a dead relative and then sit overnight in the room with the deceased to conquer their fear. Everyone in the family takes turns washing the body after it is embalmed, and it is kept in the family's home for several days. In this way, the stigma of death is abolished. Nat and Sophea

*That's second floor to Europeans and Asians, third floor to Americans.

say this is how children learn that all ghosts began as human. It is not fear they learn to feel so much as respect.

At the western entrance of Chak Angre, there is a ten-foot statue of Vishnu in the center of a roundabout. He stands benevolently with yellow marigolds at his feet, blessing passersby. Cambodians descend from ancient India, and the Buddhism they practice today is a strange blend of Buddhism, Brahmanism, and Hinduism. Draped over Vishnu's shoulders are dozens of sashes in many colors—thank-yous from the local populace for answered prayers. At times, there are so many scarves you can't see his neck, and at other times there are barely a dozen. I often wonder if there were more sashes after 2006 came around and the garment workers learned their industry wouldn't collapse overnight. Answered prayers.

Ry feels that despite the country's economic success, people like her still have to live, as she puts it, "quietly." Those with knowledge, with wisdom or education about the law, have to hide their knowledge, she believes. "I am used to danger. I have heard about it, but I have also faced it myself," Ry says. "Before, with Pol Pot, they kill us [but] they told us what we did wrong; we knew why we were being killed. But now you don't need a reason. We get killed and we don't know why." Ry isn't saying the Khmer Rouge killings weren't gruesome and wrong, she is saying that when a country is at war, or ruled by tyrants, the people understand that you must fight to survive. Today, she feels Cambodia is filled with a sort of violence that no one understands, that no one knows how to fight. No one knows where it comes from, or why, though of course many theories abound, most of which include the actions of a populace collectively living with post-traumatic stress disorder. "For me, I am not afraid of death," Ry says. "But it is most difficult for my parents because they are the ones that hurt the most." The fact that she says this, and that Sophea translates it in present tense, makes it all the more threatening. Sometimes, it is clear Ry is still haunted by the incident in 2002, and the murder of Chea Vichea, who she says she'd been friends with. Several weeks earlier a garment worker who hadn't shown up for work had been found nearly beaten to death in her room, a room very much like the one Ry had once rented. Her story had made the papers and both Ry and Nat say they know her. They'd wanted to visit her in the hospital, but Ry says they "didn't dare."

The violence is everywhere, not just in the garment industry, but it doesn't seem much different to me than the violence in the United States. Around the same time that Nat and Ry's friend wound up in the hospital, a pastor and his daughter had been beaten and killed in a suburb of Chicago not far from where I'd grown up. In the rest of the world, the violence is everywhere too but Nat and Ry—living as they do not in a land free from violence but in a land free from rule of law—feel helpless. The murdered pastor and his daughter had representatives of the law actively seeking their murderer, actively seeking justice. In Cambodia, even someone in the public eye like Chea Vichea doesn't have that. "What can we do?" Nat says. "We feel angry, but what can we do?"

Ry believes they are never really safe. Even at supposedly legal demonstrations, police often fired into the crowd to disperse them. Every time a demonstration was significant enough to make news, some leading politician or industry professional would be quoted in the local papers and warn workers that if they continued to demonstrate they'd scare away multinational buyers. The association isn't necessarily a lie, but it does rely on fear to quash dissent while at the same time placing responsibility solely on the shoulders of laborers. Ry shrugs off the threats, at least publicly. "They can swear at me, but my family is more important than a swear word," she says. "For me, I can take it. Normally, you never tell [your] family; it will hurt them if they know."

Both Nat and Ry believe that they are old women; they claim they will never look for a job in another factory because they are too old to hire—managers want young girls, pliable girls. "Under twenty-five," Nat says. Neither of them is saving money as in past years, but they are both surviving, and that means a lot. Ry sees Pov as the hope for the future just as she'd once seen the factories a decade earlier. "My generation is just after Pol Pot," Ry says. "For my daughter, life will be better than mine." Nat doesn't have children, but she looks to her younger siblings. "If I could turn back the earth," Nat likes to say, "I would turn back to the king's time" in the 1950s, a time all Cambodians, even those who weren't alive, hark back to.

Ry and Nat believe that Western countries—the United States and members of the European Union—are countries of eternal peace, from the government down to the lowliest worker. Like every single garment worker I ever met in Cambodia, they say they knew factory workers in America made $1,500 to $2,000 a month. Such a sum made their eyes dance. What never accompanies this knowledge, of course, is the price of a house, a car, a week's worth of groceries. When I first told Ry that workers in factories in the American South might have to pay $500 or $600 a month in rent or more, she told me not to tease her. When I told her that not everyone in America liked President George W. Bush, she was dumbfounded. She didn't understand what there wasn't to like about a "strong man." When I told her America had homeless people, she wondered what they "had done so badly to their families." She simply couldn't equate the problems of her own country with another; she couldn't understand how the people who could afford the clothes she made didn't have perfect lives. When I asked her once what she would talk about with Americans if she visited the United States, she said: "I would ask them where they shop for their jeans." She didn't realize, of course, that she already knew these names: Wal-Mart, Sears, Ann Taylor, Gap, Nike, Levi's.

IN FRONT OF THE UNITED ETERNITY FACTORY THERE is a spirit house, a small structure made of wood or concrete where offerings of fruit and incense and money are typically made. It stands like an oversized birdhouse on a post. In Khmer, there are multiple words for spirit, in the same way that the Inuit have hundreds of words for snow. The big trees have spirits in them, and one day a year— on the holiday called Full Moon Day—the Khmer believe that the blue fire of spirits flies from sacred Buddhist stupas to thick-trunked Boddhi trees with their heart-shaped leaves to Buddhist wats.* The spirits make their silent way through the air in sweeping triangles, hidden from mortal view. Without offerings the spirits will be eternally hungry, so families leave fruits like bananas, dragon fruit, rambutan, and longan, or small amounts of riel at altars, while they pray and light incense in the pagodas. "I think Cambodia has more spirits than other places," Ry says. "I don't know why there are more." She is thoughtful a moment. "I think it's about belief," she says. "We talk from generation to generation. We whisper."

The spirit house at the factory is unusually large, several feet tall and sitting on a thick concrete post. During the Khmer Rouge regime, the factory made mosquito nets. Ry tells me a story about the spirit house; she can't confirm whether it's true or not, but she believes it. A man worked in the mosquito net factory and one day he saw an enormous man in traditional Khmer dress standing on the street. The man was shirtless, more than seven feet tall, with a red scarf tied around his head. He was a spirit, named Neakta, who only appears to a person who is good and kind. Neakta is a powerful spirit who needs spirit houses to live, a tiny place to reside as he helps people through their troubled times. The factory worker fell to his knees and prayed. He begged Neakta to help him survive the Khmer Rouge period and promised he would build a house for him.

The man survived the regime and built the house as he'd promised. It was small, just a foot or so tall. Then, several years later, a Chinese businessman saw the spirit house and went to pray at it.

*Boddhi trees, sometimes spelled Bodhi, are members of the fig family and sacred to Buddhists, as it is believed that Buddha reached Nirvana at the foot of a Boddhi tree.

He promised that if his garment business thrived, he would build a bigger spirit house. His prayers were answered, his business became successful, and he built an even bigger spirit house—the one that's there today. Nat smiles as Ry recounts the story. When she is finished, Nat says, quietly, "Sometimes we must build a spirit house for Neakta. To control all the bad spirits."

PART FOUR

XVII

KNOCK, KNOCK, KNOCKIN'
ON FACTORY DOORS

SHENZHEN, CHINA, IS A CITY HARDLY MEANT TO BE. Twenty-five years ago, it was no more than a fishing village. Now nearly eight million people live there, evidence of the central government's carefully planned economic strategy from the 1970s.[1] I try to imagine this in terms of an American city. It's as if Chicago went from a village with a handful of cornfields to the urban metropolis of today in just half of my current lifetime. Cities, to me, aren't established in two decades, but over generations, centuries. Shenzhen, less than an hour from Hong Kong by train, was established in 1980 by Deng Xiaoping as China's first special economic zone (the country created five in total). Establishing a business here meant tax relief and investment incentives. The Chinese government also invested heavily in the area's infrastructure and encouraged foreign companies to set up shop by reducing red tape. Throughout the 1980s and 1990s, migrants from the countryside descended upon the area. In the beginning jobs were plentiful, even if salaries and conditions were far from ideal. Nearly from the time of the area's inception its economy averaged 28 percent growth annually, and in 2005 the city was responsible for 13 percent of China's total exports. The port is now the sixth biggest in the world.[2] Throughout the mid- to late 1990s however, property prices and start-up costs rose almost as fast as the city had, and low-skilled manufacturing was soon priced out of the special zone. Around the same time, China began to lose its seemingly endless low-skilled labor supply, for a variety of reasons. The one-child policy implemented in 1979 has led to an aging population. Increased demand for labor—new factories open daily in China—means migrants can be choosier about the jobs they take, and they can demand higher salaries and more benefits. Millions of young rural people are choosing to stay in school longer in the hopes of landing better jobs than merely low-skilled factory jobs many miles away from their homes and families.[3] And in 2005 China eliminated an agricultural tax, which induced many rural farmers to stay and farm their land rather than migrate to the country's manufacturing areas.[4] (On the other hand, some statistics suggest as many as one million manufacturing jobs are lost annually, mostly to technology advances.)

The earliest factories began to move farther and farther out from the city center, giving way to three- and four-star hotels, tourist attractions, and highrises. These days, technology parks dominate the inner circle of the special economic zone. But Shenzhen remains home to many of China's notorious factory sweatshops, the majority of them now in the surrounding suburbs of the city. As salaries have risen, however—by as much as 40 percent since 2000—workers have started to agitate for better conditions and higher wages. Though underreported by the Western press, strikes are frequent in China. Nearly every week thousands of workers protest their working conditions. Signs of improvement are slowly emerging. Minimum wage in China is set regionally, and for Shenzhen, in Guangdong province, it is US$100. China's suffering from its substantial labor shortage in low-wage industries like textiles and factories is forcing the country to recognize that creating conditions to keep workers around is simply sound economics. Most factories must agree to allow major buyers to dictate codes of conduct and acceptable working conditions, and for the past decade a new system of social compliance has begun to take shape both in multinational corporations and in their contracted manufacturing partners across the globe.

One morning, I took the train from Hong Kong to Shenzhen to meet a team of Vendor Compliance Officers (VCOs), as they're called, for Gap Inc. (which also owns Banana Republic and Old Navy). Like most major buyers these days, Gap has an extensive list of reforms that factories must follow in order to get contracts. Gap works with roughly 280 factories in the Southeast Asian region, including forty to fifty in Cambodia, and it's not above revoking contracts with factories that don't follow its protocol. It is no secret that extensive labor abuses and terrible conditions in a series of factories under contract with Gap, Nike, and others in the mid-1990s created public scandals resulting in significant revenue loss and consumer boycotts. Many people remember Kathie Lee Gifford's 1996 teary apology on national television after abuses were discovered in her Central American factories. A call for corporate reckoning and a new age of social responsibility by multinational firms soon emerged, though Levi's had an ethical workplace program in place long before the scandals, and companies like Patagonia and Esprit have built their brands on environmental prudence and ethical sourcing. International corporations, along with a handful of what are commonly called third-party auditors or certification groups, have now spent the past decade wending their way through this new reality. On one hand, it seems redundant even to *have* a corporate social responsibility, or CSR, department. Shouldn't CSR just naturally be in our business practices? Unfortunately, it seems, the abundance of terrible factory conditions that still exist today dictate the need for such administrative departments and activist groups.

While no one from any of the industry sectors claims sweatshops aren't still rampant, some companies are making substantial inroads. Like others, Gap has had a difficult time rehabilitating its corporate image, and perhaps as a result, the company is skirting a line between being naturally timid and increasingly transparent. In 1995, the National Labor Committee, led by Charles Kernaghan—a man who has probably done more to illuminate the horror of sweatshops than anyone else in the past century—organized a tour of the United States for two Central American teenage factory workers who were making clothes for Gap at 12 cents an hour. Their tour marked the beginning of the emergence of the sweatshop story. Gap responded by revamping their corporate guidelines, guaranteeing workers' rights in their factories around the world, and establishing independent monitoring by third-party auditors (and by their own VCOs). They were the first major buyer to list, in 2004, all the countries they operate in. In 2005 Nike went further by listing its factories, and others followed. Prior to this public disclosure, corporations had long maintained that this was proprietary information. Gap also was the only major brand that took great pains in scheduling me to go along on a factory audit (Levi's theoretically agreed, but we were never able to schedule it in time for my book deadline). Typically, no one is allowed on these audits, which can last anywhere from a few hours to a few days. Even the International Labour Organization and the Cambodian ministry of labor never allowed me to accompany their monitors. While Gap did have some requests—they asked me not to name the factory, or the VCOs, or any employee I spoke with directly—they were otherwise surprisingly open, particularly given that factories today continue to operate under shrouds of secrecy. It is a secrecy that brands are happy to exploit under the guise of "competition." Over and over I was told by various brands I contacted that they'd be happy to have me go into their factories, but it was the factory owners who were skittish (factory owners say the brands are skittish). Or I'd hear something about how they'd love to let me in if only their corporate competitors could be trusted not to swoop in and steal the factory contract out from under them—this was a particularly fun excuse, given that everyone involved in manufacturing already knows what factory makes what and for whom. Even I, in my limited experience, could walk a tourist down a street in Cambodia and point out factories that sew for Wal-Mart, Disney, Gap, Levi's, and H&M. The truth is that even in this age of burgeoning corporate social responsibility, factories operate inside fortresses behind concrete walls topped with razor wire and patrolled by armed guards. This is the transparency that exists today.

In the end, though, the factory I visited with Gap's VCOs asked that I use the facility's real name—Lever Shirt—and Gap agreed. The factory was understandably proud of the work they were doing. I don't want to suggest that I had free rein, but the VCOs I was embedded with, I came to learn, are far from seeing their role as merely a job. Instead, they believe they are, in one VCO's words, "on a mission."

Jerry, a forty-year-old VCO who exuded the air of a college student with his backpack, white golf shirt, and Gap jeans (relaxed fit, slightly faded), was charged with leading the audit the day I went. Short of stature, with close-cropped hair and a cheerful demeanor, Jerry wore the sort of funky round eyeglass frames I've seen in pictures of T. S. Eliot. We met at Shenzhen's main train station along with his boss, Peter, who also acted as a translator when necessary (Peter: pinstriped pants from a local designer and Gap button-down shirt. "Are you wearing Gap?" one of them asked me later in the day.) We drove an hour outside town in a minivan, well beyond the special economic zone.

On the way, we passed a tourist park where the world's greatest monuments stood in resplendent replica: the Eiffel Tower, slightly shorter, the Taj Mahal, slightly rounder. Skyscrapers gave way to concrete block apartment towers. Billboards lined the pristine highways, advertising luxury residences and manufacturing tools—forklifts, widgets, cranes. Blue trucks carrying goods to the port or returning for new loads inundated our periphery as we drove. Like a lot of China's factories, ours was a wholly unremarkable five-story white-tiled building inside a gated compound.

Monitoring has been criticized as merely a way for corporations to make consumers feel good about their purchases. It sometimes falls short when it comes to real change—a fact most managers acknowledge. The truth is that in the garment industry, layered as it is with subcontractors and vast interconnected geographies, monitoring may never allow multinational corporations, even those with the best of intentions, to fully know what goes on when they're not looking. Naysayers believe multinationals have only managed to create low-wage jobs in unskilled sectors while at the same time creating a whitewashed, Americanized global monoculture. Others believe these corporations have introduced technologies, management, and international business and cultural connections that would otherwise have remained unavailable to most in the developing world. In fact, corporations probably offer both. At a conference on corporate social responsibility in Hong Kong in September 2006 Paul Wolfowitz, the then head of the World Bank, said that corporate for-profit business is a greater poverty alleviator than donor funding. It's a belief that is fundamental to companies like Edun, who may not carry the economic weight of a corporation like Gap, Inc., but certainly influence the world's multinationals.

I had no illusions about being taken to a factory with sub-par conditions, but what I found was even beyond the best I'd seen in Cambodia. Later, I learned it was one of Gap's model factories (managers accuse Gap of having some of the strictest professional standards—a fact other buyers benefit from). Lever Shirt, a family-run outfit begun in Hong Kong in 1956, employed five thousand people between this factory and another compound several hours away. The CEO was a tall, funky Gen-Xer who'd graduated from the Wharton School at the University of Pennsylvania and returned to run the family business. When I met him, he was sheathed in premium denim and a button-down patterned shirt and looked as if he'd be well received on a nightclub junket with Lindsay Lohan. In fact, he'd just come from having lunch with five of his factory floor workers who'd been recognized for their productivity. They were awarded a meal away from the canteen in the trendy administrative offices with their boss. Not a bad incentive, overall. Such lunches apparently occurred a handful of times throughout the year.

The administrative offices had a series of glass-walled meeting rooms or managerial offices around the circumference. In the center of these meeting rooms were dozens of modern office cubes with half walls covered in electric blue cloth. Oversized artsy photos on the walls showed individual threads and shirt weaves magnified many thousands of times, as if you were viewing them through a microscope. Even the bathrooms featured natural slate and freestanding cobalt sinks. Later, when we walked through the factory, which of course didn't have quite the same funked-out feel of the offices, I felt air-conditioning. It remains the only air-conditioned factory I've ever visited.

Of course, it would be naïve to suggest that problems, generally termed noncompliance, were not still rampant in the industry as a whole. Numerous examples of child labor, forced labor, abhorrent conditions, and abysmal pay abound. In the spring of 2006, the National Labor Committee put out a report on widespread industry abuses in Jordan in factories that contract with Wal-Mart, Kmart, Kohl's, Gloria Vanderbilt, Target, and Victoria's Secret, among others. The report cites instances of forced labor, indentured servitude, physical and mental abuse, rape, mandatory pregnancy testing (mothers-to-be are often fired so the factory won't have to pay maternity costs), withholding payment, and unsanitary conditions. Of 60,000 factory workers in Jordan's export processing zone, more than half are immigrants (often illegal) and thus particularly vulnerable. Jordan also receives preferential access to the U.S. consumer market as part of the U.S.-Israel free-trade deal. The report told of workers locked in a single room at night and forced to work until 2:00 or 3:00 A.M.; factories had withheld meals and in one case punished a handful of workers by locking them for several hours in a deep freezer.

Levi's actually first drew my attention to the report as proof that they and their industry colleagues were looking closely at their own Jordanian contractors. Gap, too, has been up-front about the fact that noncompliance is an issue that they try to tackle as they discover it. "We're still in a mode of actually trying to teach our team to find as many issues in a factory as we can find," said Dan Henkle, Gap's senior vice president for social responsibility. "So we actually view success based on—this may sound strange—success to us would actually be increasing our findings of some of these harder-to-spot issues." In other words, the more problems they weed out, the more they believe their system is working. Gap killed contracts with over seventy factories in 2004 for not meeting its basic compliance requirements—including three in the Middle East—and more than one hundred the year before. In general, Henkle said that "philosophically, we do not like to move to what we call 'revocation.' We really believe [that] what's in the best interest of all concerned is to fix a problem that crops up." Each year, when Gap publishes its annual report, Henkle and his team are keenly aware of how increased noncompliance may look to the outsider, but it doesn't seem to faze him. What matters is that while problems may be on the rise, the kinds of problems they're seeing have to do with things like overtime policies or grievance procedures, as opposed to child or forced labor. "I really believe there's not a silver-bullet solution here," Henkle said. "It's more like a puzzle, and we're playing certain roles, certain pieces of the puzzle . . . Someone from the ILO did a presentation for our team and they said, 'You know, guys, this is all just one big bowl of spaghetti. Everything is tangled together.' You can't just fix one thing and not have some impact on the other things. And that's exactly what we're seeing."

MY VISIT BEGAN WITH A BRIEF PRESENTATION ON the company, by a young Scottish-Chinese marketing manager just four months out of Edinburgh. It wouldn't be a stretch to see him in a Guy Ritchie movie. Urban hipsters who'd be at home in London's Brick Lane or New York's East Village are not exactly what comes to mind when I envision factory managers, but such is the pull of Shenzhen, migrants and managers alike are drawn to the place. Men's formal shirts are 45 percent of their business, he said, while a PowerPoint presentation showed graphs of the company's annual revenue, along with stylish photos of their products. Behind the screen, real-life examples of those wares were folded and propped up like statues, each in its own white cube, and spotlighted individually; stars in their own tiny production. We sat in modern, blue-padded chairs around a circular table that separated into four parts. "In 2006," the marketing manager said, "sales will be eighty million. We hope to see an influx of orders after 2008." Then he said: "We expect to double our business."

For all the worrying I've heard in Cambodia and Italy and Azerbaijan, and all the other smaller countries I've followed on trade and industry Web sites, I never thought about just how much China is waiting for 2008 to end. While I've generally assumed Cambodia would be all right in the long run—one of the winners, to some degree—it wasn't until this moment that I began to understand just how terrified Cambodia and the others were, and why. The shift of business wasn't going to evolve slowly; nor would it happen in a vacuum. Everyone in China seemed wholly open not only about their expectations for 2008 but also about what they viewed as the rest of the world unfairly holding them back from their full capability. For all the dread that Cambodia and its industry allies felt, China was feeling similarly put out by trade rules and stopgaps. If the industry was a massive sand hill, China was a funnel at the bottom.

Gap has been Lever's longest-running contract, and 65 percent of what they made went to the States. The factory also made shirts for Abercrombie & Fitch, American Eagle, Miss Sixty, Ann Taylor, Land's End, Eddie Bauer, Next, Ben Sherman, Benetton, and a handful of others. "In the past twenty years, there's been very little growth," said Joe Yuen, the executive director, once the marketing presentation had finished. Very little growth in the context of China, presumably. He believed that the beginning of 2009 was really "when the playing field will be leveled."

For all the competitiveness, though, Joe and the Lever factory have done far more than most factories in Cambodia who comply with the strict labor codes. Recently, Lever became one of the roughly hundred and thirty factories in China to receive what is called an SA 8000 certification. SA 8000 is a relatively new program in the industry that seeks to certify individual factories. The program, whose name derives from a group called Social Accountability International (SAI), certifies companies as well. Eileen Fisher, which makes upscale women's fashions, was the first—and remains one of the only—brand to receive SA 8000 certification in the States, I was told. Lever hadn't received the SA 8000 rating for their other factory yet, but they told me they were planning to pursue it—probably a good thing, since many manufacturers with multiple factory locations have been accused of creating one model factory that they showed to the public while their other factories maintained poor conditions.[5] Gap contracts with thirty-five SA 8000 certified factories around the world, but it's not a requirement for them. "My wish is that it just becomes something [factories] bake into their overall system and process, and that they're doing it for the right reason, which is to improve overall working conditions, and hopefully to improve their whole business operation," Henkle said. "And they're not doing it because we're saying they have to."

Based on ILO and United Nations workplace conventions, SA 8000 has helped improve working conditions in factories and firms in more than forty countries around the world. To get such certification, a factory undergoes substantial auditing by trained professionals. In the case of Lever, the process took a year and a team of eleven auditors, and cost less than fifty thousand dollars. It's a sum Joe claimed wasn't substantial given the benefits, which he believed were a stable, happy workforce, credibility for international buyers, and increased productivity. Of course, even a well-regarded factory in Cambodia could never afford such fees. "We faced some challenges with SA 8000," Joe said. "Some workers didn't know about social compliance. There was a problem with controlling overtime, [but] we wanted to be among the pioneers for social compliance. In the long run, we see it as a competitive advantage."

SAI says they have created a global standard to improve the conditions of workers around the world through SA 8000. In some ways, what they do is the next phase of corporate social responsibility. It nullifies the common criticism that having a buyer do its own audits is like having the police policing themselves. SAI claims that once factories are certified the benefits are significant, including "improved staff morale, more reliable business partnerships, enhanced competitiveness, less staff turnover and better worker-manager communication."[6] Factories who sign on to participate in SA 8000 and who operate in a country where unions are outlawed—like China—are required to create alternatives to unions, much like Lever has done with a team of workers' representatives. The process can be arduous, even for a factory like Lever that was in decent shape before it received certification. Among others, factories are required to adhere to the United Nations charters on child labor, forced labor, women's rights, and debt bondage (when a factory worker is forced to pay a manager or agent for her job). Such "debt" can cost workers thousands of dollars, and arrangements like these permeate the garment industry.

SA 8000 organizes and vets consultants in the countries in which they work; the consultants then conduct ongoing audits. Factories are required, among other things, to appoint both a senior manager to be the point contact for all SAI-related materials, guidelines, and activities, and a workers' representative who understands the requirements for ongoing certification. In this way, SAI manages to include workers, a practice that Michael Kobori, the head of social compliance for Levi's, feels is the real key to change.

SA 8000 has certified factories in fifty-five countries and fifty-eight industries, the majority from apparel and textiles. Italy leads, with nearly four hundred certifications, followed by India, with 141. China is third, with 129. All told, roughly half a million people around the world work in factories under SA 8000's umbrella of good working conditions and respected workplace rights. In operation for a decade (SAI began in 1997), they are a good example of what can be accomplished.

Ironically, China's government is a great impediment to implementing the international codes that buyers are looking for, because it does not recognize the right to freedom of association. Joe believed that forced labor and child labor were still "quite common." These facts haven't stopped foreign firms from setting up shop in China, of course. The country does have one trade union—the ACFTU, or All-China Federation of Trade Unions—but it is widely viewed as an arm of the government. Though the ACFTU recently accomplished something their AFL-CIO counterparts in America have long failed to do by unionizing Wal-Mart employees in more than twenty of the big-box retailer's stores throughout China, such an effort must be taken with a grain of salt, given the organizing body. The ACFTU, for its part, of course has promised it will tirelessly seek better conditions and improved workers' rights. Individual factories like Lever recognize unions, and the right to collective bargaining, but, given the political situation, they've had to circumvent the rules by creating a three-person team of worker representatives for grievances and negotiations with management. There are only about a hundred and thirty factories with SA 8000 certification in China. One must presume that the overwhelming majority of manufacturers do not make grievance procedures and collective bargaining a priority.

Like the majority of countries around the world, China has a relatively detailed set of decent labor laws (in Cambodia's case, these labor laws compose about a half-inch-thick book; China's book more resembles the Bible). Around the world, the problem tends not to be creating labor laws to eradicate sweatshops but rather enforcing laws that exist. One of the surest incentives to keep monitors from taking bribes, for example, is simply to pay them well above market rates. The ILO pays its monitors in Cambodia $750–$1,000 a month—a phenomenally high salary for the country—claiming it offers a disincentive for graft.

JERRY BEGAN HIS AUDIT OF LEVER BY REQUESTING A multitude of factory records. One of the common complaints from groups like Social Accountability International and its activist community, which includes other well-known groups like Verité and Fair Labor, is that many factories keep two sets of books: one for the auditors and another "real" one. Peter admits that this has been a problem in the past and outlines a number of ways they try to weed out this practice. They compare working dates, dates of fabric shipments logged in and finished garment shipments logged out, overtime records, production records versus factory capacity, public holidays and vacation days. Even weather can be telling—during rainy season, for example, some shipments that would otherwise go out on a working day may have to go out on a Sunday, and a determination must be made about whether or not employees were used for overtime and whether that falls within their acceptable overtime limit. Gap's 2004 corporate report admits monitoring is "more art than science" and that the best monitors are the ones who read beyond the page, extrapolating from a multitude of sources and records to create an accurate picture of what's really happening.

A woman named Joyce who heads the factory's three-person social compliance department began to produce large black binders for Jerry.[7] Peter explained what the binders were: records of personal protective equipment, or PPE, which included things like masks, metal gloves for the pattern cutting section (since a band knife, which, as noted earlier, cuts through dozens of layers of cloth at once, can go through a hand like it's mayonnaise), gloves if chemicals are used, eye protectors on button and rivet machines, finger protectors on sewing machines, and other gear. Because, as we have seen, fire safety is one of the biggest hazards in textile and garment production, the codes are stringent. Lever had binder after binder with records of their fire drills, each with dated pictures showing workers walking down lighted hallways and standing in lines on the pavement outside. Drills happened day and night. There were certain people designated to set off alarms, to count worker groups, to call the fire department and police, to work the extinguishers, and to give first aid—one in every fifty workers and one per sewing line must be first-aid-certified, with updated training every couple of years. Painted yellow boxes on the floor marked areas where fire equipment was stored, and emergency lights had lists of test dates taped to them. Doors opened out. Stairs required railings. Outer escapes were to be wide enough for two at a time. The detail was staggering, and as the hours passed, the binders and paperwork surrounding Jerry blossomed and spilled onto the surrounding tables like a time-lapse garden growing on a movie screen. Jerry began to look very small in contrast. "We need to spend time with the documents," Peter said, as if each record held the symbolic power of a line of poetry (which, in some ways, it does). After three hours, I was ready to leave. This is what separates marginally lazy people like me from people like Jerry, who believes he can make a difference in a worldwide corporate revolution. I never saw him yawn. I never saw him look up from his checklist or the garden of paper encircling him, and he maintained an air of respect and seriousness throughout the day. But he also seemed like the kind of guy you hope will audit you, someone who will understand the complexity and the difficulty and still demand, in the nicest way possible, that you do things his way.

Jerry had known the people at Lever, including Joyce, for the entire six years he'd been a compliance officer for Gap. He and Peter were among the pioneers of this painfully detailed style of audit—an audit that would have taken a whole second day if I hadn't been there (they sped things up for my limited schedule, but normally they spent the night in Shenzhen and took two full days to finish). They had learned by trial and error what to include, and while Gap had dictated the overall plan, the two spoke of monitoring as a sort of global collaboration. Different geographies dictate different safety and climate standards; different products require different machines and chemicals. In this regard, the kind of auditing Gap is doing is really in its infancy. Dan Henkle told me Gap had come up with a plan that they'd titled One-Plus-One. Basically, it meant one audit, one chance to fix the problems, and one follow-up visit. In the beginning, they found that they'd audit a factory, list a dozen problems, and each time they went back two or three more things would be better. It was a drain on everybody. "This is not a game we're playing," Henkle said. Gap's stance had had to get tougher. "If we tell you that there are fifteen problems, you need to fix those problems."

Every few minutes, Jerry pushed up his glasses and shifted in his seat, but otherwise he was wholly focused. He told me that before this job, he'd been an interior designer. In 1997, when the Asian economies crashed, no one cared about design anymore and he lost many of his clients. It was terrifying for him. He was already established in his career and he was afraid to change, afraid of what sort of sacrifice that might mean. He decided that the economic crisis might actually be offering him something entirely new. "It was a difficult time for me," he said. "I was not developing. But it was a good chance for me to take a risk." He interviewed for the newly created position of VCO at the Gap, and in the interview, he was asked what in his interior design experience could possibly have prepared him to be a factory auditor. He'd designed factories, of course, along with residential and commercial buildings, though designing a factory was, in his estimation, simply "construction." Still, he gave what may well be the greatest answer in the annals of job interview history.

"We both have the same goal, VCOs and interior designers,"

he told his interviewer. "To improve the living and working environments of people."

Later, he would refer to this as the single smartest moment of his life. "I don't know where this answer came from," he laughed.

Peter pulled out the binder that recorded accidents and picked several at random. Health costs were generally picked up by the factory, though there was no health clinic on site (they plan to build one next year). One woman was burned by hot water and sent to the hospital. Another was injured by a button-punching machine. The records showed the injury report, the hospital record and bill, and the payment. Jerry meanwhile had chosen a dozen or so random employees and asked for their records. Reviewing thousands of employee records would take several weeks, of course, so they tend to choose only a sampling. He looked at their work contract, their photocopied ID cards (using fake IDs has long been a problem in China), overtime and vacation records, payment history and attendance records. Their turnover rate was only 3 to 5 percent; clearly the factory was doing something right. Two young girls were called in to help locate files as Jerry asked for them. I imagined they would spend the bulk of tomorrow refiling the papers now filling the conference room.

It occurred to me that this factory, with its unbelievably good working conditions, its global certification, and its high-quality product, is exactly Italy's nightmare. Indeed, most of the fabric came from Italy, though there was talk of moving some fabric production to China or buying more locally from factories in China already producing the fabric they generally used.

Peter, Jerry, Joe, Joyce, another administrative staffer, and I took a break for lunch in the early afternoon. Peter and Joe walked ahead of the group and I overheard Peter saying quietly that Gap could not accept anything in the way of gifts from its vendors. I presumed this to mean he intended to pay for lunch. We walked first through the workers' canteen, as some employees were then on their (hour-and-fifteen-minute) lunch break. For about a quarter they could opt to eat here daily, and there were a dozen different dishes from which to choose. The two lunchroom areas were clean and bright, with long plastic picnic tables. Peter pointed out the emergency exit doors—"They open out, see?"—and the emergency lights, and he stood on his toes to hit the test button to make sure the system worked. The lights flickered on, then off. A side window with three or four dishes offered super-spicy food. Peter explained that one of the early complaints from workers was about the food. The migrants from the interior preferred spicy food to the bland seafood offerings in Shenzhen, and the factory created this separate culinary window for them. What I thought of when I saw this was whether or not such things could be replicated on a larger scale. Lever was undoubtedly a model factory, as is New Island, the Marks & Spencer factory in Cambodia, but if they're so wonderful, why *aren't* the others following in line? Were companies like Lever and New Island the equivalent of corporations in America who went into the red to build cafeterias and gyms for their employees? Even Stanley Szeto, Lever's CEO, said that changing the factory paradigm from sweatshop to archetype comes at a cost to the general business model: Earnings have not yet materialized in a way that suggests they've mastered the balancing act.

We ate in the café of a place called Mission Hills, a brand-new complex of ten golf courses designed by players like Ernie Els and Nick Faldo. It also had luxury residences, lush tropical gardens, and elegant restaurants, and covered such a vast area that it spilled into the boundaries of two separate cities and took more than half an hour to drive across. During lunch, Joe explained how he determined the capability of the factory. Overtime had been perhaps the factory's biggest impediment to getting the SA 8000 certification. Like many brands, Gap's corporate policy allowed up to a sixty-hour work week—or 80 hours of overtime a month—but China's labor law dictated that workers could not put in more than thirty-six hours of overtime in a month. The question was whether the government's or the employer's law had jurisdiction. It is a question repeated over and over in an age of globalization, where corporations and their mandates exist in one place with one set of rules, but the corporations establish offices or partnerships in another place with another set of rules. Lever had received a government waiver to follow Gap's code from the local authorities—a common practice among manufacturers in China. "A shirt takes thirty minutes to make, approximately," Joe said. "And in this one factory we can do four hundred thousand a month." Capacity is checked on a daily basis, and the production plan is adjusted only days in advance. In industry parlance, the big goal is "lean lines," meaning sewing lines that are not only efficient but running relative to one another. Having the front part of a pair of jeans arrive at the section of a sewing line where it is joined with the back part long before the back arrives is a common problem. The big challenge is accepting enough orders to keep the factory at full capacity without overtime and still getting the shipments to buyers on time. "If there is volatility in [our] daily productivity [or] we have excess orders, I may have to use overtime as a balance," Joe told me.

By contrast, overtime in a Cambodian factory is necessary for workers to make ends meet. If the minimum wage is $50 a month, but the average worker earns $69–$71, then overtime clearly plays a role more akin to, well, plain old work time. In Cambodia, I am eternally amused by people who say that Khmer girls just *like* to work till 6:00 or 8:00 or 10:00 P.M. They tend to be the same ones who think factory workers don't like air-conditioning anyway because it's too cold.

In the café, large tables of men on lunch breaks or golf breaks ate Chinese, Thai, or Singaporean dishes and smoked. I counted two other women in total among the patrons. After a while, Joe asked me about the expiration of all the safeguards. In particular, he wanted to know what I thought the United States might use to keep China in check. "Social compliance," he asked, "or anti-dumping?" Anti-dumping is basically a trade restriction to keep any one country from selling too much of one item, or dumping it, in another country very cheaply. His question suggested to me just how much economic power America still wields through its policies.

Joe said he thought the quota system might be indirectly responsible, to a degree, for some of the labor issues in China. It kept foreign investors—particularly those in Hong Kong who could have made a difference—from investing in the country. I told him I didn't quite buy that argument; it placed the blame for the abuses that are allowed to flourish on a group of people who weren't even there. The real blame, I said, should be on factories and governments willing to overlook rabid abuses. Hong Kong investors may well have created better working environments, but thousands and thousands of factories in China and elsewhere had still been built on the backs of a desperately impoverished citizenry. Joe didn't disagree with this. He suggested that politically China was making inroads to democracy, that the younger generation would eventually replace the elder statesmen and embrace democracy. Someday they would approve the right to establish unions, engage in collective bargaining, and enjoy freedom of association, all of which would be the key to honest economic growth in the country.

XVIII

A VIEW OF ONE'S OWN
FATIGUED AUDITOR

IN THE AFTERNOON, JERRY LEFT THE GARDEN OF BIND-
ers to take a walk through the factory and the dormitories. Earlier,
he had interviewed several workers on their lunch break as they
sat in their dorm room eating, mosquito coils burning under two
of the beds. The room was bright and had metal bunks for eight or
ten workers, along with lockers for their things. Each room had its
own bathroom. The beds, which had tatami mats rather than mattresses—a common preference in this part of the world—had cur-
tains drawn across them. Little stools were strewn about the floor.
One of the girls we spoke with sat on several chunks of Styrofoam
taped together. The dorms were depressing, but they were free.
Under the labor law, factories can take up to 30 percent of a
worker's salary for housing.

Jerry told them he and Peter were just like them—workers—
and so the women should be honest and not fear telling them
something negative. I wondered at this approach. Peter admitted
it had shortcomings and might not elicit the kind of information

they are looking for. He said they tried to conduct interviews off factory floors for this reason—to make workers more comfortable. Admittedly, my presence there changed some of the methods of a normal audit—they were a little slowed by my asking questions throughout the experience. "We know they might be too scared to talk," Jerrry said, but showing them that buyers care was more the point. "We cannot check paperwork for harassment or discrimination, so this is what we do to talk about those things."

That may well be true, but it's also one of the criticisms of monitoring—that it does not empower the workers to take charge of their own situation. It simply leaves their fate in the hands of others—auditors, managers, buyers. Interviews generally take just a few minutes and are often conducted on company property, as they were the day I went. Joyce stood outside the door while we talked to the workers on their lunch break, though this was also necessary because Jerry and Peter were men inside a woman's dorm. But for the most part interviews tend to happen in an environment where workers aren't likely to be forthcoming. It took me many, many months to get Nat and Ry to speak openly, and it's hard to imagine that wouldn't be the case everywhere.

Michael Kobori talked about this issue at length the day I visited him at his office in Levi's San Francisco headquarters. Levi's was the first brand to come up with a code of conduct, which they call Terms of Engagement, back in 1991. Kobori worked for a dozen years with the Asia Foundation in Thailand and Bangladesh before joining Levi's. He refers to their process of interviewing workers as cultural anthropology fieldwork. "The whole philosophy is that you go in and speak with workers informally and simply have conversations with people rather than trying to interrogate them," he said. We were drinking coffee from mugs crafted to look like Levi's jeans. Behind him was the famous Levi's red tab as big as a stop sign. "Anthropologists call it 'informants.' You're going in like Margaret Mead to gather information in the village and you develop informants. People who reside in the village who will tell you what's happening. So we develop this network of people in the factory who can tell us what's really happening. It's not about asking twenty questions."

Verité, which also works a lot in China, is so strict about this that its auditing teams are divided into those who will stick with management and administration and those who will stick with workers. "We talk to workers off-site," said Dan Viederman, executive director of Verité, "and those people should never be seen with management. They're more credible with workers [this way] and they're seen as secure." In other words, the monitors won't appear to be playing workers off management, or vice versa. They are, as Viederman put it, "untainted."

The way monitoring is often conducted leaves workers out for the most part, say critics of the process. It's useful to look at fire safety records, employee records, and so forth, but most of the time workers don't have any idea who the monitors are or why they're there. One report I read suggested that the only way real information will be dispensed in the monitoring process, at least as it pertains to workers, is to have that aspect of the monitoring conducted by a worker herself, confidentially. "Workers know the whole picture, day in and day out, visible and hidden," the report stated, "particularly if they have been informed of their rights and trained to detect violations." The report went on to say that in general, workers don't have a say in the key principles upon which codes of conduct or manufacturing agreements with buyers are made. "The implication is that workers will be protected if consumers care about their welfare, [but] this is an entirely different strategy from empowering workers themselves."[1]

AS WE WALKED THROUGH THE FACTORY, JERRY POINTED out some of the things he looked for. If someone looked very young to him, he jotted down his or her ID number and asked for employment records later. Though the factory vetted all the workers and their documentation, this vague approach seemed particularly open to blunders. He checked the aisles for obstructions, the medical kits on each floor for completeness, the safety lights and equipment records. We came to an area where new employees were training on various machines to get up to speed with those who had been there a while, and Jerry stopped for a long time and just watched from a corner. He scanned the sewing machines, making sure that any moving parts were enclosed so things like long hair and sleeves wouldn't catch. He looked for eye protection and hand protection and whether or not the employees seemed tired or just out of it. Electric outlets hung from cables high overhead, rather than on the floor. Peter saw a pregnant worker and asked about the company's maternity policy (three months' paid leave). After a few minutes, Jerry wandered into the rows and machines and bent down to talk to one girl. The ironing stations had enormous accordion pipes that diverted the steam outside. Sewing machines had small tubes that sucked the fluff from the fabric out of the room to improve the air quality. Joyce was escorting us around the factory, but if I hadn't been there, Jerry and Peter would have gone around themselves (except into the women's bathrooms and dorms, where they ask Joyce to accompany them). Jerry checked the suggestion boxes, which were kept in washrooms for privacy. He noted that emergency procedures, the minimum wage, health and safety regulations, and workers' rights were posted on each floor. At one point, he asked to see the broken needle records, and a large black binder was produced with broken needles taped to every page, accompanied by a full report of the incident—who broke it and how and when. The packaging area was a separate, closed-off room with a security guard standing outside the door. No one was allowed in or out without authorization, including the auditors. We watched for a few minutes through the large windows. Jerry had already asked for the records of fabric in and product out and they would be waiting for him in the meeting room upstairs; he kept a calendar in his head of recent holidays and Sundays.

At the ironing station, I spotted a Banana Republic shirt with a label that said "Woven in Italy" and "Made in Hong Kong." The word China didn't appear at all on the label, yet unless my geography and my passport stamp were way off, I was pretty sure that I was, indeed, in China. "That's a quota problem," Peter told me when I asked him about it. He didn't say more. It showed just how convoluted the world of "free" trade has become. In order for the country's quota of women's shirts not to exceed the allotted amount, the tag must display a country other than China. In order for this to be true, sections of the shirt must have elements that originate elsewhere—woven in Italy, for example. Sometimes the sleeves and front and back sections were sewn in one country and sent to China for final assembly. It was completely inefficient, but necessary given the trade rules. In trade circles, this haywired dance is called the "rules of origin."

In the next few years, however, manufacturers may be forced to have "vertical integration" in order for labels to claim a country of origin, meaning the fabric must be woven in the same country where the garment is cut and sewn. This is good for China, which has the best vertical integration in the world, and bad for much of Africa, not to mention Azerbaijan, Cambodia, and dozens of other countries that lay claim to just a part of the process. In order to get the "Made in . . ." label, these countries will be forced to diversify quickly. Economic diversity is ultimately necessary, of course; but it takes time and investment, both of which are in short supply.

Joyce told me that because the Lever factory now has SA 8000 certification, there were only a handful of audits a year. At their other factory, they sometimes had more than two dozen from various brands. This is one of the common complaints from factories—that every brand has its own monitoring teams, and they need staff just to deal with all the monitoring requests. This contributes to the lack of unannounced visits from monitors and puts the common criticism from outsiders—that there aren't many unannounced visits—in a bit of context. It is not improbable for monitors to overlap. Some factories are charged for monitoring visits by third-party monitors, which get fairly expensive over the course of a year (this is common in Cambodia, though Lever does not pay for its factory audits from Gap). Verité, one of the better-known third-party auditors, performs assessments that can cost roughly $3,500 each, though other, lesser-known third-party monitoring firms charge under a thousand dollars. Auditing has become a multimillion dollar business. In Los Angeles, more than ten thousand factory audits were conducted in 1998 alone. Ninety-eight percent of those Los Angeles factories were found to be not in compliance, according to a report published in 2000.[2] But "compliance" is a diffuse term. Sometimes noncompliance constitutes a major violation, like child or forced labor or physical abuse. Other times, it can mean a missing toilet seat or a burned-out lightbulb. What's worse, most buyers have their own codes of conduct. A monitor from Sears once gave me the example of a fire door—one buyer required thirty-four inches' width, the other thirty-six. In such a case, the factory would always be in noncompliance with one of the buyers. In Gap's code of conduct, where requirements differ monitors are instructed to go with the stricter of the two codes. In addition to buyers, there are also auditors from local governments, or from labor organizations, or activist groups like SAI and Verité.

Michael Kobori put it more bluntly. "We're monitoring factories to death," he said. "On average, these suppliers are being visited twenty-five times a year by brand monitors, and even if the factory has a compliance officer to help with issues, all that compliance officer is doing is taking the monitors around. And they can't work on any of the changes in the factory's management systems or labor practices that are really going to make a difference. Factories are suffering from audit fatigue." Dan Henkle agrees. So far, there are pilot projects to join forces under way in the industry. Levi's has partnered with ten other big buyers to try to implement a single system, though Kobori declined to name the other participants at this early stage. "A lot of these codes are very similar," Dan Henkle told me, "so if we could get companies starting to march in the same direction . . . I think it'll happen. It's just going to take some time."

To the naysayers who believe monitoring is largely ineffectual, Kobori, surprisingly enough, tends to agree. "My response to that is that the [factory monitoring] model hasn't failed, the model hasn't been implemented . . . the economics of the way the current system is set up is not working. It's an economically unsustainable model right now and we need to start changing that. We've disclosed our factory locations and . . . now whoever's sourcing in these factories can come and work with us so we can eliminate this duplication . . . We've all tried to get one monitoring system. We've tried that for ten years and it's failed, because nobody wants to give up their portion of it. And because the further you get from those factories, the more ideological it becomes. We don't understand the local challenges. I would say if there's one thing that we've learned over 15 years it's the fact that unless there are business consequences to the behavior you're asking [to change] it won't happen."

Besides which, in any given year there are only so many factories that Jerry and Peter can get to. On average, they try to visit each factory twice a year, but sometimes it's less. Third-party organized monitoring would likely be more comprehensive in terms of the auditing and perhaps less disruptive for factories.

We made our way outside to the chemical room. Peter said the Gap demanded its factories stop using benzene several years ago, but that it was likely still common in many other factories.* In July 2006, twenty-two people were killed and another twenty-nine injured in a fluorobenzene explosion in Jiangsu, China; the plant hadn't even opened yet, and more than seven thousand residents were evacuated.[3] Jerry asked to see the inventory and purchasing

---

*Not to be confused with benzidine, benzene is a compound derived from coal tar or petroleum and is used in all sorts of compounds, including medicinal and commercial chemicals and dyes, DDT, insecticides, fuel, and detergent.

records, as well as the MSDSs, or Material Safety Data Sheets. Here, chemicals were used as lubricants for sewing machines, in softening agents and spot cleaners, and even in oxidizing agents. Peter's area of study was environmental management, in which he holds a master's degree, and he said that he believed China was starting to get more serious about its environmental issues. The country is widely criticized for being one of the world's worst polluters, and, like the labor laws, it actually has decent environmental regulations in place. The real problem is in enforcement. Jerry checked that the room was properly ventilated, with fire extinguishers, buckets of sand to soak up liquid, eyewash, louvered windows, and an outside shower. A small, ten-centimeter-high retaining wall would, it was hoped, contain spills.

China's industrial spills are infamous—there were more than forty-nine in the country during the first four months of 2006 alone. Nearly 80 percent of China's eight thousand or so biggest polluting offenders were located near bodies of water.[4] This figure includes Shenzhen, a city known to have some of the worst air quality in a country known for its air pollution. Globally, for every kilogram of textiles made, roughly two kilograms of CO_2 is emitted into the air.[5] Peter told me that China is notorious for its sulfur dioxide emissions, which cause acid rain, in part because it utilizes mostly coal and petroleum for power. In fact, such emissions grew by more than 25 percent between 2000 and 2005, making China the world's worst polluter of sulfur dioxide, and all the while the government has vowed to cut emissions by 20 percent. A shocking third of China's land was harmed by acid rain in 2005.[6] It is estimated that environmental pollution costs the country more than 3 percent of its gross domestic product. One textile firm, Dongguan Fuan Textiles Ltd, was fined more than a million dollars for secretly releasing ten million gallons of wastewater over the course of two years through an underground pipe. Their clients included Adidas, Next, JCPenny, J. Crew, and Levi's[7]—all companies with well-respected monitoring systems in place. Nearly half a dozen of the biggest rivers in China are "not suitable for human contact," and China's official environmental regulatory committee, SEPA, reported that water pollution, or "noxiousness of water," measured by chemical oxygen demand (COD), rose by about 4 percent in 2005.[8] Issues of water—shortages from drought and mass pollution—threaten the most heavily populated areas of China and could cause significant civil unrest throughout Asia. One article warns: "China's economy could crash by 2015 as the supply of fresh water becomes critical."[9] Around the world, textiles are particularly demanding of water—about sixty kilograms of water are used for every kilogram of manufactured garments, and forty-five kilograms of wastewater are discharged into water sources (the other fifteen kilograms evaporate during dyeing).[10]

China's lax regulation is often attributed to the regime allowing local governments to control environmental standards. One article I read claimed that SEPA had only three hundred employees and was one fiftieth the size of the EPA in the United States—for a country with more than three times the U.S. population.[11] (Eleven new environmental protection offices are currently planned around China). Peter said that Lever fell under local governance but claimed the "local government here has very stringent policies on wastewater." Outside the window of the conference room in the property across the street, garbage piles as high as two-story buildings covered the lot, and towered behind several small buildings that looked like apartments. Peter suggested maybe it was a recycling center, but I doubted it and I suspect he did, too. I never saw a single bird flying in the area all day.

The factory essentially had five areas of environmental regulation according to Gap's codes. These were: chemicals, solid waste, wastewater, noise pollution, and air quality. Peter had hopes that China was developing policies for stricter local regulations, but history has suggested that practice does not always follow policy. Of all the monitoring I saw, this appears to be one of those areas, like harassment or abuse, that are the most challenging not only to combat but even to expose. In a 2004 article in the *New Republic*,

Joshua Kurlantzick may have said it best when he claimed China was "hurtling toward environmental catastrophe."[12]

People like Peter and Jerry aren't wrong to be hopeful, though. Environmental movements in China are gaining ground, and in 2005, SEPA claimed complaints from the public increased by 30 percent and more than fifty thousand protests over pollution took place in one year.[13]

ON OUR WAY BACK TO THE OFFICE, WE STOPPED IN A warehouse of items ready to be shipped. More Banana Republic shirts, boxed and waiting, stacked up a dozen high. The boxes said "Made in Hong Kong."

All in all, Jerry had just two issues from the entire day. One aisle was obstructed, and one cutting station had an electric outlet on the floor rather than overhead. He complimented Joe on the work they'd done fixing their overtime issues and keeping their records accurate and up to date. When he heard this, Joe slumped with relief in his seat. "This gets easier every time," he said. "Gap helped open my eyes as to how to move the company forward. They've been giving me good advice. There's a high level of trust between us. We don't play games; we just do the right thing."

This is perhaps one of the most meaningful gains in monitoring—the ability of a multinational brand to go beyond the local authorities, who often avoid dealing with abusive workplaces, and demand a contractor make changes or face losing business. Levi's has made this a cornerstone of its foreign investment strategy. So have Gap and many other companies.

Monitoring is the best way buyers have at the moment of ensuring that the factories they work with are responsible partners, but most everyone agrees that it is a strange development. It turns corporations into social policemen, and while the Gap and a handful of other major brands set good examples, the vast majority of buyers operate under this social accountability radar. Wal-Mart, Target, and Federated Department Stores (which owns Macy's and Bloomingdale's) have all been accused of lax enforcement or a lack of transparency in their monitoring by labor groups and activists, though they all have codes of conduct on their Web sites. Corporations—and some care more than others, to be sure—have been forced unnaturally into this role by governments unable or unwilling to do better for their own citizenry.

It's clear monitoring is really just the beginning. Getting factories to change their policies and procedures is one hurdle; getting inbred social norms to change is quite another. In many countries, the idea of a boss *not* harassing his workers, *not* threatening or manipulating or screaming, is itself a foreign concept. And these are the sorts of problems that are the slowest to change.

Jerry and I took the bus back from Shenzhen to Hong Kong together. He preferred the bus to the train because it was quicker and afforded better views. As we boarded, he made sure to seat me on the right. "Much more to see," he insisted. It was already dark outside, and he had a small family reunion to attend in Hong Kong later that night; his sister and her family were visiting from Japan. He told me of a trip he'd taken to the Angkor Wat ruins in Cambodia the year before and how he planned to return soon. He'd taken up photography recently, which was a natural fit given his design experience, and he found that framing and composing photos came easily to him.

I asked him if he really believed it was possible to change things. Relatively speaking, even given the size of Gap, it was a tiny fraction of the industry as a whole. Of the hundred and thirty or so SA 8000 certified factories in China, about four made things for Gap Inc. This didn't even include the tens of thousands of factories around the rest of the country. Between 1997 and 2004, foreign buyers had requested eight thousand SA 8000 audits; most didn't pass.[14] "You know, four or five years ago, workers didn't even know the minimum wage in their region," Jerry said. He pushed up his glasses and looked thoughtful for a moment. "If they had to sign their name to something, it was sloppy. Now they are writing more letters home and they are getting better." This is no small feat in China; handwriting artistry is a valued skill and a sign of education. Jerry, of course, recognized it as the powerful cultural symbol that it is.

"We cannot deny that the factory is paving a good road," he said. "Factory management teaches them and they learn and maybe when they return to their village they can influence others." He told me about the work he'd done in graduate school at a local hospital that specialized in occupational safety accidents. He found that for the most part, the injured workers all knew they were supposed to wear safety equipment, but they didn't like it, or found it uncomfortable. They'd known better. It was frustrating to him, and he felt it presented perhaps their biggest challenge. "Education is important," he said. "But we must figure out ways to go beyond that."

XIX

THE THIRD PARTY, EXHIBIT A:
THE TWO-SECOND HANDSHAKE

SEVENTY TO EIGHTY STEPS. IN CASE THERE WAS EVER a question, this is the requisite number of steps a person should take per minute, the spacing of them—perhaps this is common knowledge—approximately the length of your own foot. Clapping has similar adjurations. Do not cup your hands. Do not splay your fingers. Do not make a show of it. Simply bring your right fingers to your left palm, calmly, confidently. Also, joked the speaker in this training session, "I expect you to clap for me when I am finished." I was sitting in the canteen of a factory in Shenzhen, several days after my Lever visit, with two hundred garment workers.[1] They had two hours off in the afternoon to attend this workshop—one in a series of ten, most of which dealt with far graver topics, like workers' rights, HIV/AIDS, and hygiene. This one, my translator explained, was a session on "comity."

Comity.

I knew what it meant, but during the hour-long drive to the

factory from the train station, I was sure I was misunderstanding the translator. It's not a commonly used word in English, and I assumed she had been using it incorrectly. I was to attend a training session on civility? On courteousness? For garment workers in southern China?

The session was part of a mobile training program conducted by Verité. Based in Massachusetts, Verité began auditing and researching factories in 1995. Many of their clients are high-profile American brands: Timberland, Eileen Fisher, New Balance, Tommy Hilfiger, Edun. Verité started the program's mobile training in 2000 and it has evolved over the years. In 2003, the company gathered local doctors and incorporated SARS (severe acute respiratory syndrome) prevention into the general hygiene and infectious disease courses in Chinese factories. Another outbreak, this time hepatitis B, in the Guangdong area of China, led to more training and prevention sessions. Verité conducted these monthly mobile training sessions over the course of a year. The workers had been asked what sorts of things they wanted to learn about, and this was high on the list. Verité began to see that in addition to teaching labor rights, employees in many of the factories also needed basic life skills. Hygiene, communication, nutrition, women's health, occupational safety, and infectious diseases all became topics. Workers in most of the factories around the world were young and uneducated and came from cultures where many of these topics were never discussed. "These migrants are out of place, with few social resources to draw upon," said Dan Viederman, the executive director of Verité. "Having them take these classes or have these experiences gives them confidence [and] standing in the factory."

The factory has a large concrete courtyard at its entrance and a koi pond with dozens of fish. We had been led into the canteen, where thirty or so metal fans whirred far overhead, and we sat on round, sky-blue plastic stools affixed to Formica tables. The room was like a warehouse, with two pool tables and a Ping-Pong table

in front and a set of bookshelves that held a dozen or so magazines—all of which were dwarfed by the the room. Comity. I had
no idea what to expect.

The workshop's leader was a young schoolteacher in her mid-
twenties who occasionally took time off to participate in these
sessions. She wore a tweed skirt, white pumps, and a beige lace
top. Though it was cloudy, she deployed an umbrella anytime we
went outside. The session opened with a critique of how the workers had all streamed into the room and taken seats, boys in the
back, girls in the front. They'd come in quickly, loud and chaotic,
with no grace at all in their entry. I sat to the far left in front, with
a factory manager next to me who unabashedly watched every
word I wrote. To her immediate right was a girl who looked about
ten. No one was here to weed out underage workers—that was left
for the audits. This session was meant to empower them. With
comity. Still, I asked the manager what the minimum working age
was for garment workers.

"Eighteen," she said. (She was wrong. It's sixteen.) Then she
turned to the young girl beside her and asked her age.

"Twenty," the girl said.

Later, my translator said she thought there were many, many
thirteen-year-olds working all over Shenzhen. We think it's dread-
ful in the West, but no jobs means poverty here, for the children,
for their families. I'd seen plenty of kids in Cambodia living atop a
massive trash heap on the outskirts of the city, digging for tin cans
with their families. This girl—whether she was ten or eighteen—
had it better. No one in the West is advocating for the trash heap
kids to have better working conditions.

Fifteen years ago, two Bangladeshi factories under contract to
Levi's discovered a whole group of underage girls working for
them. Rather than fire them, the typical procedure, Levi's decided
to pay the school fees of all the girls. The factory management also
continued to pay their salaries so long as they stayed in school. If
there was no school nearby, Levi's found a room and hired a
teacher. In each case, the factory held onto the jobs for the girls

until they'd completed their educations—and they tracked the girls over the years. Some returned to the factories and were promoted to supervisory positions. Some married and began to raise families. A small number even went on to universities. But perhaps more importantly, the Bangladesh Garment Manufacturers and Exporters Association, along with a group of other local nongovernmental organizations, managed to set aside one million dollars to educate seventy-five thousand underage girls who had been found working in factories.

IN THE CANTEEN, THE SWEET SMELL OF RED BEAN paste suddenly filled the room. The teacher asked the audience to evaluate her, to shout out words they might use to define and categorize her. Of the two hundred in attendance, the boys were nearly equal to the girls, which was surprising given that young women are the demographic of choice in nearly all garment factories. A few brave souls began to shout out words: language, activity, humor. Despite the fact that they worked in a garment factory, not one of them said clothes.

"Language, clothes, conduct, and performance," she said, "are the four keys." She was smiling, pacing back and forth. Her lecture included instructions like: sit straight up, cross your legs, keep your knees touching at all times. If the sofa is lower than the chair, offer the sofa to the girl. When you go to the temple, do not fidget. When you rise from a seated position do it smoothly, in a single motion. She called up a boy and a girl and asked them to demonstrate a proper standing position. They weaved, giggled. The boy put his hand on his hip. She told them they were ill-mannered ("bad conduction," my translator called it). "Pay attention to your abdomen," the teacher said. "Be like a tree with straight shoulders. Breathe from your diaphragm. It's hard, but you must get used to it."

I was suddenly reminded of the scene in Hitchcock's classic film *The Birds* where Tippi Hedren is expected to saunter gracefully in her fitted green suit and high heels through the fine beach sand, all the while not spilling a drop of her martini. When she stops her perambulation, which is really more of a wobble, she turns to her companion, pulling her ankle in, posing like a fashion model. I can only imagine how many times they may have reshot that scene, watching her bobble in the sand with her pumps and her cocktail. This was what the comity lesson seemed to me. It was both fascinating and a little absurd.

When I asked my translator about all this, she told me I simply couldn't understand; it was something about Chinese culture. Later, trying to put it all in context, I called half a dozen university professors. Surely I was missing something. Did factory workers really need to learn that boys who chewed gum while ballroom dancing weren't worth their time? The professors, for the most part, thought it lacked any far-reaching cultural implications. But they also said since they hadn't been there to witness it, perhaps it was something they couldn't comment on with any assurance either.

But the more I thought about it, the more it was intriguing to me. These workers—girls and boys alike—no doubt had great fun in the session. They laughed, they blushed, they clapped, and they *attended*. For the most part, they were all migrant workers who would perhaps never have an opportunity to ballroom dance, or offer the sofa to a girl. But, if they were ever to get that chance, surely Shenzhen would be the place. Their lives in the countryside hadn't prepared them for job interviews, for how to sit up straight and cross your legs and not fidget—but in Shenzhen those lessons would mean something, would mean the difference between a poor job interview and a decent job interview. When the United States plans training programs for women who are getting off welfare, they often include sessions on how to conduct oneself in an interview, and how to dress and how to communicate. Was this really any different? Dan Viederman said workers helped design the workshops. "Our view is that it ought to be a hard-hitting intervention in a downtrodden people who don't have tools to fight back. We give them an element of that. But we try to meet them where they want to be met. You have to talk to them about things they care about. True transformation requires people to take responsibility for themselves."

Then I remembered how Jerry, the Gap monitor, had talked about the handwriting of the factory workers—how such improvements held symbolic weight for him, proof that they were growing in experience, in knowledge, as their handwriting grew more beautiful. Wasn't this the same thing?*

"Hands," said the teacher, "are an expression of yourself. Use them when you say hello and good-bye." She demonstrated proper waving methodology with a controlled whisper of movement, the hand not to be raised above the head, fingers together. She wandered into the crowd, picked what looked to be the shyest boy in the room, and shook his limp hand. He looked as if a sharp pain has just entered his gut. "Grasp the hand firmly, shake up and down once. If it's too long," she advised, "you're in trouble. No more than two seconds." Smile, look directly at them as you shake, say hello.

Then she posed a question. If a young man and a young woman meet, who should be the first to offer a handshake? I thought again of Tippi Hedren, figured the answer would be the young man, but the teacher surprised us all. "Girls should shake first," she said. "They should have some control. If a boy is interested, he must wait for the girl. Also," she advised the boys, "these days you shouldn't tell a girl she's beautiful first. Instead, tell her she is knowledgeable, or has personality."

*I also learned from a friend about the Chinese American Etiquette Association in San Francisco, which seems to offer similar workshops to members. For example, a session called "Menus Don't Scare Me" is offered for visitors to America, though having visited China and been offered duck stomach and duck esophagus, I wish I'd have had some scary menu training myself.

The lesson went on for another hour in the same vein. She told them not to dress like others, but to have their own style. She told fat girls not to wear horizontal lines, and all girls to use cosmetics lightly, "not like an operation." She advised them all to stay out of the sun, to wash their faces twice a day. She discussed the T-zone of oily/combination skin, told them to brush their teeth after every meal, that tomatoes were good for you, that you mustn't interrupt without saying "excuse me," that if you have an accident, you should be positive and not cry because it's not useful. "Some people may say, 'I am so lucky, I only lost my leg. Others might have lost their bodies,' " she offered by way of example. She gave a full ten-minute discourse on what it means to wear a ring and warned not to pick the wrong finger or you'll be sending the wrong message. A ring on the right thumb means you are very rich; a ring on the left pointer finger means you are single and available. A ring on the middle finger—she held up her middle finger to the room—means you are falling in love with someone. (Of course, this wasn't exactly the meaning I surmised when someone gave me the finger.) Wearing it on the pinkie means you are single but don't want to get married or have a partner.

Finally, she said, and most importantly, was language, or communication. "And that," she smiled wide and curtsied, "will be left for our next session."

The factory workers moaned and then applauded wildly. Afterwards, dozens came and thanked her. They couldn't wait for their lesson on communication.

XX

THE THIRD PARTY, EXHIBIT B: THE LAST-MINUTE ORGY AND OTHER SHOPPERS' DELIGHTS

IN THE EARLY TWENTIETH CENTURY, THE NATIONAL Consumers' League tried a certification process for factories in America. Sweatshop conditions had compelled a handful of activist women like Florence Kelley, who'd begun the league in 1899 and served as its president for more than three decades, to bring both the public's and the federal government's attention to the plight of factory workers in the United States. The certification movement was unofficially called the White Campaign. Though it'd begun as a way for consumers to identify retailers with decent conditions, it evolved to include the manufacturers as well, mainly through the use of white labels that NCL-vetted industries could carry on their products. They required their clients to meet just four conditions: 1) laws of the state had to be followed; 2) products had to be manufactured on-site and not subcontracted out; 3) no overtime was allowed; and 4) no one under age sixteen could be employed.[1] Cotton mills and textile factories were the focus of NCL activities during much of their heyday. The NCL managed to break down the customs of child labor, excessive overtime, and workplace rights for women. They first lobbied to have female factory inspectors as early as 1917. And they first made the link between ethical consumerism and factory conditions. ". . . the responsibility for some of the worst evils from which producers suffer rests with the consumers, who seek the cheapest markets regardless how cheapness is brought about," said Josephine Shaw Lowell, president of the Consumers' League of New York, which began in 1891 and merged with the NCL in 1899.[2] Getting consumers to use their spending money thoughtfully became a benchmark for NCL campaigning during the early part of the twentieth century. But even at the height of their White Campaign, the NCL only managed to certify sixty-nine factories before abandoning the program. The reason wasn't that it hadn't been worthwhile, though most agree that it did little to change employer practices. The reason was that the group simply didn't have the resources to keep up with the inspections.[3]

The NCL never stopped appealing to shoppers, however, or trying to create socially conscious consumers. NCL literature that describes the long hours and drudgery of factory work, the abuse of workers at the hands of unscrupulous employers, and low wages and dangerous conditions might well be talking about conditions across the world today. (Admittedly, I haven't seen any activity that would trangress early NCL statutes prohibiting children from "appearing publicly as acrobats.") "The public bought the product of the children's labor and asked no questions as to conditions under which they had been manufactured," according to a history of the NCL. "Shoppers rejoiced when prices were low, and did not dream of the social cost of these conditions."[4]

The league even drew attention to the "season of wariness" for factory workers. They meant Christmas, not because of holiday preparations for their families but because of the "shopping public's universal habit of indulging in a last-minute orgy of holiday buying."[5] Excessive work during this period often led, the NCL claimed, to grave illness and even death. Today, one can still chart this sort of excessive holiday work, the crunch time coming in late summer for Asian countries and in the fall for Latin American ones.

On the eve of World War I, the NCL had garnered significant public and political support. They had successfully lobbied to eradicate mandatory overtime and nighttime hours for working mothers and child labor. They were working on getting a minimum wage set, and many states had capped the work day to eight or ten hours. During the league's eighteenth annual meeting, they invited the secretary of war, the Honorable Newton D. Baker, to address the participants in Baltimore. "What we actually do is to go out into the life of America and find those things which are costing us more than we can afford to lose," he said. "Things which cannot be counted in dollars and cents. . . . We get those deadly costs and drag them into light and place them within the horizon . . . so that after awhile what has been discovered by some such society as ours as a neglected social duty comes to be recognized as an unescapable social obligation."[6]

Baker believed that even while world events threatened to redirect the focus of the country, the NCL and the American public should remain steadfast about protecting rights of industrial workers. He managed to show the relevance of the cause of fair labor to the war.

This is the moment when the imagination of the American people is most likely to fail. . . . They are most likely to demand goods in increasing quantities and not to stop to ask the cost of them.

Employers who have contracts with the government or with the allies, or who make things more or less necessary to the life of the people, are constantly saying to themselves . . . : "This is not a time to enforce these laws about children and women and their hours and condition of labor; too large and momentous events are moving now for anybody to stop with these things."

. . . it does us no good to be able to call ourselves free and to describe our land as the land of the free unless we have all the component parts of real freedom. And that means the political liberty to recast our industrial life so that it will really be a life of opportunity to the least person who lives under it.7

Of course, he was referring to Americans, but his message seems no less significant a century and many more geographies later.

All apparel companies will eventually have problems no matter how hard they work to eliminate the most grievous cases. The supply chain is so long and so involved, with so many built-in layers, that to have a perfect record without revolutionizing the entire system is simply never going to be possible. For every Nike and Gap and Levi's under the microscope, there is a company flying under the radar. "Monitoring is just information," Dan Viederman of Verité said. "A company's ability to act on that information is constrained, to a certain extent, by the sociopolitical environment, by their own resources and will, by conflicting agendas between sourcing and social compliance. I'm not ignoring the systemic nature, and the fact that companies ought to be held responsible. You want them to be ambitious about what they change. [But] companies ought to be judged by *what* they change."

Though its early prestige began to wane somewhat through the twentieth century, the NCL was resuscitated in the 1990s by the sweatshop scandals that erupted during that decade. In the New Deal era, they believed consumers could be convinced to use their dollars to support employers who respected their workers; their belief in the ability of ethical consumption to drive a market is still relevant today. Even now the fundamentals of the organization haven't changed. "Charity by way of alms could have been doled out to starving workers," stated an early history of the league. "Medical relief to consumptive sweatshop toilers could have been extended to a few. But such palliative measures would have been of small permanent value."[8] What the league was really after was addressing the root of the problem. For them, this meant addressing the habits of the consumer and the practices of the employer.

Or, as Edun puts it today, ". . . an attempt to help deliver the fishing rod, rather than the fish."

XXI

THE GUARDIANS OF EDUN

THE EDUN OFFICES ARE A MINIATURE UNITED NATIONS.
There are thirty-four employees, representing Korea, India,
Turkey, Colombia, Nepal, Japan, Puerto Rico, Canada, Ireland,
Vietnam, and the United States. The company's clothes are made
in Peru, India, Tunisia, Lesotho. Their CEO is a Canadian in Paris.
Their boss is Irish. Their offices are in New York and Dublin.
Scott Hahn says each person has his own story, that such a multi-
national production army underscores part of the point. They're
everywhere, and everywhere is them.

Rogan Gregory and Scott Hahn were a good fit for Ali and
Bono Hewson. Not many designers who are socially conscious and
environmentally concerned are also well respected in the high-end
fashion industry. "I think in a way, [Bono] and I associate with
each other," Rogan said one afternoon. He was enjoying a quiet
moment in his office—his desk was peppered with energy bars.
One of the books on his shelf was called *The Tragedy of Industrial
Forestry*. It sat next to one of *National Geographic*'s photography
books. Balance. "He's a very talented musician, but he's interested

in everything. I'm not really a clothing designer, I just happen to be doing this. I have varied interests."

This is not a misstatement. Rogan's also a surfer (in New York—not an activity for the faint of heart), a sculptor, an environmentalist, a rebuilder of many strange and varied things. Surfboards, for example. The first time I met him, his eyes swept past me and he did not say hello. Instead, he said, "There's my skateboard. I've been *looking* for that thing forever!" I didn't know yet that he had many many more than that one. Then he said hello. He has a dry sense of humor, and though he is creative director, he seems not to claim ownership of those things that come from his own mind, at least so long as they pertain to clothing. A design, for example, never finds its way to the rack of a store without a thousand "What do you thinks" being asked of the people who work for him, and even occasionally of the visiting interloper. He is a communal sort of guy in this way. Masterful without being a Master.

From time to time, he appears in pictures next to Bono or Ali Hewson or some other celebrity associated with the couple's many initiatives, and in these he sometimes looks mildly uncomfortable. His face is long and bearded and he looks a little like he's just come from Yak, Montana, and someone's thrown some clothes over him and stuck him there, in a picture with superstars. You'll come across a picture with Bono bending forward, hamming it up, arms splayed and maybe grinning wildly, or in profile to the camera, and there Rogan will be, closemouthed, unsmiling. After I began to recognize him in photos, I wondered whether he was mentally redesigning all the cameras in front of him, big black boxy things that they are. It'd be the sort of thing that'd cross his mind.

ONE AFTERNOON, SCOTT WALKS OUT FROM BEHIND A half wall in the main workroom. Sunlight tidals through the enormous windows; dozens of hoodies and jeans on portable racks stand sentry around the floor. The tags of one of Rogan's brands says: Drive Off Evil. Their Loomstate T-shirts often have sociological missives buried in them: All Together Now, The Sound of Things, Passion, Point of View, It Happens. The smell of curry wafts from the conference table—delivery of strange and wonderful food is a daily occurrence here, organic soba noodles and fresh edamame and marinated seitan and ginger candy—and somewhere in another office down the hall I hear "Sewanee River" playing on someone's radio. Rogan sits in a black office chair, wheeling it in for closer inspection, and says, "Oh, Daddy! You look hot!" Scott does a 180. He's wearing a pair of prototype jeans designed by Rogan.

"What do you think?" Rogan asks. He hasn't used the terms "lumpy" or "mushy" yet to describe the jeans, but he will.

"Are these higher or lower than the ones I was wearing?" Scott asks. The two of them, along with a handful of other employees, use themselves as models for the clothes, to test the fit, the comfort, the feel, the look.

"Those loops are no good. Those loops are loopy!" Rogan had said earlier in the day at a denim mini-skirt fitting with a woman who works for him who is so utterly beautiful that it's difficult to look away from her.

"It's bootilicious," she laughed.

"It's *so* booty," he said. Then he frowned.

It's as if there are always two parallel conversations going on with Rogan, the sometimes silly thing he's saying out loud and the alternate conversation he's having in his own mind about everything that's wrong with what he's seeing in front of him. Everything means the design, the details, but also the inefficiencies—like trade rules run amok, or environmental mismanagement. For Rogan, the message is as much about efficiency as anything. He uses this word almost like a mantra. Why aren't we all driving hybrids when they're so much more *efficient*? Why choose SUVs that are inherently *inefficient*? "You don't want kids making clothes for your kids. That's kind of warped. Don't you want to know that the cotton where you get your garments isn't contributing to the poor health of the environment or people? Isn't that important?" he asks. It's a question of logic and common sense, of "highlighting," as he puts it, "things that are pretty obvious."

The question, of course, isn't so much that we don't want these things. The question is whether we're willing to pay for the alternative.

While Rogan and Scott ask this question all the time—and do hope to make inroads into the larger, less expensive markets someday—in balance, it's a question they ultimately hope will be answered by consumers. "There are places in the world that are really screwed," Rogan says. He's speaking of Africa, but he could just as easily be speaking of Cambodia, or Azerbaijan, or even of pockets of the industrialized world. "Places where just because of a [tariff] or just because a politician changes his mind, all of a sudden production is gone . . . Once it's gone, it's never coming back."

This, perhaps, is the most indisputable truth in the manufacturing trade.

Once it's gone, it's never coming back.

Christian Kemp-Griffin, the Canadian CEO of Edun who is based in Paris, says Edun often finds a factory they like, with decent managers and owners who share their vision, and they'll spend the time training them how to do something. This reverses the traditional business model, in which a company goes in search of a factory that already has a certain expertise. "It's a bit of a hassle, but the rewards are great," Kemp-Griffin says. "One factory we worked with [in Peru], we'd gone through an agonizing procedure, but in the end you end up getting a good product and the second round doesn't cost that much time and money. If you want to help a nation get out of the position they're in, you can't have an on-off switch. You need to work with them, be involved with them, bring in partners."

Edun is building not just partnerships in factories but partnerships with individual farms willing to grow organic cotton even before they can afford the certified organic rating, which can cost upwards of US$60,000 for certification from Europe and the United States. "If they're taking the leap of faith to do it, you need to support that," he says. "What farmer can spend twenty-thousand dollars or [more] to get certified? It's the certifier making the money. My philosophy is, if you know you're doing the right thing, then just do it."

Kemp-Griffin says he commends the Gap for the work they've done with their contracted factories. If he finds a factory that is Gap-compliant, he has confidence it's a decent place to do business. In all fairness, the sheer difference in size between companies like Gap and Edun make factory monitoring and logistics for Gap far more challenging than for Edun. With all the new attention paid to corporate social responsibility, Scott says the people who monitor the factories are never the same people negotiating prices or purchase orders, and the seeming contradiction between these end goals will always create tension. He believes the responsibility, though shared, rests mostly with management, which buys goods from factories and then uses those contracts to leverage one factory against another. The tactic puts the factories at a disadvantage and ultimately probably affects workers more than anyone. It also often pits the buyer's agent against the buyer's own corporate social responsibility department. "So you have this conflict that exists," he said. "Hopefully at some point consumers will become educated enough to see this disconnect between people trying to be nonsweatshop and the fact that [the consumers] are flooding into Wal-Mart and Target and all these great retailers that make up the U.S. economy and buying jeans for nineteen, twenty dollars and T-shirts for two dollars or three dollars. Where do they think that stuff is coming from? Who do they think is making it? If they're not paying for it, someone, somewhere down the line is—somehow."

Edun takes its fair share of criticism over pricing. Not many people make the connection between higher production costs and higher prices at the cash register, if Internet blogs and anecdotal cocktail party chatter are any indication. Consumers are so used to cheap goods, to bulk, to stuffed closets and packed shelves and instantaneous consumption, that we don't make the simple calculations ourselves. Scott spells it out for a pair of $200 Edun jeans. At that price, they'll wholesale for $84. Fabric will run roughly $11; the actual cutting and sewing, $14; washing and finishing, $15–$20; trim, meaning zippers, buttons, and rivets, $4–$6. The grand total for production—$44—leaves them with $40, from which they pay salaries, overhead, design costs, marketing, and advertising.* Scott said a good target for net profit is 13–15 percent, but 10 percent is a decent average. "We've never made that," he said. (Edun won't discuss financial figures specifically. One magazine I came across said Loomstate would gross twenty million in 2005, but the figure was unverifiable.) "We hover around break even. We're working hard to make our business not lose money. We're perceived as these guys who are very successful. We're partners with a rock star—one of the biggest ever. I'd have to be part of a really profitable business to judge what's reasonable, because I'm still at that stage of desire. I don't know what real profit is, [except] on a spreadsheet."

Fundamentally, Scott says, his job is to worry. "And I do. That's *all* I do."

PERHAPS THE QUESTION OUGHT NOT TO BE WHETHER consumers will absorb the extra costs of social and environmental

----

*The breakdown costs for an average pair of five-pocket jeans are both widely available and widely variable on the Internet, but generally speaking it costs between $8.00 and $15.00 to produce a single pair. Edun would be higher than, say, Levi's or Target not only because the fabric, dye, labor, and design costs are higher, but because they don't receive the same volume discounts for cotton, fabric, manufacturing, or transport costs that a larger manufacturer would receive.

responsibility, but whether consumers can curtail their desire for more. After all, buying five pairs of jeans at Target may be the equivalent of one pair of jeans at Edun. But what other things, beyond seams and zippers, are bought into?

And who needs five pairs of jeans anyway?

Scott says he's deflected criticism like this since the beginning. Gap, for example, is a decent model of social accountability and affordability. They also aren't organic, though like many other mass marketers, they're using a small percentage of organic as a cotton blend and they say they're interested in increasing this. They also have volume to bring costs down. Edun, comparatively, is tiny. "We're fortunate to be in a premium market to be able to put another dollar on our price, and pass it along the [supply] chain," Scott said. "Where it's challenging is with the low-priced products, all the disposable clothing . . . For us it's about having relationships with factory owners. Knowing their values, their commitments. They'll tell us what they're going through, why they can't give us a certain price."

While factories who work with Gap and Nike and Levi's are required to be in compliance with their code of conduct, their workers are also typically being paid minimum wage plus bonus, if they're lucky. Rogan and Scott's factory workers earn between $270 and $300 a month—well above the minimum wage for, say, Lesotho and Tunisia. "When Rogan and I were first starting the company, we'd get asked how we can sell jeans for 260 dollars," Scott says—forgetting the obvious, of course, that Scott and Rogan don't set the retail price of their jeans. "We'd say, 'How many times do we change our jeans?' We're making the perfect jean that we love to wear, and there's a value associated with that. We wear them for six months straight. For us it's real. We don't change our jeans. We wear them." Then he concedes that growing up, he also wasn't necessarily "the guy who could have afforded what we make."

Scott says what alarms him is a trend he sees of people who can easily afford Edun buying $1,800 Chanel coats and $29 H&M

jeans. People who don't need a bargain. "People with money want to feel resourceful as well," he says. "It's about the behavior of consuming."

- -

SOME OF BONO'S CHARITABLE CAMPAIGNS, IN WHICH Edun is involved, have been criticized for catering to corporate greed by increasing profit as much as humanitarian aid. The (Red) campaign, which launched in the fall of 2006 in the United States, partners with Motorola, American Express, Armani, Gap, Converse, and others—retailers who have been accused of raising prices on their (Red) products to increase their bottom line. Half of all (Red) proceeds go to fight AIDS in Africa, but one editorial claimed that a $50 pair of Gap jeans had been raised to $198 when repositioned as a (Red) product.[1] If it were true, the price hike would leave the company $50 in the black. "If profit has a negative air about it, it is probably because companies or owners are valuing profit before they're valuing the lives of people in the majority of cases," Scott says. "The locus of control resides in the owners."*

At Scott's fitting, Rogan is studying the jeans along with several designers and fitters on his team, all of whom are focused right now somewhere near Scott's rear end. Most everyone on the team, except Rogan, has a Blackberry with a clubby ring tone, and they go off intermittently and consistently throughout the day, like there's a DJ standing behind the drywall screwing around.

"What would you change?" Rogan asks Scott ("pinging" ideas

---

*But it's important to remember that those on the receiving end of aid efforts hardly care one way or another whether the help originates with multinational corporations, with religious institutions, or with unaffiliated nonprofits. What matters is that it comes at all. Criticism and the moral high ground come, of course, at the luxury of never having to be in the position to ask for help.

off him, Rogan once called it). Rogan's wearing Moroccan slippers with pointed toes and fluorescent orange crosses on them because they are comfortable and because he is always slipping in and out of clothes in various stages of design. Also, his own loft is in this same building, and so technically he hasn't left home.

"I'm worried about the pitch a little," Scott says. "The shank . . ."

"Well, you're going to have that problem," Rogan says. "You've got a big ass."

Scott yanks on the pants and studies them in the mirror. The back pockets are beautifully subtle, disappearing into soft lines like an infinity pool. Scott is more serious than Rogan. I once tried to tally the number of times he said environment and organic in the passing conversations of a single day, but I lost count after forty-five. Cotton might be his particular vehicle of environmental expression, but he knows the particulars of making ethanol, and the intricacies of how wind and solar power work, and even the many uses of recycled cooking fat.

When Rogan designs he starts with an existing style, then works with a fabric that fits that style. After that he makes a prototype, and from the prototype he makes adjustments to the shape or the silhouette, as it's called in industry lingo. The adjustments are why everyone is currently focused on Scott's bottom half. This particular pair of pants is approaching "blueprint" status, Scott says.

Rogan tells Scott to pull the pants down to where he'd naturally wear them, and then decides they need to be cut to come down half an inch. "They're in preproduction right now, right?" Rogan asks. One of the fitters confirms this. "It doesn't look bad. It's just not right. Is this going to make them upset?"

Scott wears a white Edun T-shirt, fitted around the chest, looser around the waist. Its white, short sleeves have a design of swirling vines, a trademark for the brand that he calls a flourish. Jeans, Scott has said, and clothes in general are simply a wrap. "They're the product and the product is just skin," he believes. "The soul of a [pair of jeans] is something just beyond. In real life, it's a kind of armor. That's what it *does*, but there's so much more to look at. It's about digging a little deeper." The product, the clothes, are simply a vehicle for these much more compelling, much more important, stories.

Scott and Rogan are a fraction of a $400 billion industry, and thus a fraction of a much larger set of stories, of course. Yet this doesn't seem to overwhelm them. "Nature is the inspiration," Scott says. "If you keep that in mind, a lot of hard decisions are made for you." Scott was invited once to a photo shoot for a 2006 *Vanity Fair* spread: the hot young denim designers and their muses. Nicole and Michael Colovos of Habitual brought Mena Suvari. Jerome Dahan of Citizens of Humanity brought Cindy Crawford. Scott Morrison of Earnest Sewn brought Kirsty Hume. Scott Hahn brought Mother Nature, a Japanese sweet gum tree, a muse he prunes and waters with the care of a new parent. It lives with him in his Brooklyn apartment. When he goes away for a few days, its leaves sag.

"I think if we can, we should give them to Scott," Rogan says of the prototype jeans. He means as testers, for Scott to wear around for a few weeks. Diondra, the fitter, says it's fine. She doesn't need them.

"I think they're long," Rogan says. He and Scott wear the same size, which is a little shocking because Rogan is taller and thinner than Scott. He tends to have them both try on clothes to get an idea of how they exhibit on different body types. Then he says it. "The embroidery looks lumpy." To me, of course, it all looks perfect. Someone comes in with an armful of papers and asks Rogan a question apparently about a T-shirt design with dolphins on it, because his answer is: "Who doesn't want to wear dolphins? Dolphins are such friendly animals." Scott does several half turns in the mirror and tugs at the back pockets.

Rogan sits quietly for a moment, slumped down hipster-style in his chair, mulling over the jeans. Diondra is jotting down notes, a measuring tape wrapped like a scarf around her shoulders. Even when Rogan sits still, he carries the illusion of movement. Both

Scott and Rogan have the unusual gift of soft, almost mesmerizing voices; the kind of vocal acoustics that quietly and insistently make people listen.

"I want to make the leg straight," Rogan says, suddenly.

Diondra looks up with a pained expression on her face. "Today?" she says.

Rogan doesn't answer. His mind is already creating new mental imagery. A straighter leg, a different jean.

"Can't it wait till next season?" Diondra says.

Of course, everyone, including her, including me, already knows the answer.

ONE OF THE MOST SIGNIFICANT ASPECTS OF HAVING A company as small as Edun is the ability to control, even from many thousands of miles away, things that other companies struggle with. The day after I met Rogan, he was leaving for Tunisia, which happened to be just after Scott returned from Peru. Their factories are small, in the dozens or low hundreds of employees. Their reasons for going are many. Sometimes, they are simply taking what Rogan calls "inspirational" trips. Sometimes they're checking on the factory, or how the more complicated orders are coming along. Sometimes they just need to further establish the relationship. Every factory they work with is vetted by one or both of them. "We won't do any work unless you kick the tires," Scott says. We are at a cocktail bar around the corner from Edun's offices. The multistory ceilings have enormous, colorful maritime balloon animals; koi, stingray, and whales hang menacingly above us, swaying gently, while we eat tiny, tiny bite-sized hamburgers on tiny, tiny bite-sized buns. Suddenly, the scale of everything seems off. "Kids in America" by Kim Wilde is the soundtrack.

Though Rogan claims to have a "finite tolerance" for travel, he gets a sense of energy just by being at a factory. "I like to see the way things are actually done; I don't like someone else's explanation," he'd said to me earlier. The fact that he and Scott personally visit their factories several times a year sets them apart from most other designers. "If you're able to see what people's natural tendencies are, you can design into them, instead of requiring them to do something that's foreign to them, which in the end would be much more difficult for them."

They say they're determined to stay in the factories they're in with Edun's line, even if it increases their cost. Bono, even as a brand, is surprisingly not a sure thing, just like trying to eradicate sweatshops in exchange for profit isn't a sure thing, or focusing on the design and manufacturing reputation you've long had isn't a sure thing, and having the desire to just get in and play the game isn't a sure thing. In 2006, some newspaper articles suggested Edun's designs lacked fresh style. And their fabric costs more, the design costs more, the salaries of factory workers are higher, and the transport costs—trucks, cargo ships, trains—all carry increased fuel costs. Like practically everyone in the business, they're also not using organic washing and finishing, which leaves them open to even more criticism. "There are stages to any effort you're making," Scott says. "People are getting smart, saying 'what's so great about an organic jean that you're flying the fabric in a jet airliner all the way across here?' These are the contradictions that are woven into our lives right now. For us, the root of that story is agriculture."

Perhaps the most difficult job for Scott—indeed for any responsible company involved in overseas manufacturing—is the myriad decisions that come from working outside your own culture, your own language, your own ideals and choices. There is a part of him that empathizes with the factory owner who just shuts down, pulls out, gives up. The point for Rogan and Scott is to commit to a country, to start small and be effective, and continue to bring work there so a community can establish itself. The profit isn't inconsequential, but they want it to be secondary on their value chain. "Any decision that's going to affect anyone other than yourself is a hard decision," he says. "But it gets easy to make a hard decision when money becomes the hinge." In other words, when a factory owner starts to see red, suddenly the livelihood of all those working for him becomes far less compelling than his own livelihood. This is the difference Scott sees between himself and so many others, that when he starts to see the red in his own accounting books, he won't split. "I have to have faith in human nature, but there's so much evidence you can't," Scott says. "Most people don't have the bandwidth. They'd rather zone out in front of the television. When you get fatigued at your own life, you kind of acknowledge what needs to happen, but getting to the acting stage to do something about it . . . that's where the courage comes in. The moxy."

Still, there are decisions that haunt you, people who come and go and then become part of a very different story. Mexico was like this for Scott. He went down once, early on in the Loomstate evolution, to check out a factory that was supposed to sew their jeans. "This factory was not ready to be a factory yet," he says. It had only natural light, and twenty sewing machines set up in one end of the enormous warehouse. The owner talked to Scott about a code of conduct, about how they really wanted the work and how they had every intention of getting up to code. "I didn't have the confidence that the product would be what we needed it to be and the conditions would be to our standard," he says. "It felt wrong. 'Getting up to code' was what I kept hearing, but it was a good year away from happening." They nixed the contract before any sewing had been done.

This is the crux of the story—how to know when to give someone a chance and when not to; how to know when to walk away and when to stay. Nearly all of their competitors are in China and Scott says they're all doing great. By comparison, he thinks their business models are so much less complicated, so much more— here's the word—*efficient*. The Mexico factory haunts Scott; he second-guesses his decision still, because behind that owner and all his promises were people desperate for work. "Nothing serves you better as a business owner than visiting your suppliers, and understanding the needs and constraints on someone else's business," he says. "When I look back on that decision, I wish I'd spent more time there."

What frustrates Scott is what he perceives to be his own inability to convey the message that he's not just selling clothes, soulless covering for our own flesh and bone, but that he is trying to provide "something that has value beyond keeping you warm and dry," he says. "The substance of the garment isn't just the fabric, the sewing. It's the people behind it. It's not a criticism; it's just a message to say pick your head up. Slow down."

Scott tells the story of a former CEO at one of the high-end department stores who came to the design offices of Edun before, as Scott puts it, "we were at the point of knowing the aesthetic ourselves." The man came in and looked at their color swatches and design boards and started asking where their "tonnage" was. In retail terms, tonnage is product you move into the store by the truckload; as items fly off the shelf more are right there ready to be restocked. Tonnage is what Target and Wal-Mart and Macy's and other department stores are built upon, but it's not part of Edun's mission. "He was like 'tonnage! Where's the tonnage?' " Scott recalls. "I think we all just looked at him."

ONE AFTERNOON, SCOTT WALKS ME AROUND TO ROGAN'S new concept design store. It's a small space with soft amber lighting, groovy music, and concrete floors, where limited-run designs are tested. Scott calls it a "lab of experimentation." Everything from the clothes to the lights to the furniture to the accessories—which are random things like wallets, corkscrews, and knives—are designed by Rogan. He was an experimenter, a tinkerer before anything else, before the clothes and the New York life. One of his early memories, he once told a reporter, was being covered in sawdust in his dad's workshop.

"As one big monster, this can all be a little overwhelming," Scott says as we wander around the store, looking at the elements that have undergone the Rogan metamorphosis—knives, lighters, chairs. "But you break it into pieces." The responsibility of all this, he meant, not just what they were doing, but how. And with whom.

Their main wholesale sales offices are nestled in the back of the store. We skirt a 120-year-old wood table from the Philippines and an enormous helicopter blade sitting in the middle of the floor. (I am suddenly reminded of Mehman's snakes hissing forth from cotton bales. This could be a story of the things that must be avoided.)

Colleen, a member of the sales staff, is sitting behind her desk when we walk in. Earlier in the day she'd explained to me how real denim should never be machine-washed. To freshen it, she suggested hanging it outside or throwing it in the dryer with a softener sheet for a few minutes. Like many of her colleagues, she is a denim purist. Her own jeans have already begun to bear the singular marks of her life. How she sits, how she walks, the folds and creases a pattern of her habits.

Scott gets some sales figures he needs from Colleen and we walk back outside, across the street and to Loomstate's showroom, which was once an apartment he shared with Rogan. The Rogan/Edun/Loomstate offices are housed in three different places in Manhattan, in an area that straddles Chinatown and TriBeCa. It is quiet, late in the day, and no one is in the showroom. It is clear Scott still has some lingering attachment to the place. "When you get to a quiet place, outside the city, you can still hear the hum in your ears," he says. "It takes like a day to get rid of it. But the white noise is part of your experience." We are talking about his having lived in the midst of noisy Manhattan and how he could always hear the garbage trucks and the deliverymen day and night. But it felt, for a moment, like the sentence meant as much about a place in the world that had nothing at all to do with geography.

It has only been the last three or four years that Scott's family hasn't run the marina at the Sunken Forest on Fire Island. After a drawn-out battle that lasted several seasons they lost the contract, having decided that the terms of the bidding were beyond what they were willing to sacrifice. Scott's grandfather hadn't lived long enough to see it taken away, but Scott believes his mother had been profoundly saddened by the loss; he'd called the place her "life's work."

Scott lost other things on Fire Island, too. A mentor named Casey Morano had taught him that you could invent the life you wanted. Casey had been a thousand things, a restaurateur, a farmer, a motorcycle manufacturer, a television producer. He'd created the world in which he'd chosen to exist in a way that few people do. Casey died of a heart attack at forty-five while he was still involved in a project with Scott. "He taught me you didn't need anyone to tell you how to do anything. You could go seek the answers, find the right people to help you do it, be resourceful. And don't take no for an answer," Scott says. "Casey taught me that something's not going to be handed to you; you have to create it."

We talk again about Fire Island, how he remembers seeing the world through the people who came to the park. "We're all products of our own environment," he says. "We can take very little credit." Then he stops a minute, smiles, amends that thought. "We can take some."

Fire Island was open to the public and still is, of course, but for Scott it is a private place. "I could go out there anytime," Scott says. "We could go." And he does, occasionally, mostly to surf with Rogan on the weekends. But the connection doesn't seem what it was once, like visiting your childhood home and finding it both familiar and strange, always smaller than the memory you hold of it. To confront what *was* would likely be far less useful to him than to figure out what *is* anyway.

Protect the imperiled forest.

Protect the factories, and the cotton and the fabric; protect the investment and the backers and the employees, and even yourself a little. "I used to think that for every one good person, every solid karmic soldier, there were nine bad guys," Scott says. "Rogan and I were talking about it and he was like, 'No. It's not like that. For every bad guy, there's one good guy and eight apathetic people.' " Scott likes that. He always remembered it.

Rogan and Scott are trying to do it all in a way no one else really is. Others are involved in elements: No Sweat and American Apparel both claim to be "sweatshop-free" employers, both have posted profit, but they aren't organic. Scott and Rogan are navigating the trade rules, treading lightly on the environment, creating fashion-forward garments, and providing a better life for people, a life with a financial legacy. And they're doing it all in the most public of partnerships, under the watchful gaze of industries beyond the industry, under the watchful gaze of a bevy of demographics and professions. They didn't just follow a decent corporate code; they attempted to go beyond that, by visiting factories themselves, by paying very good salaries, by buying organic cotton. But choosing this path had been difficult, and while everyone put forward a hopeful, determined, even brave front, the truth is no one knows if what they're attempting can be done long term, or if it can work in other places, or with bigger corporations. SweatX, an antisweatshop brand begun by one of the founders of Ben & Jerry's ice cream, had quit after two years of operating in the red. Rogan and Scott were trying to protect all these things they touched. But in the end, that would have to include themselves as well.

Scott knows the stories of those who have come before him; he knows the odds may not be in their favor, but karma certainly is. "Life is a mental leap in a lot of ways," he says, at the end of the day. It's dark outside and nearly everyone has gone home. Somewhere several buildings away Rogan is catching up with those employees he didn't have time to see during the day when they ran from room to room in their eternal search for him. A pattern that will be repeated the next day, and the day after, and the day after. Scott smiles. "The only boundaries that exist," he says, finally, "exist in your own mind."

EPILOGUE

AT THE LOCAL SOS CLINIC IN PHNOM PENH, CAMBO-
dia, where most of the expatriates seek medical care, I noticed a
framed quote on the wall one day: "What you wear thirty years
from now won't matter, but what you learned and how you used
your knowledge will." It was an odd piece of décor for this particular country. It occurred to me as I sat there that perhaps my
greatest hope for this book might simply be to offer a counter-
point to the sentiment expressed in that saying.

As I wrote the book, I found it oddly difficult to talk about.
Authors are always told by people in the know—publishers, other
authors, teachers, and so forth—that they should be able to
describe their book in one or two sentences. I could never do that
with mine, at least not in any way that captured what it was about.
If I said "global garment industry" people's eyes tended to glaze
over, and I didn't blame them. Mine would have done likewise had
the roles been reversed. If I said I was writing about garment
workers, it kept the designers out of the picture; if I said designers, then the garment workers were nixed. Factory monitors or

cotton classers required their own lengthy definitions and still left my answer far too narrow. Saying the book was about changing trade rules or globalization felt too generically academic, and didn't capture the voice or the people I followed. The book is, in part, about all these things, but they all seem so much grander and so much less tangible to me than the human lives and struggles I've tried to depict. After a while, I took to joking that my book was a story about the people in our pants. That presented its own dilemmas, but at least it usually led to a lively conversation.

More than a year went by before I realized that it didn't matter what I said, because people invariably responded in one of two ways. Either they would nod and say something like, "Ah, yes. Sweatshops!" or they'd ask me where they should be shopping, which so often seemed like a bid for me to help them *feel good* about their purchases. Of course this second response presupposes that we are all both motivated and fulfilled by the same desires when we shop.

Still, both responses gave me hope. For starters, the fact that people knew about sweatshops meant hard-won success for the writers, academics, and social activists who had worked to get that message out. I don't cover sweatshops in *Fugitive Denim* not because they don't exist but because I felt the individual lives so affected by globalization hadn't been explored as well as many of the cultural, economic, and political issues had been. What I wanted to do was find the complex humanity in the world of manufacturing—beyond simply the good factories and the bad, the making and breaking of rules, and the unwieldy negotiations of trade deals, I wanted the struggle illuminated in the people who lived between all these extremes. Because the truth is, sitting in Pascal's fabric booth, or Ry's rural home, or Scott's trendy office, what gets talked about so often isn't the latest hiccup in G8 negotiations. What gets talked about is food (cheesecake in Azerbaijan, harvests in Cambodia, salami in Italy, or organic curries in New York). What gets talked about is commuting, or the difficulty of deadlines, the exhaustion of full-time work, the latest movies or sports scores, new colors of lipstick, music, ghosts, and family sagas, and what to do in your free time with your friends. What gets talked about, ultimately, is the details of the life you're living. That's what mattered to me.

When people gave me the second most common response, asking me where to shop, I have little doubt that my response wasn't what they were looking for. The idea that the shopping question was asked at all, however, suggested a growing thoughtfulness among consumers. While many expected me to denounce Wal-Mart, I do believe there is a small economic need for the Wal-Marts of the world. What concerns me more about the low-cost mega-chains is how they incite our overconsumption. Throughout my research, people involved in the industry often discussed environmental and economic issues in terms of expanding the use of organic cotton or decreasing the use of chemicals, improving working conditions or raising the minimum wage. They were focused on how to meet our apparently endless desires, rather than how to tailor those desires to what the world has the reasonable ability to offer. And so I've come to answer the shopping question ultimately with more questions. Is it economic progress that we used to own four T-shirts and now we own twenty? Are we a greater economic success because we are able to buy so much stuff cheaply? Where is our strength?

What western Europe and the United States have, frankly, is the greatest consumer market in the world. They have you and me. If those stores where we shop know that we demand decent labor conditions—good wages, worker's rights, functional unions—if the corporations know we demand transparency, they in turn will demand it of their contractors, and they will offer it themselves. Governments, businesses, and, yes, workers, all have some power to change things, but so do consumers. In the end, the real power may lie with us.

Few in the industry are willing to predict what 2009 will hold. It is entirely possible that a new set of stopgaps will continue to keep China in check and the rest of the garment-producing world unnaturally afloat. Some experts believe the ending of the quotas won't truly be felt until 2015 or later, when all possible trade restrictions under the current system will have been exhausted. In the spring of 2007, the United States opened up the possibility of putting tariffs on many Chinese goods, including textiles, under the guise of China's granting "illegal" subsidies in some of their manufacturing industries; how that will unfold remains to be seen.[1] For now, though, things seem to have settled into an uneasy calm. Many countries that were expected to falter have done extraordinarily well in the U.S. market, including Bangladesh, Cameroon, Venezuela, Syria, Lebanon, Ghana, and of course China. Others, like Pakistan, India, and Honduras, are holding steady. Still others have textile industries clearly in decline, like Panama, Uganda, Kazakhstan, Iran, and Bolivia.[2]

AND THEN THERE ARE THE STORIES THAT I COULDN'T include. I had to cut an entire section on shipping, a topic, I've come to find, that deserves books of its own—and has a few already. I spent over a week at the Long Beach port and several days at the Singapore port. One afternoon, I went out with a small contingent from Jacobsen Pilot Service, a family-run operation since Long Beach's first days as a freight destination. Jacobsen's pilots are ferried two miles out to sea in small boats so they can board the massive container ships and maneuver them into the port (United States law dictates that international vessels inside port breakwaters must be driven by a pilot with an American license). Basically, it's parallel parking for giants. In ties and dress shoes these guys clamber up rope ladders dangling down along the clifflike sides of cargo ships. It's a lot like rock climbing. In wingtips. While the rock face bobs up and down in front of you. Also, you're untethered and wearing a clip-on tie.

Another afternoon on the water I was treated to a series of

full-throttle tugboat donuts by Foss Maritime's new high-tech craft just before they guided a ship carting more than five thousand containers into port. Perhaps the greatest testimony to the sublime grace of these boats is the fact that as someone who is susceptible to motion sickness while doing sit-ups in the gym, I survived the 360°s without a single wave of queasiness. In the parlance, this five-thousand-container vessel had been merely a medium-sized freighter. Now, new ones are being built to hold ten or twelve thousand containers—ships so enormous that the Long Beach port, along with many others around the world, aren't even equipped to handle them yet. Every year somewhere between ten and fifteen thousand containers are lost at sea because of big waves or storms. Eight feet wide and up to forty feet long, they tend to have quite a lot of air in them, so they float in the water, wreaking havoc on small boats and local fishermen before they sink to the ocean floor—filled with our computers, our dishware, our jeans.

There is also lots of chatter these days about the environmental consequences of our "food miles," how far our fresh fruits and vegetables must travel to get to us, but "clothes miles" are almost surely higher, given that fabric has a much longer shelf life than, say, grapes. It is a discussion that must begin, and the most obvious place is within shipping, an industry that not only grows exponentially as our consumer desires grow but that also, as my friend Elizabeth Becker pointed out in an article for the *New York Times*, is perhaps the greatest symbol of our growing trade deficit. As the ships come in to U.S. and European harbors too small to manage their ever-expanding girth, those same ships leave a day or two later half empty and bound for Asia, for Latin America, for Africa, where they'll stuff themselves once again and head for our shores.

Ultimately, the shipping section was cut not for lack of fascinating characters or complexity; it was cut because it seemed to me the one place where someone's hands weren't physically touching—planning, designing, sewing, packaging, monitoring—our garments. So it didn't make the book; but it's stayed with me nonetheless.

My focus on the rest of the world, similarly, doesn't mean I am unaware of the bleak prospects for manufacturers and their employees in the United States or the European Union. In truth, the manufacturing decline in these areas began long before the birth of the WTO or the ending of the quota system. A lobbyist in Washington, DC, once told me that union activists for the textile trade in the United States weren't fighting for jobs for workers anymore; they were fighting for the machines that took over those jobs. Whether or not this is true will be left to other books, but one thing did strike me throughout my research—and it will come as no surprise to the historically astute. Simply, that we are living in an era of both great worry and great opportunity. While manufacturing may no longer be a central part of the diverse economies of the industrialized world, certainly there is room for technological advancement in any number of businesses. I thought about this cycle often as I read of the fear the English had when cotton from the new colonies began to replace wool, and then when machines in the cotton fields of the South began to replace human labor, and especially when the Industrial Revolution spurred technological advances that became the economic foundations of western Europe and the United States today. Call me an idealist, but I see this moment as a great opportunity for countries that can no longer rely on manufacturing but remain filled with human ingenuity and resources nonetheless.

For those around the world who did make it into the book, I did not set out to look for symbols of the whole in Rogan, Scott, Pascal, Mehman, or anyone else. I set out to look for two things: connections and compelling stories. How did political, economic, cultural, and social forces connect one of the richest rock stars in the world to a seamstress in Phnom Penh, a cotton classer in a little-known country to an Italian denim designer, a factory monitor in a prefab urban landscape to a New York designer melding high style and social development?

Pascal and Ariana met me on my first morning at Legler. They'd been charged with finding out what I wanted to write about and who might be appropriate for me to interview. After several days of touring the facilities with them, it occurred to me that *they* were the ones I'd been looking for; their lives captured the complexities of operating in a globalized world. For Mehman, it was the same thing. I went to visit his lab on my first morning in Baku and was instantly intrigued by his humor, and by the way he looked out at the world through the push and pull of desire versus tradition.

In this way, he mirrored Nat and Ry in Cambodia. There, I had an almost endless array of women to write about, not only because I'd lived there for several years but because I'd met so many garment workers on previous story assignments. Nat and Ry were different. They approached me, which is unusual. They asked questions about my experiences and about women I'd met in other countries. We spoke often of stories I'd written on women in Niger and Afghanistan for a U.S. magazine. They had a curiosity that I didn't often find in other workers, and I sensed an authenticity in how they described their lives and their struggles, as opposed to workers who are too often influenced by the non-governmental organizations charged with helping them to use the word "exploited" in describing their lives—most often within the first few seconds after you meet them. This is not to say they aren't exploited; but it does suggest to me they have been unwittingly coached to view themselves as outsiders often view them. Nat and Ry weren't like this; they weren't victims. They saw positive change in their own lives right alongside those things they *wished* they could change.

Scott and Rogan actually displaced another company and set of designers I'd planned to include. While I myself knew nothing about what they really did in the world of fashion, I understood that for a tiny company they wielded enormous influence. But they also represented a hopeful future. Even if you remove Ali and (Sir) Bono from the equation, Scott and Rogan had been charting their own complicated course—not only within a foreign world of manufacturing but within a foreign world of aid and development. Many of their peers had chosen careers where human rights played a tertiary role to the religion of fashion, but Scott and Rogan seemed determined to put the human and environmental implications on equal footing with the fashion. I spent far less time with them than I did with others in the book—having a common first language made my time there more fruitful—but Scott in particular seemed a mixture of idealist and shrewd businessman. Edun doesn't have the sorts of established rules for their factories that larger brands have, but they are able to do what many others cannot. They can actually know on a personal basis the people working in their factories; and sometimes this matters as much as or more than the exacting standards for light and ventilation. The question is how they'll maintain this personal connection to their suppliers as their brand grows.

As of this writing, I've learned that Mehman has left Intertek and taken a job with CTS Agro, the gin where he warned me to watch out for snakes. Ariana is happy in her new job and spending more time with her daughter. Pascal remains at Legler. Nat and Ry have held on to their jobs and, in fact, are part of a growing workforce in Cambodia that by March 2007 had 350,000 textile workers in nearly 300 factories. The industry was up by nearly 20 percent over the previous year, and the Trade Act had been reintroduced in Congress. Scott and Rogan were part of a team from Edun engaged in a pilot program in corporate social and environmental responsibility for business school students at an Ohio university, and they were looking for ways to support partnerships with organic cotton growers in Africa. And Vasif? I tried for over a year to contact him, to find out if he'd run in his local election and if he'd won. No one was able to get ahold of him. Once again, it seems, he's disappeared.

AFTERWORD

IN THE WINTER OF 2008 SOPHEA AND I DECIDED TO spend a Sunday afternoon looking for Nat and Ry because we'd lost them. Neither had ever had a mobile phone, but we used to get hold of them by leaving a message with Nat's brother. Since a Khmer speaker usually signaled a wrong number to me, I'd worked out a system with Ry to call me. Before saying "Hello," she was to say "Khmow." Khmow was the name of our dog. Anyone calling to say "Khmow" could only have been Ry. And then I'd either speak to her in my broken Khmer or have Sophea call her back. For a long time, the arrangement worked, though she called only on rare occasions. But then time passed and neither Sophea nor I heard from them. I got pregnant, gave birth to a daughter in Bangkok, spent a couple of months in the United States and England, and still we hadn't heard from them. Sophea tried to call a few times, but no one ever answered the phone. Then one night someone climbed through Sophea's window and snatched her mobile phone, and all her phone numbers vanished along with it. Whatever imperfect and occasional contact we had had with Nat and Ry disappeared.

We'd heard Ry had bought her own house and that both women were working at new factories. Nat's mother's house had been down a tiny, dirt alleyway that looked like hundreds of other dirt alleyways in Phnom Penh. The times we'd visited, Nat had waited for us on the main street, then walked us in. When I began *Fugitive Denim*, Chak Angre was the outskirts of the city; but by late 2008 the city had grown so rapidly that places like Chak Angre were folded solidly inside it, no longer the distant suburbs they'd once been.

The day of our search, Sophea was five months pregnant with her second son and wore a white frangipani flower barrette in her hair. She was enthusiastic, jumping out of the car when an alleyway looked familiar. But no one knew whom we were talking about. There were tens of thousands of girls in Chak Angre, all working at factories.

Nat and Ry weren't the only ones I'd lost. Mehman was gone, too. If he was still at CTS Agro, he didn't answer my e-mails or phone calls. The Italians, Pascal and Ariana, were gone, too. Pascal had left Legler in late 2007, as the company's fate seemed to grow increasingly dire. Shortly after, the couple had given birth to a son. But that was the last I heard of them.

As I drove, dodging bicycles and pedestrians, food carts and remorques on the slow-moving highway, Sophea looked for signs of familiarity. Had that pagoda been across the street from Nat's alley? Had the half-built white building been next to their factory? We couldn't remember the color of the factory gate across the street from her. We couldn't find the sidewalk restaurant where I'd first met them. Finally, we passed an alley that Sophea thought looked familiar.

"They all look familiar," I told her. "They're identical."

She laughed. She didn't dispute this, but she still jumped out of the car and made her way down the alley. While I waited, a little girl jumped up and down in front of the car, waving her arms wildly, as if I was a block away, instead of directly in front of her. Westerners were still an oddity in this part of town. Westerners behind the wheel of a car were even more rare, since so many have drivers. And I may well have been the first foreign woman driving a car that she'd ever seen. I smiled. Sophea returned within two minutes and said she'd found Ry's old landlord, who remembered Ry because of the missing fingers on her hand.

"The landlord said Ry was working at Kin Tai factory last she heard," Sophea said.

Five minutes later, having spoken to the security guard at Kin Tai, who made a call to the administrative offices, we had Ry's mobile phone number in hand. Such is the way of the globalized world. Mehman, Pascal, Ariana, Nat, Ry . . . they could never really disappear into the world. They'd always be findable. No one, no matter how off the map, is ever really more than a thirty-minute search away anymore. The difference was mostly geographical; I was still in Cambodia, a twenty-minute drive from Chak Angre. I didn't doubt that a quick trip to Italy or Azerbaijan would bring the reemergence of those I'd lost track of. So what really amazed me wasn't that we'd found Ry so easily. No. The part that stayed with me was Sophea saying she had Ry's number. Ry's. Number.

Ry had a mobile phone now.

IN THE FALL OF 2008, THE FINANCIAL WORLD BEGAN to resemble a house of cards. The global meltdown had left countries from Italy to Cambodia, Azerbaijan to France, the United States to Bangladesh, and even China and India, struggling to maintain growth or in some cases just stay afloat. Factories in every country closed. Workers by the hundreds of thousands lost their jobs. And the worry that Cambodia had always carried multiplied into what was beginning to look like the country's worst-case scenario. Every day the news seemed worse. In decades past it would have taken years for a tiny developing country like Cambodia or Azerbaijan to be affected by the fallout from a U.S. recession; but now everyone was so interconnected economically it was a matter of weeks. Whatever U.S. consumers did, Cambodians felt in an immediate ripple effect. If a headline in the *New York Times* talked about the retail sector tightening, the *Cambodia Daily* or the *Phnom Penh Post* would run a story a week later about factories closing or workers losing their jobs or export numbers falling. The election of Barack Obama to the U.S. presidency seemed to buoy everyone's spirits, however. One senior minister in the Cambodian government sent me an e-mail three days after the U.S. election: "I am dancing," he wrote. As a senator, Obama had cosponsored Cambodia's Trade Act, now called the New Development Partnership Act, though, like its predecessor, the bill was stagnating in congressional committee.

The numbers are ominous. China closed more than 67,000 factories in the first half of 2008. Significant labor shortages and rising costs have begun to take their toll on China's explosive growth, and Vietnam is emerging as the next big "it" country for manufacturing. Sweatshops have again been in the news, with big multinationals like Tesco and Asda being put on the defensive. A spokesman for Tesco claimed that all forty-eight of their factories in Bangladesh, where the sweatshop allegations originated, had been audited within the past year—a claim I find dubious.* What makes situations like this even more frustrating is that corporations like Tesco and Asda all belong to ethical and environmental initiatives. They all claim to monitor their factories, to respect labor standards and environmental standards. But when they're publicly accused, most often they cite irregularities with the facto-

---

*When I brought this up with Dan Viederman at Verité, he said he didn't doubt at all that the company had audited all its factories in the past year. Generally speaking, he told me, companies really were auditing all the time, and though he couldn't speak specifically of Tesco, he said the problem was that not enough companies were taking action when their audits elicited only glowing reports. From his perspective, knowing what the industry does about working conditions, particularly in Bangladesh, any company that gets a green light on *every single factory* should recognize that it has received falsified reports or conducted ineffectual audits.

ries they're using. Those factories, they say, are illegally subcontracting to others. Or the abuses began just after an auditing session. But the truth is that factories generally don't abuse workers because they don't know better, or because they are immune to human suffering. Factories generally abuse workers because they feel they have no choice. Because they feel pressure from the buyers, who in turn complain of pressure from consumers. Or because they live in a world of insecurities, a world with no rule of law or respect for human rights.

Predictably, Cambodia was in an even more precarious situation. Twenty factories—out of three hundred or so—had closed in the first half of 2008, and more than twenty thousand workers had lost their jobs. Another thirty-five factories were threatened with closure in late 2008. Two-thirds of those factories fled without paying final salaries. What had been double-digit growth for nearly a decade in the industry had slowed to a trickle and then stopped altogether. At the time of printing, the industry had begun to contract. The Ministry of Commerce said exports had fallen by 46 percent in the fourth quarter of 2007, but a year later, despite a clear downtown, the prime minister claimed the country would remain "on target" with garment industry exports. Despite this public assertion, the consumer spending slowdown in America and Europe was hitting countries like Cambodia harder and harder each month. Cham Prasidh, the minister of commerce in Cambodia, felt battered. Not only was all his lobbying for tariff-free access stagnant in Congress, but he claimed that least developing countries in Africa had begun to lobby the United States *not* to give tariff-free access to Cambodia, or their own markets would be hurt. "They fight Cambodia rather than China," he told me. "We perform. Why penalize those who are successful?" Several people in the industry claimed that Bangladesh and Vietnam had become the newest Asian powerhouses for garments, despite the fact that neither had the labor standards of Cambodia. At the time of printing, the international trade division at the U.S. Department of Commerce maintained that the safeguards put on China would expire as planned at the end of 2008 with no current plans for renewal. It would, even with the rising costs and labor shortages, certainly give China a boost. So the question in Cambodia would seem to be why keep it up, why keep putting all this effort into a system that is not nearly as successful as, say, that of Bangladesh, where the international press reports workers toiling in sweatshops even in the twenty-first century? Why keep it up when the industry talk is all about decent labor practices and environmental sustainability but conditions on the ground in every other country are suspect? Bangladesh's growth rate has been greater than 8 percent, while Cambodia's industry shrinks. It doesn't bode well for corporate social responsibility and ethical consumerism.

Plus, some in Cambodia's garment industry believe the country is backtracking on some of its fair labor practices. To many, it seems there are more protests and an increase in worker intimidation. Adding to the tension is a documentary in the works about the murdered union leader, Chea Vichea—a topic that makes everyone in the industry so nervous that no one will talk about it. Entitled *Who Killed Chea Vichea?*, the film is a four-year investigation by director Bradley Cox into Chea's assassination. It will be released in the summer of 2009. As of this writing, two men who are almost surely innocent have been charged—though both have solid alibis—and they continue to languish in a Cambodian prison. The trial is set to begin in late December 2008. One factory manager, who asked not to be named, said of the growing tension, "Everyone knows what's going on. The buyers know. The government knows." Then he added, "It was the system that killed Chea Vichea."

One of the more surprising changes, however, is Rogan and Scott's split with Edun and Bono in January of 2008. All parties claimed it was mutual. In part, it had been a matter of schedules and logistics. Rogan was stretched designing for so many different lines, and Edun's offices were scattered all over the world, which always creates inefficiencies. But Edun's vision of designing high-end fashion in Africa was a huge challenge, and they had scaled down their line so drastically that they reinvented the company as a T-shirt and jeans outfit. While the company had never been more than a fraction of one of the big fashion powerhouses—usually earning under ten million a year, though exact figures are not made public—Rogan found that it was difficult to find factories in Africa that could provide the quality and intricacy that his designs demanded. When one of their managers at the Lesotho factory died of cancer, they'd eventually had to pull out altogether when they couldn't find anyone with the same level of quality control to replace her. Scott said no matter how much they'd tried, you just couldn't ignore China. You couldn't *not* compete with China, especially now that the country was getting better and better at high-end fashion and design of their own garments. Some of Scott and Rogan's stuff was even made in Hong Kong now (and anything made in Hong Kong means, of course, southern China). "I don't think it's impossible to create business in Africa, especially with Bono involved," Rogan told me. "It just has to be conceived and executed in the right way. I'm convinced it can be done. Maybe in the beginning China has to be a component of it."

One of the new directions for Scott and Rogan, ironically, has propelled them into the mainstream in a way that they never had been with Edun, or with any of their other brands. In partnership with Target, Rogan designed a collection called *Rogan for Target* that was the chain's first run of organic cotton at the scale with which it was executed—half a million to three-quarters of a million garments. "The potential to build something that will affect the conventional cotton industry is exciting," Scott said. "We'll be able to have a meaningful conversation with the industry around it. Rogan and I want to make a big difference in the world." And, they said, there are future fashion lines in the works with Target.

Scott believed, in spite of the state of consumerism and failing economies, that "the wave of consciousness is upon us." He thought the financial crisis would make people really think about what they were buying, how they were buying, and why they were buying. It's what we should all be doing anyway, he said. The shake-up might just be what the industry and consumers need. Rogan, too, saw the economic challenges in terms of his own vision. The smaller players, the less authentic designers and companies, he felt, would be weeded out by those willing to work harder and longer, those who were purists like him. "If you're clever, you can do a lot," he said. He'd even begun to define his vision in a way that he hadn't been able to in the past. "Soulful minimalism," he called it, and he was looking forward to working in the mass market again, with Target certainly, but also with anyone else who might come calling who was willing to work within his parameters of sustainability, efficiency, and aesthetics. "The Target thing was great," he said. "One of the biggest organic runs ever in fashion. Maybe the biggest. That's what I call real change."

There had been positive movement in other aspects of the industry, too. The ILO's Better Factories program in Cambodia, now called Better Work, had grown into programs in Lesotho, Haiti, Vietnam, and Jordan, with other countries to follow. The ILO, in partnership with the World Bank's International Finance Corporation, has taken the initiative to move the industry past the model of simply monitoring and into a much more comprehensive system that would actually be cheaper to implement in the long run for buyers, factories, and local governments. The key, Ros Harvey told me, was making sure the buyers, factories, unions, and local governments were all involved and had input into building a consensus. Monitoring factories had grown over the past decade in part because local governments didn't enforce labor standards and union bargaining was traditionally weak or nonexistent. Buyers like Gap, Nike, Timberland, and Levi's stepped into the monitoring role in the absence of local governance. What they'd learned from Cambodia, Harvey said, was that this model wouldn't work in the long term in part because you need local governments, factories, and unions to be involved. "Factories don't live in isolation," she said. "They live in the context of laws and the country. Say your factory is great, but outside the factory there's no rule of law. It creates fear in the community. All of us are realizing we have to have a way to move forward at the enterprise level, but it's got to be broader than that. You've got to build the nations' ability to run good labor standards and industrial relations. You cannot disempower at the national level. That's exactly the opposite of what we want."

The other big challenge, she said, was learning to take a valuable and successful project like Better Work in Cambodia and scale it to lots of countries, often with much larger industries. "You have to be able to talk about millions of workers if you're going to have an impact," she said. By separating the initial costs of development, which the ILO and IFC get through grants and partnerships, and the costs of sustaining the Better Work program, which are covered by fees from the participating entities, they've managed to build a base for the individual country programs, which, she is convinced, will be financially viable in the long term. It costs seven to ten million dollars over the course of five years to set up the Better Work program and train all the participants and staff. Half that money comes from donors for development; the other half comes from fees charged to the factories, buyers, unions, and local government. It might sound expensive, but, factoring in the huge costs for factories associated with monitoring, this new system is actually much cheaper. In Vietnam, Harvey said, Better Work will cost approximately $1.42 per worker, whereas the current monitoring model costs upwards of $50 per worker. It would take a long time, of course, to bring the Better Work program to the many dozens of countries around the world involved in manufacturing, but it's a start. "Change is not instantaneous," Harvey said, "but we are committed to building labor standards in supply chains. Over time we will achieve this through action, discussion, dialogue and debate."

Buyers, it seems, are all beginning to think of ways to move beyond the model of simply monitoring. It remains to be seen what innovations will emerge in the field of corporate social responsibility in the coming decades. Dan Henkle, at Gap, said the company had begun looking into putting more information about each product on the label, "not to market, but to educate." If a certain pair of jeans has come from a factory with SA 8000 certification, for example, should that information be shared? If you label the washing or treatment systems that go into a pair of jeans, will consumers care? He told me about a company out of Switzerland that had begun to include a code on the care label of every garment they made so that consumers could go to the Internet and use the code to see exactly where the product was made. They could go inside the factory, learn about compliance and certification, and actually see the workers. "It's not just about transparency," Henkle said. "It's about traceability, too. . . . I'm not saying we've arrived, but we're on a journey. Brand by brand."

IN LIGHT OF EVERYTHING, NAT AND RY WERE LUCKY to still have jobs, though of course they never saw themselves that way. Sophea and I finally met them after work on a Saturday afternoon. Ry was standing in front of the small gate at Kin Tai garment factory and she directed us to Nat's alley, just up the road. Nat had gained weight and looked considerably healthier, but there was tension between the two of them. They barely looked at each other, and Nat hardly spoke at all. Sophea told me that Nat's relatives in the United States had been sending the family money and that everyone was healthier, happier. She said Nat had stopped talking to Ry because she had begun to see herself as better than her fellow garment workers. This was Ry's take on it, anyway. I didn't know for sure what had happened, but it was clear that their friendship was no longer what it had once been, and it saddened me. If Nat had once been the sole person in the world Ry trusted, where did that leave the two of them? More alone than ever in the world, perhaps. The price of progress seemed painful when Culture reared its head in this way. When you had precious little in a place like Cambodia, status—even under the somewhat hazy pretense of poor and slightly less poor—could be everything. It depressed me.

We drove to Ry's house on the edge of the city, ten or fifteen minutes from Chak Angre, where many of the roads were still unpaved and electricity was sporadic. We had to park the car at the entrance of a dirt track that led to Ry's house. She lived on the edge of a small lake surrounded by one- and two-room brick houses with kids running up and down the yards and chickens wandering around. It was peaceful and people smiled as we walked past. It seemed idyllic, really, but Ry wasn't happy. She'd begun to build her small house—a single room set back in the yard about twenty feet from the track. The yard was just dirt now, but someday it can be used as a small garden. She'd managed to get the bricks and mortar up, but then she'd run out of money to plaster or paint, so she lived there in that little brick room. Still, it was hers. She owned the land. She owned the bricks.

The worst time, she told me, was when United Eternity closed down. She and Nat and all their fellow garment workers had lost out on owed wages, and for a long time she couldn't find work. She knew lots of others who'd never returned to the factories, but she and Nat were lucky. Nat now worked at a place called U.S.A. Factory, but they were not supervisors anymore. Their salaries were low, $70 to $90 a month, and they didn't work as much overtime as they'd have liked, but it wasn't all bad.

We sat on Ry's wooden platform bed and talked. She held my daughter in her lap and Nat stood at the foot of the bed, not really joining in the conversation. On the brick wall was a series of phone numbers written in permanent marker: friends, family, work contacts. One corner of the room was a small kitchen with a hot plate and a wok and a few utensils. In another corner a bathroom was hidden behind a doorway. Inside it was light and breezy and I noticed that Ry had bought herself a fan. I asked if she remembered telling me how she'd said someday she'd buy a fan when she was rich. She laughed and nodded. It was starting to get dark outside and a gaggle of children had formed in the doorway and at the window to listen as we talked. Ry's daughter was still in school and living with Ry's parents. Her English, Ry said, was getting better and better. Then she asked me for another copy of my book.

"I can't read it," she said. "But someday my daughter will be able to."

ACKNOWLEDGMENTS

WRITING AN ENTIRE BOOK IS CHALLENGING, BUT THE possibility of forgetting to thank someone who's been pivotal in one's professional or personal life is a whole other level of agony. I feel as if I understand the tears behind Oscar acceptance speeches in a new way; it's not about the honor and glory, it's about the terror of forgetting to thank your grandmother's neighbor. Or worse, your barista, which in my case happens to be my partner, Paul Burton, who woke me each morning for two years with the gentle wafting of Illy cappuccino and who supported me in ways I never imagined I'd need. He allowed my career to dictate our changing geographies with extraordinary patience. To him I owe something far beyond words. I'm hoping an infinite number of Earl Grey morning teas will begin to suffice.

A number of people were supportive of this project early on and answered numerous emails and phone calls from me, including Ken Loo at the Garment Manufacturer's Association of Cambodia; Michael Lerner at the Arbitration Council; Sandra Polaski at the Carnegie Endowment for International Peace; Axel Mangenot at Emerging Textiles in France; Fairchild Publications and *Women's Wear Daily*; Pam Devolder at the U.S. State Department; Pete Daniel and Peter Liebhold at the National Museum of

American History in Washington, DC; Lynda Grose; Ros Hibbert at Line Consultants in England; Beatrice Le Pechoux at Cotton, Incorporated; Amy Hammonds at AATCC; Ros Harvey at the ILO; Eileen Kauffman at SAI; EJ Bernacki and Michael Kobori at Levi's; Karen Kyllo at Intertek; Adrian Ross at New Island Clothing; and Christian Kemp-Griffin and Bridget Russo at Edun. Dan Henkle at GAP and Dan Viederman at Verite made the impossible possible in Shenzhen and Hong Kong; and Dave Kelly at the Library of Congress not only helped me find research on everything from the molecular structure of chemicals in fabric dye to doggie yoga—which is cause enough for thanks—but also occasionally drove me home in inclement weather, kept me in music with many gifts of CDs, and even made sure I had enough pocket change for snacks through some long days of research. His fellow librarian, Cheryl Adams, was always cheerfully helpful as well, as was Barbara Van Woerkom at the National Press Club library. Harry Mercer of Indigo Blue was kind enough to read for accuracy on the chemical and dye sections of the book; and Scott Wagner at Cotton, Incorporated made sure I had the processes of cotton dyeing and weaving correct. Though I tried to think of someone to take the blame for any mistakes I may have made here, I found no willing participants (apart from my dog, Khmow, who would do anything for hunks of meat), so any mistakes herein are mine alone.

Four readers and dear friends were pivotal in making this book far better than it may have otherwise been: Arin Farrington, who shares my love of jeans and canines; Wynne Cougill, who not only provided dozens of wonderful meals but also shared her home for over a year while I was in the States researching this book—and shared it not just with me and with Paul but also with Khmow, who bravely made the trip all the way from her Cambodian birthplace, Ann Maxwell, my sister, my friend, and perhaps the person in my life more than any other who compels me to be more curious, more thoughtful, and more compassionate than I feel myself capable of being; and especially David Corey, who has answered frantic, zany writing phone calls from me since our graduate school days at Emerson College twelve years ago.

I also owe gratitude to Liz and Dan Mohler, who have offered their Los Angeles guest room to me for over a decade; Jane Alexander and Steve Carr, who offered me help and friendship in England and who initially introduced me to Mehman during their Azerbaijan tenure; Joyce Neal, who provided me a temporary office in her Phnom Penh home; Andre Dubus III; Caroline Alexander; Elizabeth Becker; Sarah Koenig; Ira Glass; Tap and Mia Jordanwood; Lisa Arensen; Kris LeBoutillier; Gayle Forman; Alison Brower; Nancy Updike; Samantha Brown; Don Rutledge; Julie Gibson; Yasmina Kulauzovic; Charles Pearson; Loung Ung; Vera Titunik; Grace Ko; Kim Oldham; Carol Glowacki; Ambereen Sleemi; Rick Whitney; Tom Parks; Heide Bronke; Karen Lowe, Sue Hendrickson; the Overseas Press Club; the Conrad Hotels; the National Press Club in Washington, DC (where parts of this book were written over plates of cheese and fruit); Dana Points (the first editor to publish me); and Gianofer Fields (the first producer to put me on the air). Two wonderful assistants aided me along the way: Yelena Dontsova in Azerbaijan who is an excellent journalist herself, and the extraordinary Sophea Seng in Cambodia.

I have long been lucky to have family who always encouraged me, from my mother, Gail Margery Lee Snyder, who made me keep journals from the time I was old enough to write, to my grandfather, the poet and writer Charles Lee, and to my cousin, the poet Lance Lee, whom I never met face to face until my early thirties and who has become a pivotal person in my life and my heart. I would also like to thank my brother, David Jonathan Snyder, a better writer and thinker than I'll ever be, and Erma Butman, Robert Carp, Saskia Coenen, Richard and Barbara Snyder, Wesley and Barbara Snyder, John Snyder, Joshua Snyder, Katherine Doyle, Alyssa Lee, and David Levy.

I wanted a home at W. W. Norton long before they'd ever heard of me, and Brendan Curry eventually made that happen believing in this book. He talked me down from literary cliffs and laughed at my terrible jokes before he'd even received a finished manuscript. Finally, Susan Ramer at Don Congdon and Associates took me on two months after I finished graduate school, and years before I was ready to be an author. Her patience is far beyond what any agent should be asked to give, yet she never stopped believing me capable of having a life as a writer. To her I owe much gratitude.

Finally, the people in this book deserve far more credit than they are likely to get: Mehman, Vasif, Ganira, Rogan, Scott, Nat, Ry, Pascal, Ariana, Jerry, Peter, and the thirty million-plus workers involved in the global garment trade today.

NOTES

I. THE SUBVERSIVE ECOSYSTEM

1. See http://www.nps.gov/fiis/naturescience/index.htm.
2. Edward Gresser, "The End of Textile Quotas Will Redistribute Pain and Gain," *Yale Global*, June 10, 2004.
3. Elizabeth Becker, "Textile Quotas to End, Punishing Carolina Towns," *New York Times*, November 2, 2004.
4. Phone interviews with Sandra Polaski of the Carnegie Endowment, August 2004, and Pam Devolder, Economic & Labor Officer, U.S. Embassy, Phnom Penh, Cambodia, June 2004.
5. Evan Clark and Kristi Ellis, "Let's Make a Trade Deal: U.S.-China Sign Accord to Limit Surging Imports," *Women's Wear Daily*, November 9, 2005.
6. See www.agoa.info.

II. THE VEGETABLE LAMB
CONQUERS THE WORLD

1. Interview with Vasif Iruizou, Bilasuvar, October 21, 2004.
2. Liverpool Cotton Association, as of October 2004.

3. Interview with Rovshan Aliyev, Baku, November 3, 2004.
4. Ibid.
5. See http://www.cottoninc.com/cottonfacts/.
6. Maria Leach and Jerome Fried, *Funk and Wagnalls Standard Dictionary of Folklore, Mythology and Legend* (New York: Funk and Wagnalls, 1949), 254; C.A.S. Williams, *Encyclopedia of Chinese Symbolism and Art Motives* (New York: The Julian Press, 1960), 99; Wilhelm Max Müller, *Egyptian/Indo-Chinese Mythology* (The Mythology of All Races, Vol. XII [Boston: Marshall Jones Co., 1918]), 299–300; Hartley Burr Alexander, *Latin-American Mythology* (The Mythology of All Races, Vol. XI [Boston: Marshall Jones Co., 1920]), 27; Vergilius Ferm, ed., *Encyclopedia of Religion*, Vol. I (New York: The Philosophical Library, 1945), 189.
7. B. A. Botkin, *A Treasure of Southern Folklore* (New York: Crown, 1949), 20.
8. Maciej Adamczyk, *Cotton Markets*, The Gdynia Cotton Association course handbook, 2004.
9. Interview with Vasif Iruizou, Bilasuvar, October 21, 2004.
10. Mark Elliott, *Azerbaijan* (Surrey, England: Trailblazer Publications, 2004).
11. Interview with Rovshan Aliyev, Baku, November 3, 2004. The half-million figure is based on estimates received from the ministry: there are 230,000 field workers, roughly, with another 210,000 seasonal workers like cotton pickers estimated.
12. Ibid.
13. Valmont has not independently confirmed this deal to me. A company called Caspian Energy reported a MKT / Valmont deal on its Web site: http://caspenergy.com/36/2005_36_07e.html.

III. WHITE GOLD AND ALL-TEX QUICKIE

1. Adamczyk, *Cotton Markets*.
2. Interview with Vasif Iruizou, Bilasuvar, October 21, 2004.
3. In 1793, the year the gin was invented, the United States had exported 487,600 pounds of cotton and was home to a slave trade that was not only dwindling in size and economics but had come to be viewed as unfavorable in society. A year later, when Whitney's gin—short for engine—became standard at cotton farms, the slave trade had seemingly overnight begun to boom again, and the United States had exported 1.6 million pounds of cotton. The next year it burgeoned to 10 million pounds. F. Ewart Storey, *All About Cotton* (Philadelphia: The Storey Cotton Company, 1901), 10.

4. T. A. Heppenheimer, "The Machine That Killed King Cotton," *Invention & Technology* (Summer 2004): 39.
5. James H. Street, "Mechanizing the Cotton Harvest," *Annual Report of the Board of Regents of the Smithsonian Institution*, 1957, 422.
6. Ibid., 423.

IV. THE LITTLE VOLCANOES WE CARRY

1. Transparency International, "Corruption Perception Index, 2004," http://www.transparency.org/pressreleases_archive/2004/2004.10.20.cpi.en.html.
2. See http://www.cottonsjourney.com/Storyofcotton/page5.asp.
3. National Institute for Occupational Safety and Health, "Pesticide Illness and Injury Surveillance," http://www.cdc.gov/niosh/topics/pesticides/.
4. This could not be verified by the World Bank's representative in Baku.
5. See http://www.ewg.org/farm/persondetail.php?custnumber=001347872&summlevel=detailbyyear.
6. See http://www.ewg.org/farm/persondetail.php?custnumber=001598946&summlevel=detailbyyear.
7. Evan Clark, "Bush Moves Against Cotton Subsidies," *Women's Wear Daily*, July 6, 2005.
8. See www.georgiacottoncommission.org/index.cfm?show=10&mid=6.
9. See http://www.ewg.org/farm/progdetail.php?fips=13000&progcode=cotton.
10. Stephen Yafa, *Big Cotton* (New York: Viking, 2005), 168.

V. THESE GALOSHES WERE MADE FOR WALKING

1. Yafa, *Big Cotton*, 203.
2. Pesticide Action Network North America, "Problems with Conventional Cotton Production," www.panna.org.
3. Carl Smith, "Pesticide Exports from U.S. Ports, 1997–2000," *International Journal of Occupational and Environmental Health* 7 (2001): 272.
4. Somini Sengupta, "On India's Farms, A Plague of Suicide," *New York Times*, September 19, 2006.

5. Pesticide Action Network North America, "Problems with Conventional Cotton Production."

6. Marla Cone, "EPA to Ban One Pesticide, Lets 32 Others Stay in Use," *Los Angeles Times*, August 4, 2006.

7. Pesticide Action Network North America, "Problems with Conventional Cotton Production."

8. Ibid.

9. See http://www.pesticideinfo.org/Detail_ChemReg.jsp?Rec_Id=PC33392.

10. Pesticide Action Network North America, "Organophosphates," www.panna.org.

11. See http://pmep.cce.cornell.edu/profiles/extoxnet/haloxyfop-methyl parathion/methyl-parathion-ext.html and http://www.pesticideinfo.org/List_Chemicals.jsp?.

12. Cone, "EPA to Ban One Pesticide," and HealthDay News, "Controversy Surrounds EPA Review of Pesticides," *Forbes*, August 2, 2006.

13. Smith, "Pesticide Exports from U.S. Ports, 1997–2000," 269.

14. See http://www.organicexchange.org/Documents/marketreport_2006.pdf.

15. See http://www.nike.com/nikebiz/nikebiz.jhtml?page=27&cat=ogcotton &subcat=commitment.

16. See http://www.walmartfacts.com/FactSheets/12272006_Sustainability.pdf.

17. International Cotton Advisory Committee, "Limitations on Organic Cotton Production," *The ICAC Recorder*, March 2003, 3.

18. Ross Tucker, "Cotton's Organic Debate," *Women's Wear Daily*, July 11, 2006.

19. Marcia Gibbs, Rex Dufour, and Martin Guerena, "Basic Cotton Manual," Sustainable Cotton Project and National Center for Appropriate Technology, January 2005, www.sustainablecotton.org.

20. Pesticide Action Network North America Corporate Profile: Monsanto Company, www.panna.org.

21. Yafa, *Big Cotton*, 284.

VII. GOD'S NECTAR AND OTHER DENIM YOU DON'T KNOW YOU WEAR

1. His name has been changed.

2. Statistic from the Istituto Nazionale di Statistica (Istat) in Rome.

3. He was referring to denim fabric, not finished jeans.
4. Her name has been changed.
5. For a great description of these, read Naomi Klein's *No Logo* (London: Flamingo/HarperCollins, 2000).
6. It claimed to be the second largest employer in the area (though the biggest apparently has 17,000 and Legler's Ponte San Pietro location has just 600). In all, Legler claims to have 1,400 employees, though it officially has 900. Regardless, it might fall well below the top employer, but it's a significant player in an area hard hit by Italy's recession.
7. Legler did not release specific numbers to me, and since it is a private company, there is no accurate way to find them, but a significant downturn in their revenue was confirmed to me in several interviews with two of Legler's chief operations managers.
8. "Addio, Dolce Vita," *The Economist*, November 26, 2005.
9. "Structurally Unsound," *The Economist*, November 26, 2005. All statistics in this paragraph come from this source.
10. There are lots of specialty types of spinning as well, but they are not as commonly used in denim.
11. This shouldn't be confused with tinting, which often leaves pockets and labels dyed, too.

VIII. URINATING ON YOUR JEANS JUST MAKES GOOD SENSE

1. J. N. Liles, *The Art and Craft of Natural Dyeing: Traditional Recipes for Modern Use* (Knoxville, TN: University of Knoxville Press, 1990), 55.
2. Philip S. Clarkson, *Indigo MLB: A Handbook of the Practical Application of Synthetic Indigo* (New York: H.A. Metz & Co., 1904), 1.
3. Arnold Krochmal and Connie Krochmal, preface to *The Complete Illustrated Book of Dyes from Natural Sources* (Garden City, NY: Doubleday, 1974).
4. For the results—Dia also claims that the most-used color on the World Wide Web is blue—check out http://www.diacenter.org/km/survey results.html.
5. Visit to Cotton Incorporated, Cary, North Carolina, November 2005.
6. Wastewater pollution from Brooklyn dyehouses, in fact, wiped out oyster harvesting in New York in the early twentieth century. See www.colorantshistory.org.

342 | NOTES

7. R. M. Christie, R. R. Mather, and R. H. Wardman, *The Chemistry of Colour Application* (Oxford, England: Blackwell Science, 2000), 91.
8. Ibid., 17.
9. "Q & A: REACH Chemicals Legislation," BBC News, November 28, 2005, http://news.bbc.co.uk/go/pr/fr/-/1/hi/world/europe/4437304.stm.
10. See http://www.greenpeace.org/international/news/eu-reach-chemical-law-vote131206.
11. The United States Mission to the European Union, "Ambassador Gray Discusses EU's REACH Chemicals Proposal," June 8, 2006, http://useu.usmission.gov.
12. Albert Roessler, "New Electrochemical Methods for the Reduction of Vat Dyes," PhD dissertation, Eidgenössische Technische Hochschule Zürich, Switzerland, 2003. Abstract.
13. E-mails and phone calls to UNEP could not independently confirm this.
14. Conversations with Harry Mercer conducted by phone, May 11, 2006.
15. Melody Kemp, "Resistance to Occupational Safety," *The Jakarta Post*, November 10, 1997.
16. Dr. Mitchell Hecht, "Link between Chemical Exposure, Bladder Cancer," *Knight Ridder/Tribune News Service*, reprinted from *Times-Picayune*, June 2, 1999.
17. Judy Mann, "A Hard Look at the Health of Working Women," *Washington Post*, September 18, 1998.
18. Confirmed by Manfred Wentz, phone conversation, May 24, 2006.

IX. HOW THE WEST WAS WON

1. Katherine Weisman, "Vive Le Jeans!" *Women's Wear Daily*, May 18, 2000.
2. David Little and Larry Bond, *Vintage Denim* (Layton, UT: Gibbs-Smith, 1996), 37–38.
3. Barbara Fehr, *Yankee Denim Dandies* (Blue Earth, MN: Piper Publishing), 27.
4. Koju Hirano and Luisa Zargani, "Foreign Intrigue: The Yanks Were Coming and Their Duffels Were Stuffed with the Makings of Worldwide Dungaree Envy," *Women's Wear Daily*, May 18, 2000.
5. Valerie Steele, *Encyclopedia of Clothing and Fashion*, vol. 2, *Fads to Nylon* (Farmington Hills, MI: Thomson Gale Publishers, 2005).
6. Hirano and Zargani, "Foreign Intrigue."
7. Little and Bond, *Vintage Denim*, 14.

X. A SOCIETY OF THE MIND AND OTHER ATMOSPHERIC CONTAMINANTS

1. From a 1548 dyeing manual courtesy of AATCC historical archives.
2. Mark Clark, *Dyeing for a Living*. (Research Triangle Park, NC: AATCC, 1998), 4.
3. Ibid., 5.
4. Ibid., 6.
5. See www.colorantshistory.org.

XII. IN THE LIVING WE LOSE CONTROL

1. Ellen Israel Rosen, *Making Sweatshops* (Berkeley and Los Angeles: University of California Press, 2002), 57–58.

XVII. KNOCK, KNOCK, KNOCKIN' ON FACTORY DOORS

1. Michael Schuman, "The Birth and Rebirth of Shenzhen," *Time*, Asia edition, August 14, 2006.
2. Ted C. Fishman, *China, Inc.* (New York: Scribner International, 2005), 93.
3. Thomas Fuller, "China Feels a Labor Pinch," *International Herald Tribune*, April 20, 2005.
4. See http://www.asianews.it/view.php?l=en&art=7688#, November 7, 2006.
5. Fishman, *China, Inc.*, 95.
6. SA 8000 Overview, www.sa-intl.org.
7. Her name has been changed.

XVIII. A VIEW OF ONE'S OWN FATIGUED AUDITOR

1. Jill Esbenshade, "The Social Accountability Contract: Private Monitoring from Los Angeles to the Global Apparel Industry," *Labor Studies Journal* 26, no. 1 (Spring 2001).
2. Ibid.

3. Stephen Frost, "China View," *CSR Asia Weekly*, vol 2, week 31, August 2, 2006, 7.

4. Jim Yardley, "Rules Ignored, Toxic Sludge Sinks Chinese Village," *New York Times*, September 4, 2006.

5. Julian M. Allwood, Søren Ellebaek Laursen, Cecilia Malvido de Rodriguez, and Nancy M. P. Bocken, *Well Dressed? The Present and Future Sustainability of Clothing and Textiles in the UK* (Cambridge, England: University of Cambridge Institute for Manufacturing, 2006), 16.

6. Yardley, "Rules Ignored," and Science News, "China Fails to Cut Pollutants: Government," *Scientific American*, August 30, 2006.

7. Frost, "China View," *CSR Asia Weekly*, vol 2, week 39, September 27, 2006, 7.

8. Science News, "China Fails to Cut Main Pollutants: Government," *Scientific American*; Joshua Kurlantzick, "Purple Haze," *The New Republic* online, August 23, 2004; and Elizabeth C. Economy, *The River Runs Black* (Ithaca, NY: Cornell University Press, 2004).

9. Richard Welford, "Tackling Asia's Water Crisis," *CSR Asia Weekly*, vol. 2, week 36, September 6, 2006, 3.

10. Allwood et al., *Well Dressed*, 16.

11. Yardley, "Rules Ignored."

12. Kurlantzick, "Purple Haze."

13. Yardley, "Rules Ignored."

14. Dr. Jing Leng, "The Emerging Discourse of CSR in China," *CSR Asia Weekly*, vol. 2, week 37, September 13, 2006, 9.

XIX. THE THIRD PARTY, EXHIBIT A: THE TWO-SECOND HANDSHAKE

1. I was asked not to mention the factory by name.

XX. THE THIRD PARTY, EXHIBIT B: THE LAST-MINUTE ORGY AND OTHER SHOPPERS' DELIGHTS

1. *The National Consumers' League, First Quarter Century, 1899–1924* (New York), 3.

2. Ibid., 1.

3. Landon R. Y. Storrs, *Civilizing Capitalism* (Chapel Hill: University of North Carolina Press, 2000), 20.
4. Ibid.
5. Ibid., 8.
6. *Industrial Liberty in Wartime: Address of the Hon. Newton D. Baker* (Baltimore), November 14, 1917, 2.
7. Ibid., 3–6.
8. Ibid., 16.

XXI. THE GUARDIANS OF EDUN

1. See http://michaelmedved.townhall.com/blog/g/942a7a01-7d02-4a72-8232-606c7adf80ee.

EPILOGUE

1. Steven R. Wiesman, "In Major Shift, U.S. Imposes Tariffs on Some Chinese Paper," *New York Times*, March 30, 2007.
2. See http://www.otexa.ita.doc.gov/MSRCTRY.htm. All import shipping numbers from this Web site.

INDEX